A Manager's Guide to Leadership

A Manager's Guide to Leadership

Mike Pedler, John Burgoyne, Tom Boydell

The **McGraw·Hill** Companies

London Boston Burr Ridge, IL Dubuque, IA Madison, WI New York San Francisco St. Louis
Bangkok Bogotá Caracas Kuala Lumpur Lisbon Madrid Mexico City Milan Montreal
New Delhi Santiago Seoul Singapore Sydney Taipei Toronto

The **McGraw·Hill** Companies

A Manager's Guide to Leadership
Mike Pedler, John Burgoyne, Tom Boydell

ISBN 0077104234

 **Professional**

Published by McGraw-Hill Professional
Shoppenhangers Road
Maidenhead
Berkshire
SL6 2QL
Telephone: 44 (0) 1628 502 500
Fax: 44 (0) 1628 770 224
Website: www.mcgraw-hill.co.uk

British Library Cataloguing in Publication Data
A catalogue record for this book is available from the British Library

Library of Congress Cataloguing in Publication Data
The Library of Congress data for this book has been applied for from the Library of Congress

Text design by Gray Publishing
Cover design by Ego Creative Ltd
Printed and bound in the UK by Bell & Bain, Glasgow

Contents

Preface

The philosophy of this book

This book is an active guide to leadership rather than a stock of knowledge. Its message is simple: if you wish to contribute to leadership …

Decide on the most significant challenges facing your organization, determine what needs to be done about them and then do something that leads to a useful outcome.

If asked to think of times when we were proud of ourselves, most of us can give examples of when we took the lead. These stories may come from work, family life or outside work activities, but they all tend to be about times when we did something useful in difficult or testing situations.

Leadership is a doing thing; a performance art. It is not defined by any set of personal qualities or competencies, but by what we actually *do* when faced with challenging situations. These challenges come from life and work, from the wider world and from our own questions about ourselves. Leadership is what we do when we acknowledge and respond to these challenges.

Why is leadership so important now?

Leadership is likely to be playing a more important part in your life now because it has become a matter of pressing importance for organizations, communities and societies. Good leadership overlaps with, but is different from, good management. Management efficiency and effectiveness have long been the hallmarks of organizational success; but this is no longer enough. Something else is needed.

If your organization has only one leader, then it is almost certainly short of leadership.

Gerard Egan

Whether you work in a hospital or a large company, in a school or a local business, you have probably noticed this new concern with leadership. Your boss is talking about it, the Government says how important it is, the newspapers deplore the lack of it – you may even be on the receiving end of initiatives to improve it. What people are saying is that:

- Organizations are massively challenged by change and need more leadership.
- Good managers are always important, but the ability to lead in the face of the critical challenges of the day is what makes the vital difference.
- In the past leadership has been seen as the preserve of the few; today leadership is needed 'at all levels' – in all situations.

Most organizations and communities are short on this sort of leadership. Leadership development programmes have been set up to meet this demand, but such programmes tend to focus on the next set of top people. The talents and potentials of the great majority of people are neglected.

Taking part in leadership

The talents of the many are ignored because of a strongly entrenched view that leadership is the preserve of the few. Organizations and communities are full of talented individuals, and the potential for leadership is widely distributed amongst them, but they do not always work well together.

Yet the challenges that we face demand a concerted effort by everyone in the situation. Enabling talented people to work better together is a critical leadership task in any organization. As Peter Senge says, 'leadership is *the collective capacity to create something useful*'.

To achieve the collective capacity to create useful things, we need a different image of leadership. This is an image that emphasizes the individual person as connected with others in a collective effort. In this view, the unit of analysis for leadership is not the heroic individual, or the undifferentiated community: *it is the connected individual creating a better world in good company*.

A challenges approach to leadership

This book is based on the assumption that:

Leadership is about recognizing and responding to the CHALLENGES facing us in our organizations and communities.

As good leadership has become more important, the need for a challenges approach has become clearer. Leadership means moving towards difficult and challenging situations, rather than avoiding them, even when we have no clear idea of how to proceed.

Most leadership development programmes are based on teaching people skills and knowledge, which – by themselves – do little to encourage action on the key challenges facing the organization. The challenges approach to leadership development puts the emphasis upon action and learning in order to move forwards in company with your colleagues. It is the nature of these collective leadership practices that shapes the meaning and relevance of our individual skills and knowledge.

This book will help you to prioritize the critical leadership challenges facing you in your situation and help you to get started on them by providing ideas, tools and resources for action and learning.

How to use this book

This book aims to be a useful and friendly guide to the challenges approach to leadership. It encourages you to take action and to learn from that experience to develop yourself, your colleagues and your organization. Inputs of knowledge and ideas are kept brief and are illustrated with stories and case examples. The self-development and action learning philosophy of the book is apparent in the diagnostic activities and tools which carry the message: *'here is a challenge – appraise it, act on it and learn from it'*.

In this book there are chapters on each of the *21 Challenges of Leadership*. Each is designed to identify the challenge and to provide ideas and resources for tackling it. All of the 21 chapters are designed as provocations and calls to action and learning, and are not intended as comprehensive or exhaustive treatments of these major themes of 21st century organizational life. Whole books and even literatures are available on each of these themes and it is not our intention to replace or rival these offerings. Such treatments rarely act as spurs to action. In conditions of uncertainty and confusion, where there is no ready-made solution to hand, it is action that creates the information and learning that enables the next intelligent step. Each of these chapters will help you to get started on the action and learning cycle of leadership.

Whilst being friendly and accessible, the tone is assertive. Our message is that leadership is everyone's business and that we should all get on with it. We are impatient with patronizing views about special people or specific qualities of leadership. We encourage everyone to seek good advice and expertise from colleagues rather than relying on experts. There are no experts in leadership, and it is best to put your faith in those people who want to change things and who are able to learn in that process of change.

Contents

The book is in three parts. Part 1 describes the model and provides the argument around which the book is structured. Parts 2 and 3 divide *The 21 Challenges of Leadership* into two: Part 2 deals with the more personal leadership challenges, such as facilitation and using power, entitled *Core Leadership Practices*; Part 3 focuses on the more organizational challenges, such as mergers and major change, entitled *Key Leadership Challenges*.

Chapter 1 introduces the model of *The 21 Challenges of Leadership*, which is then employed in Chapter 2 to create *The Leadership Prioritizer* – a diagnostic framework to help surface your most important leadership challenges. This chapter helps you takes stock of the position of leadership in your life and provides guidance on the use of the rest of the book. Part 1 concludes with the first of the core leadership practices: Leading Yourself, which underpins everything that follows.

The six chapters in Part 2 cover the other *Core Leadership Practices*:

Practice 2: On Purpose
Practice 3: Power
Practice 4: Living with Risk
Practice 5: Challenging Questions
Practice 6: Facilitation
Practice 7: Networking

Part 3 consists of 14 chapters on the *Key Leadership Challenges*:

Challenge 1: Developing Direction and Strategy
Challenge 2: Creating a Learning Organization
Challenge 3: New Organizational Structures
Challenge 4: Powerful Teams
Challenge 5: Crafting Cultures of Innovation
Challenge 6: Fostering Diversity and Inclusion
Challenge 7: Promoting Partnerships
Challenge 8: Improving Work Processes
Challenge 9: Streamlining
Challenge 10: Encouraging Social Responsibility
Challenge 11: Mobilizing Knowledge
Challenge 12: Leading in Networks
Challenge 13: Managing Mergers
Challenge 14: Making Major Change

Chapters 1 and 2 introduce you to the model of the *21 Challenges of Leadership* and help you to choose your route through the book.

Acknowledgements

There are many people whose ideas have contributed to this book. Ideas and stories have been gifted, borrowed and blended and frequently emerge all in 'a knot of one another's labours'. First amongst these many friends and companions are:

Kath Aspinwall, for her wit, erudition and wide reading of the leadership literature – and for supporting Mike when he most needed it. Also for telling us that the book felt 'grown up'. At last! Kath contributed to many chapters, read the whole book and did a lot of revisions.

David Wilkinson, Mike's partner on long walks, for being the inspirer of new learning and, together with Margaret Attwood, for championing Ronald Heifetz in spite of ill-informed objections.

Phil Radcliffe, for wisdom about learning, change, mergers and lots of other things. Phil read a number of the chapters in draft and his advice was always spot on.

Chris Bones for his customary brilliance and generosity in making time to talk when doing two jobs (at least).

John MackMersh never fails to inspire, in this case, especially around power, networks and working with teams. Thanks, John, for the ideas, energy and humour.

David Casey for his clarity, generosity of spirit and encouragement just when it was needed.

Janet Atkinson for her thinking on the responsible use of power and her model in Chapter 5.

Maxine Conner for her insights into process mapping, networks and lots of other things.

Elizabeth Michel-Alder for her gripping story of streamlining in a Swiss Hospital.

Barry Lowe for sharing his powerful experiences of owner-managing a rapidly growing business.

Mark Gamsu for his story of service redesign in social services.

David Percy for his story in Leading Yourself.

Barrie Oxtoby for his account of the Rover/Honda partnership.

Bob Fryer for his favourite after-dinner story about organizational restructuring in Chapter 12.

And certainly not least, Elizabeth Choules, our Editor at McGraw-Hill, for helpful feedback and support during a time which was sometimes difficult for her.

Thanks finally to all those others, including reviewers, who freely gave of their ideas, who helped us to get stories straight and who gave permissions to use them.

Part 1

A Challenges Approach to Leadership

The 21 Challenges of Leadership

This chapter outlines our ideas about leadership but, before this, you might like to pause and jot down your own views on these two questions:

■ What do you think leadership is? And how does it differ from management?
■ What do you think is the best way to learn about leadership?

This book is based on a framework of the *21 Challenges of Leadership* drawn from recent research, our working and consulting experiences and a wide reading of the leadership literature. This chapter introduces the framework and our key assumptions about the nature of leadership. But first, where do you stand on this question?

Are you part of leadership?

If you are a professional or a technical expert, perhaps an engineer, a pharmacist or an accountant, you may find yourself handling a lot of people and projects in your work. Perhaps you grumble about this – it is not what you were trained for – but it means that you are becoming a leader. You probably had a long period of education, training and development to acquire your professional expertise – what help can you get with becoming a leader?

You may have the word *manager* in your job title, but find that *leadership* is talked about as something beyond managing and even more desirable. In the BBC there is a slogan: 'Manage well; lead more'. What is the difference? Although they overlap and are linked, leading is more concerned with finding direction and purpose in the face of critical challenges, whereas managing is about organizing to achieve desired purposes – efficiently, effectively and creatively. The focus on choice and purpose is a reminder that leadership has a moral aspect and is never value-free. Choosing this rather than that involves judgements between what is right and what is wrong.

Managing is more about bringing order and control and implies systems and procedures that you may both welcome and find restrictive at the same time.

In the creative professions and the public services, management can sometimes be a dirty word, with those things done in its name seeming more hindrance than help. This surfaces a puzzle: to be responsive and innovative, enterprises rely more and more upon their professionals and knowledge workers, but such people often resist being managed by others and prefer to manage themselves. For these people to work well together, rather than as isolated individuals, calls for less control and more high-quality leadership.

Leadership is less easy to spot than management. Its presence or absence in a situation is less obvious than the more specific activities of management. Leadership is more sensed or felt, as in, for example:

- Do you feel part of this – project, organization, network? Or not?
- Do you have a sense of collective purpose, a shared understanding and a commitment to what is being done? Or not?
- Do you feel proud of the work you are doing? Or not?

Leadership creeps up on you. Whatever leadership means to you, unlike the promotion to manager, it arrives not with a big bang on a particular day, but almost unnoticed. Leadership creeps up on us because we may not notice the extent of the difference that it makes.

So, are you part of leadership or not? If you are not leading, then what are you doing? – supporting, resisting, bystanding, undermining, cheerleading, … or what? Leadership involves everyone; and everyone involved is doing *something*.

A leadership model

Leadership is a contested issue. It is much discussed and debated, both practically and theoretically, and means different things to different people in different contexts. There is no one correct definition of leadership, or any one set of personal qualities or competencies that characterize leaders. Despite this, most approaches to leadership development are based on personal competency models and focus upon the individual.

Our model of leadership has three domains (see Figure 1.1), where:

- CHALLENGES are the critical tasks, problems and issues requiring action.
- CHARACTERISTICS are the qualities, competencies and skills that enable us to contribute to the practice of leadership in challenge situations.
- CONTEXT is the 'on-site' conditions found in the challenge situation.

All three domains are important: without challenging tasks there is no call for leadership; challenges make great demands on the qualities, abilities and skills of the people in the situation; and leadership is always situated in a particular

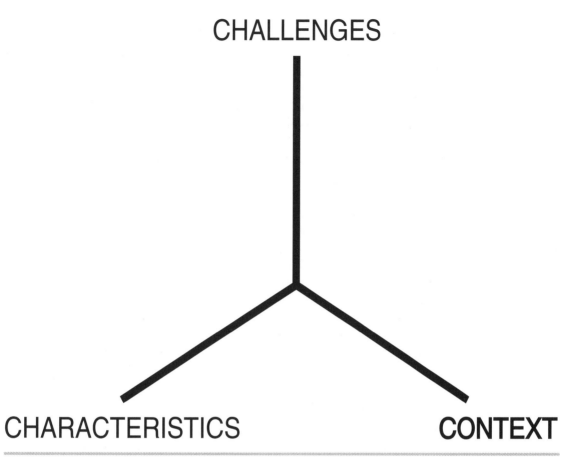

Figure 1.1 The three domains of leadership

context. Because of the complexity of these contexts, there is no one best style or approach that fits all situations.

What are the implications of the three domains for your leadership development?

The domains of leadership: characteristics, contexts and challenges

The characteristics domain

Many leadership development programmes focus upon personal characteristics. The qualities, abilities, competencies and skills of people are of great importance in leadership situations, but this domain is usually overemphasized. This is partly a legacy of the 'Great Man' era that saw leadership as the province of outstanding individuals with rare personal qualities. This still pervasive tendency is allied to a training tradition that focuses on individual knowledge and skills. Together, these two traditions conspire to encourage an individualistic and one-size-fits-all approach to leadership.

Leadership development based on models of individual characteristics or competencies is often helpful for personal development, but does it lead to useful action in the organization? These characteristics matter, but take their meaning from our ability to contribute and participate in leadership practices with others.

The context domain

This domain is generally neglected in most leadership programmes. Yet leadership is always situated: always done *here*, with these particular people; it is always local and contextual. Context is vital: what works here and now may not work in another place and at another time. There is no right way to lead: if you do get it right here and now there is no guarantee that this will work in the same way in another situation, or even in the same situation some time later.

Generic leadership characteristics are context-free, but leadership challenges are always contextual, always situated with particular people in specific circumstances. Context emphasizes the collective nature of leadership; it is about working with others in a concerted endeavour to create something of value.

The challenges domain

Although acknowledging the importance of context and characteristics, this book emphasizes the domain of *Challenges*. Leadership is principally concerned with recognizing, mobilizing and taking action in the face of critical problems and issues. In this view, leadership is defined in action, by what people do in the face of the challenges that they face at home and at work. It is thus a performance art, measured on what we *do* in this situation, here and now, and not what we are or what we know.

The *Challenges* domain puts the spotlight more upon the task and the concerted effort at leadership and less upon the individual. Leadership challenges in organizations and communities are usually collective ones, faced by all those in the situation. Although it is individuals who spot and raise challenges, and individuals who make heroic efforts to resolve them, few big challenges are met by one person acting alone. The urgent need is to mobilize the people in the situation, to engage colleagues, networks, communities and whole organizations in the effort to meet and overcome challenges.

Leadership as the collective capacity to create things of value

Look back at Figure 1.1 and place yourself in the centre. Now move out along the arms. As you move towards the *Characteristics* pole, you move towards the individual and their personal qualities. Move now towards either *Challenges* or *Context* and you move towards a more collective and situated view: what can we do about this challenge here and now?

Organizations and communities rarely lack talented individuals, but frequently fail to bring those talents together to create a powerful collective force. In part this is due to old-fashioned thinking. We still seem to think that progress is only made when we have a 'leader with vision' who can show us the way. This persistent image damages the collective capacity to do better things.

This image persists because there are so many aspects of life – politics, religion, business, sport and so on – where the leader stands out in front. No wonder then that leadership programmes are modelled on heroic individuals with futuristic visions with the rest of us following on. Does this fit with your view of what is needed in your situation?

Thinking of your own view of leadership, do you see it more as the province of outstanding individuals and heroes? Or as more of a collective spirit, emerging from teams and committed groups? The Challenges approach to leadership sits slightly differently. In seeking to encourage people to tackle their tough problems, the emphasis is not upon the heroic individual, or upon the undifferentiated team or community, but on the *connected individual creating a better world in good company*.

This puts the responsibility for leadership on you as a person, but in company and relationship with other people. This concept of leadership is more appropriate to the daily complexities of running businesses, services and societies than that of the heroic and isolated leader.

However, there is a snag here: with the heroic leader, when things go wrong it is obvious where the blame lies. With heroes around there is little need for the rest of us to take much responsibility. On the other hand, if leadership is the collective capacity to do valuable things, we can all claim the credit when things go well, but when things go wrong we also have to accept responsibility and seek to learn from the mistakes in order to do better next time.

The *21 Challenges of Leadership*

This book is designed around the *21 Challenges of Leadership*. These are the problems and opportunities of the day which call for good quality leadership (Figure 1.2).

This figure has two zones: the outer zone consists of *14 Key Challenges* that are typical of the kinds of organizational challenges that you are likely to face at work; the inner zone of *7 Core Practices* contains the more personal, inner challenges that you face when you engage in leadership. These inner challenges or practices are about action – what you do (and need to do skilfully) – but they are also ways of being – of who you are, and of how you do what you do. The *7 Core Practices* link us as individual people to the outer organizational challenges through our actions. It is the quality of your responses to both inner and outer challenges that makes the difference between good and bad leadership.

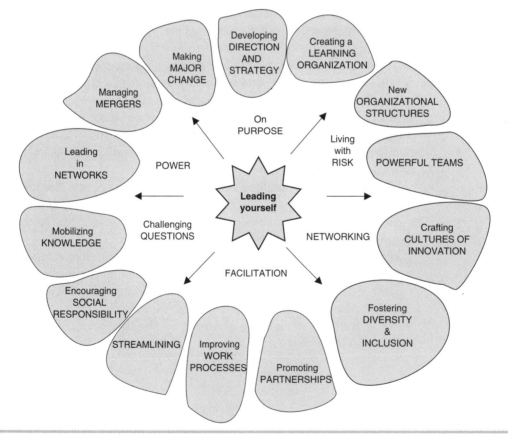

Figure 1.2   The 21 leadership challenges

The 14 Key Challenges

The *14 Key Challenges* are representative, but not exhaustive, of the most important leadership challenges of the current era. We have chosen these 14 on the basis of our combined experience of consulting and working with people in many different groups and organizations, and supplemented this by a wide reading of the huge and expanding leadership literature. We have also drawn upon the empirical research on management and leadership conducted by the Council for Excellence in Management and Leadership (CEML), where one of us was Policy Research Consultant.

However, none of this means that these are the right challenges for you. Although they are typical and representative of what we know, your organizational challenges in particular may well be different, and they will certainly be more specific and varied in context. What will be the same is the Challenge approach on which this whole book is based. This holds that leadership is defined by moving towards the challenges that face you and your colleagues, and not by moving away from them or hoping they will go away.

Each of the *14 Key Challenges* has its own chapter in the third part of this book. Each chapter provides a template for analysis and action and contains stories, cases, models and tools that will help you and your colleagues get started on these challenges. Even if your particular challenge of the moment is not listed amongst the 14, it is likely that you will find materials here that will help you move towards it. This is not a book to be read respectfully from front to back, but a guide to action. So, use it to pick and choose, to pick and mix, and to take from it whatever you want and can apply.

The 7 Core Practices

The *7 Core Practices* (Figure 1.3) are the inner challenges of leadership because they are more personal than the outer challenges. They link us as a people to any organizational challenge through the actions we take. We approach these challenges through our leadership practices – as a builder tackles the building of a house through the laying of bricks, or a doctor practises medicine in the face of illness.

The *7 Core Practices* are the core challenges because they all relate to a greater or lesser extent to all those organizational challenges in the outer zone. It is difficult to think of a significant challenge that will not, for example, require you to ask challenging questions or to use your power wisely. The seven chapters contain stories, models, ideas and strengthening *activities* for the development of your leadership practice. They are development challenges in themselves.

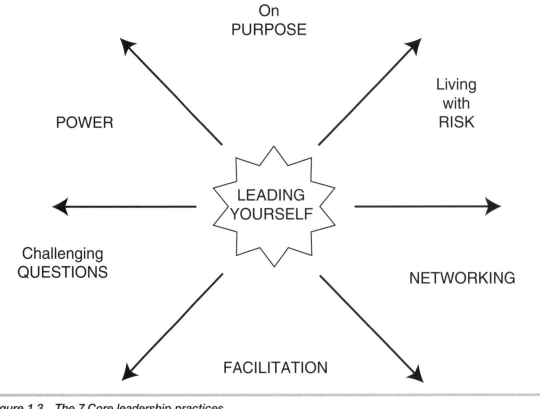

Figure 1.3   The 7 Core leadership practices

Your leadership practice

The word *practice* has important implications that make it a much better concept for thinking about leadership than skill or competence or personal characteristics. Practice is a 'doing' word, it is what you or I do as a leader. Because it is what I do, it is also a key part of who I am: as a teacher, plumber or financial controller, to a lesser or greater extent, I *am* my practice.

However, practice is also a connecting concept, and this is what makes it so appropriate for the idea of leadership. Practice connects the person with a wider group and to the outer challenges in the world:

■ MY practice: my personal way of working
■ OUR practice: the professional community of practice
■ THE practice: a recognized service for particular human purposes.

The next chapter is *The Leadership Prioritizer*, which will help you decide which of these challenges are most important for you. It also acts as a guide for making the best use of the rest of the book.

2

The Leadership Prioritizer

This chapter will help you take stock of the challenges in your situation and establish your priorities for action and learning. What are the challenges facing you now? And which are you likely to face in the future? How well do you understand these challenges? And which strategies can you develop to deal with them?

Sorting out the challenges to which you want to give priority will help you to make selective use of the rest of this book to extend and enhance your leadership capabilities.

How this chapter works

This chapter works 'from the outside in' and starts by asking you to review the challenges that you have faced in the past, are dealing with now and may be dealing with in the future. It is in two parts, Part A, which concerns the outer *Key Challenges*, and Part B, which covers the *Core Practices* of leadership.

After first assessing the outer challenges that you may be facing, now and in the future, the chapter goes on to help you assess the areas of practice in which you are experienced and capable and those where you could further develop your capabilities. The next step is to make your priority lists of challenges and practices in the light of your analysis. You can then use these lists to choose those parts of this book to which you want to give most attention.

Part A

Assessing your leadership challenges

In this book, we argue that leadership is situational, contextual and relational. What we mean by good leadership varies with the task or challenge and is profoundly affected by the wider context in which it is exercised. Leadership is best thought of not as individual activity based on skill and competence, but as a practice, or set of practices, carried out by and between people in work situations.

As the world is constantly changing and evolving, the leadership challenges also change, as do the practices that help meet the challenges. As individuals, we can lead ourselves and contribute to good collaborative practice in our own work situations through our own personal leadership practice. There is nothing fixed about the future, but it will, in part, be shaped by how we practice leadership with one another.

To develop your own contribution to leadership, begin with the challenges that need to be addressed in your situation. Below you will find brief descriptions of the *14 Key Leadership Challenges* featured in this book.

Work through each of these descriptions and assess:

the extent to which you face them *now*
whether you have experienced them in the *past* … and …
whether you are likely to face them more in the *future*.

Then, using the simple rating scales, make a judgment about the importance of each challenge and your abilities to deal with it.

C1: Developing direction and strategy

Historically, management arises as an intermediate function between the owner and the workers of a business. Managers were the overseers and organizers of the production process, whereas the owners continued to direct their businesses. As organizations have got bigger and ownership has become more diffuse, institutional and less personal, a role for leadership has emerged as distinct from managing. This is expressed in the need to create and find a sense of organizational direction in the form of a mission or vision for a particular context. Given the direction and the objectives, the management task is one of planning, establishing, operating and overseeing the activities needed to achieve them.

Most definitions of leadership include the core characteristic of giving direction, setting strategy or pointing the way to the future. Choosing strategic direction in a rapidly changing world whilst drawing on a deeper sense of purpose and values is a key part of this territory.

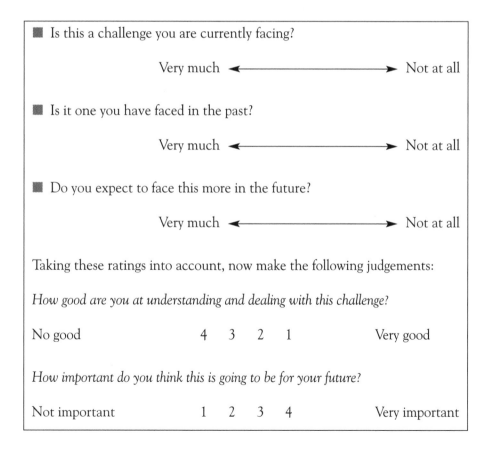

■ Is this a challenge you are currently facing?

Very much ◄——————————► Not at all

■ Is it one you have faced in the past?

Very much ◄——————————► Not at all

■ Do you expect to face this more in the future?

Very much ◄——————————► Not at all

Taking these ratings into account, now make the following judgements:

How good are you at understanding and dealing with this challenge?

No good   4   3   2   1   Very good

How important do you think this is going to be for your future?

Not important   1   2   3   4   Very important

C2: Creating a learning organization

Over recent years it has become apparent that organizations need to become capable of continuous change and learning. However, change for change's sake is not a good idea, as many changes can have undesirable or even disastrous consequences. Being a learning organization is about making the right changes continuously – both to adapt to new circumstances and to create new ones.

Much more is known now about how to do this. It involves creating learning opportunities for everyone in the organization and devising means of learning as a whole organism. Leading the learning organization means applying this understanding to specific situations. From this perspective, leadership is about creating the kinds of processes, structures, procedures, cultures and relationships that make this continuous learning possible.

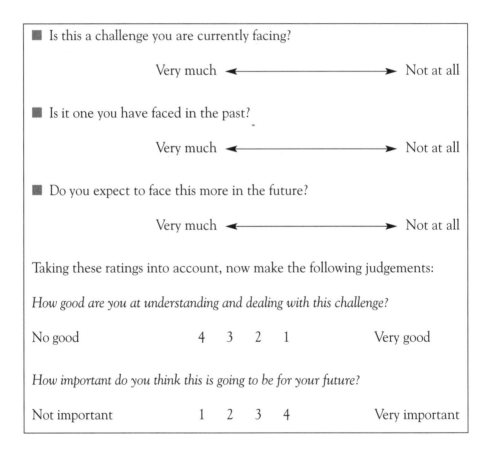

■ Is this a challenge you are currently facing?

Very much ◄————————► Not at all

■ Is it one you have faced in the past?

Very much ◄————————► Not at all

■ Do you expect to face this more in the future?

Very much ◄————————► Not at all

Taking these ratings into account, now make the following judgements:

How good are you at understanding and dealing with this challenge?

No good   4   3   2   1   Very good

How important do you think this is going to be for your future?

Not important   1   2   3   4   Very important

C3: New organizational structures

Most people in management and leadership roles these days experience more or less continuous 'restructuring' as organizations are streamlined and adapted to fit changing priorities and circumstances. We tend both to be on the receiving end of this – trying to understand and influence where (and sometimes if!) we fit into things – and also to have to work out and implement the new structures or roles and relationships for the domains for which we have responsibility.

In addition to the main organizational structure, there are usually other alternative structures stemming from various projects, partnerships and other initiatives. These project and network structures sometimes involve people across very different parts of the same organization or from a variety of agencies. Here, finding an appropriate and temporary structure is a major element of successfully doing the work.

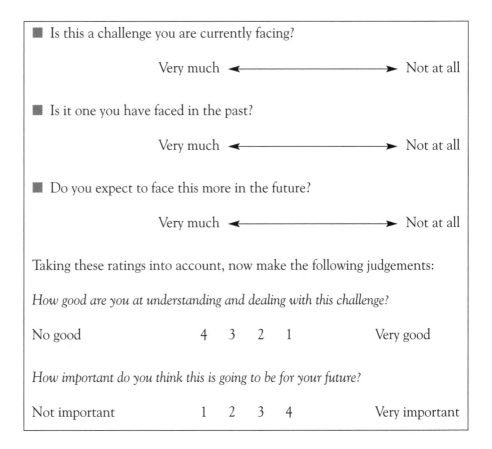

■ Is this a challenge you are currently facing?

Very much ⟵————————⟶ Not at all

■ Is it one you have faced in the past?

Very much ⟵————————⟶ Not at all

■ Do you expect to face this more in the future?

Very much ⟵————————⟶ Not at all

Taking these ratings into account, now make the following judgements:

How good are you at understanding and dealing with this challenge?

No good   4   3   2   1   Very good

How important do you think this is going to be for your future?

Not important   1   2   3   4   Very important

C4: Powerful teams

One very important aspect of leadership is about getting teams and groups to work well. Project teams are an increasingly common way of organizing work and the quality of this work depends on team performance and not just on talented individuals. Is this a high-performing team, or are they just OK or even struggling?

Increasingly, teams and project groups have complex sets of stakeholders to please rather than a single sponsor. With the trend towards autonomous and self-managing teams, it is even more vital to ensure that their activities fit with overall purposes and are co-ordinated within the shifting network of other projects and teams. Many groups and teams have irregular and floating memberships of people who come and go and who belong to a number of other teams and groups at the same time. Additionally, today's teams are often led 'remotely' and meet via a mixture of face-to-face and 'virtual' working through electronic communication.

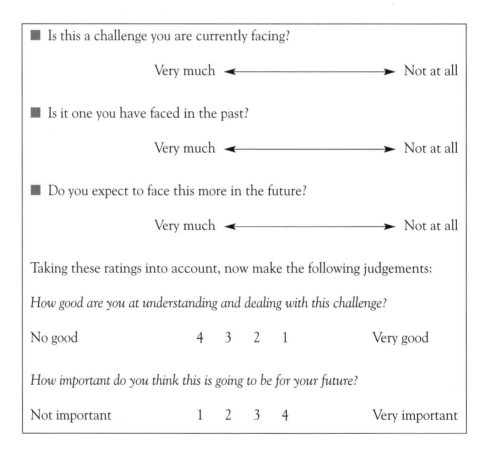

■ Is this a challenge you are currently facing?

Very much ◄—————————► Not at all

■ Is it one you have faced in the past?

Very much ◄—————————► Not at all

■ Do you expect to face this more in the future?

Very much ◄—————————► Not at all

Taking these ratings into account, now make the following judgements:

How good are you at understanding and dealing with this challenge?

No good   4   3   2   1   Very good

How important do you think this is going to be for your future?

Not important   1   2   3   4   Very important

C5: Crafting cultures of innovation

One of the main reasons for the new preoccupation with leadership is that innovation, and innovative cultures, are better achieved through leadership than management. There is considerable emphasis on innovation in contemporary organizations, both public and private sector, as the key for achieving success and effectiveness. Leading and keeping up with innovation are taken as a key factor for organizations to survive and succeed.

Leaders may well benefit from being innovative in themselves, but even more important is their ability to lead others in bringing about innovation both individually and collectively. Innovation needs both space and freedom for creativity, but also the capacity to turn individual creativity into collective creativity, and creative ideas into innovative action. An innovative 'culture' is one which provides the best conditions for these processes, and the leadership task can be seen as creating and maintaining this culture.

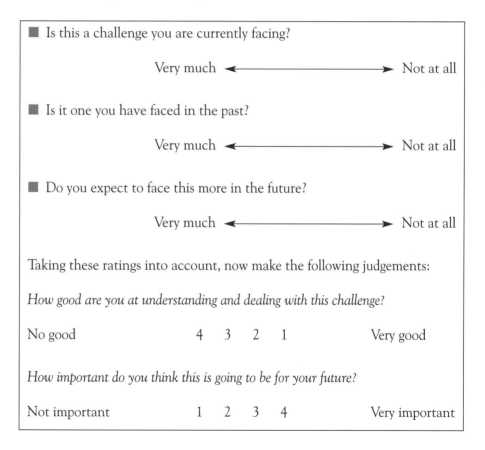

■ Is this a challenge you are currently facing?

Very much ⟵——————————⟶ Not at all

■ Is it one you have faced in the past?

Very much ⟵——————————⟶ Not at all

■ Do you expect to face this more in the future?

Very much ⟵——————————⟶ Not at all

Taking these ratings into account, now make the following judgements:

How good are you at understanding and dealing with this challenge?

No good   4   3   2   1   Very good

How important do you think this is going to be for your future?

Not important   1   2   3   4   Very important

C6: Fostering diversity and inclusion

Ashby's law holds that the internal variety of a system must match the variety present in the environment. Attending to diversity and inclusion is a growing issue for organizations. Diversity is about using and working with the different kinds of people in the population, society and the economy. This concern covers many different things and many motivations and possible actions. Gender, race, age and disability are some of the kinds of difference most often considered, but the dimensions of difference are themselves multiple and complex.

Inclusion is the related notion that those who are affected by organizational decisions should also have access to and participation in these decision-making processes. The stakeholder concept is particularly important here. The concern with diversity and inclusion is populated with ideological argument in addition to making business cases and the need to respond to new rules, laws and policies.

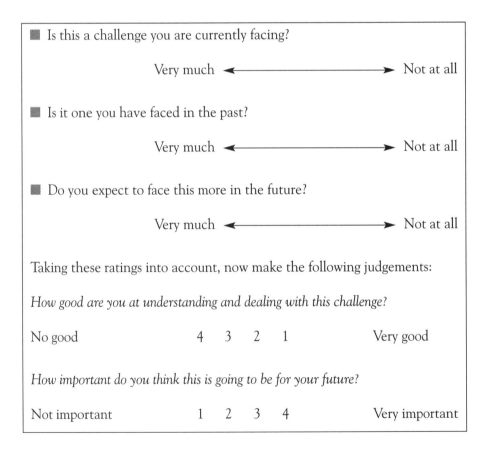

■ Is this a challenge you are currently facing?

Very much ⟵—————————⟶ Not at all

■ Is it one you have faced in the past?

Very much ⟵—————————⟶ Not at all

■ Do you expect to face this more in the future?

Very much ⟵—————————⟶ Not at all

Taking these ratings into account, now make the following judgements:

How good are you at understanding and dealing with this challenge?

No good   4   3   2   1   Very good

How important do you think this is going to be for your future?

Not important   1   2   3   4   Very important

C7: Promoting partnerships

In the current era, few organizations do it alone. Much organizational work involves working in partnerships between individuals, groups and teams and whole organizations. In the public sector, there is the call for 'joined-up government' and 'seamless services' so that the public can get an integrated service. In the private sector, more and more firms are going for niche markets, concentrating on their core business and locating themselves with other organizations in a supply chain network. Smaller businesses often supply specialist support within larger projects involving many organizations. It is increasingly recognized that industrial clusters, often geographical, are a major driver of economic growth.

All these developments create the demand for effective partnership working. Partnerships are arrangements where no party has strong control or authority over another. Working collaboratively, and through influence, understanding and negotiation are where leadership can really make a difference.

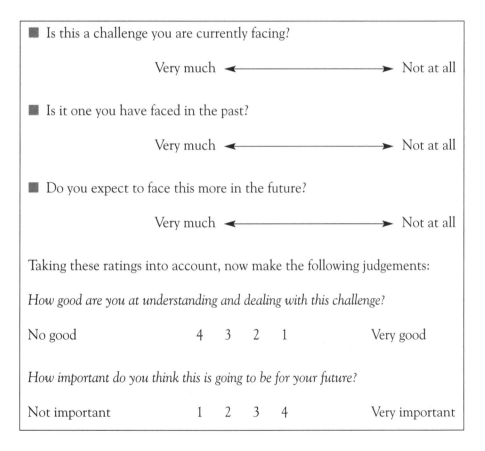

C8: Improving work processes

All contemporary organizations must improve the quality and efficiency of their services to clients, customers and users. At the same time, businesses and organizations are becoming more complex in function and configuration. Many jobs, including senior leadership, and units, can become detached or distant from the core value-creating processes of their organization.

Improving work processes involves mapping the value chain across the boundaries of organizational functions and units, assessing the constrictions and bottlenecks and then moving resources and 're-engineering' processes to speed up or improve the flow. Finding lines of influence from leadership roles to the core processes of an organization, and using them constructively, are a key challenge for leadership.

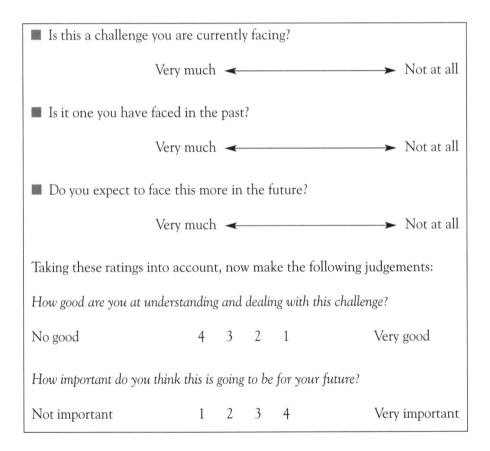

■ Is this a challenge you are currently facing?

Very much ←—————————→ Not at all

■ Is it one you have faced in the past?

Very much ←—————————→ Not at all

■ Do you expect to face this more in the future?

Very much ←—————————→ Not at all

Taking these ratings into account, now make the following judgements:

How good are you at understanding and dealing with this challenge?

No good   4   3   2   1   Very good

How important do you think this is going to be for your future?

Not important   1   2   3   4   Very important

C9: Streamlining

Development and cuts-back run together in business. Organizations seek to expand here and contract there, in whole or in parts, and often at the same time. The need for speed and competitive advantage in the private sector and the pressure of demand in the public sector mean that organizations are either expanding flat out or contracting as fast as possible to cut losses on abandoned or obsolete projects. It is like driving flat out on the accelerator or hard on the brake, with very little in between.

Leadership textbooks are better at the expansion than the contraction aspect, but if everything that goes up must come down again in the long term, contraction is an important part of the business cycle. Smoothing this process and streamlining the organization through managing development and contraction together constitute a critical and neglected leadership challenge. It is usually harder to end a project than to start one. Managing contraction and streamlining the business, helping people cope with the change involved, minimizing pain and the waste of resources and seeking creative ways of reallocating people and resources are all aspects of this important role.

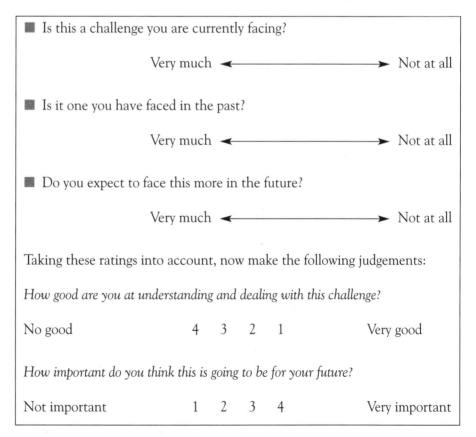

■ Is this a challenge you are currently facing?

Very much ←——————————→ Not at all

■ Is it one you have faced in the past?

Very much ←——————————→ Not at all

■ Do you expect to face this more in the future?

Very much ←——————————→ Not at all

Taking these ratings into account, now make the following judgements:

How good are you at understanding and dealing with this challenge?

No good   4   3   2   1   Very good

How important do you think this is going to be for your future?

Not important   1   2   3   4   Very important

C10: Encouraging social responsibility

In addition to the instrumental aspect of leadership, which is concerned with making things happen whatever, there is also an ethical element – working out what is 'right' and 'good', and pursuing this. The growing size and wealth of some corporations have given them a power and influence to rival elected government and the place of such organizations in society is increasingly subject to new scrutiny and critique. Generally, there is a new concern with corporate social responsibility (CSR) in an age which is more ethically, socially and environmentally aware.

Although much neglected in leadership theory and writing, social responsibility in organizational life is becoming an important element for leadership. This challenge requires corporations to define what their social responsibility actually is in specific situations, and to consider carefully the extent to which it is both a good thing in itself and also a contributor to other goals such as profitability and effectiveness.

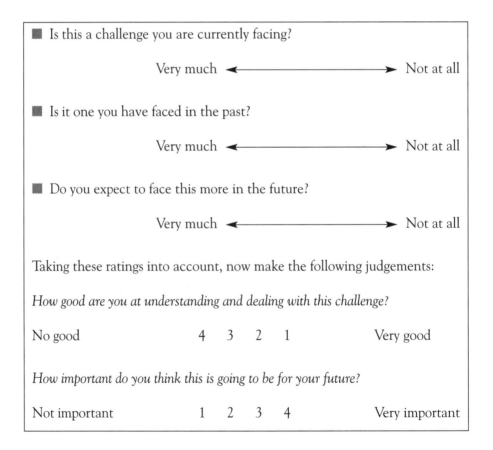

■ Is this a challenge you are currently facing?

Very much ◄——————————► Not at all

■ Is it one you have faced in the past?

Very much ◄——————————► Not at all

■ Do you expect to face this more in the future?

Very much ◄——————————► Not at all

Taking these ratings into account, now make the following judgements:

How good are you at understanding and dealing with this challenge?

No good   4   3   2   1   Very good

How important do you think this is going to be for your future?

Not important   1   2   3   4   Very important

C11: Mobilizing knowledge

Knowledge is a crucial asset and essential resource in organizational functioning. The growth of the 'knowledge economy' and the 'information era' is a trend likely to continue into the future. Under pressure to become more adaptable and innovative, firms are increasingly aware of the value of specialised know-how and also of sharing this knowledge throughout the business. Advances in computing provide some of the tools for generating learning from practice and then for sharing and spreading knowledge within the organization.

One of the new leadership challenges is to visualize the kind of knowledge system that would be useful in a particular setting or situation, and bring it into being. This is likely to include the 'hard systems' that capture, disseminate and give access to information and explicit knowledge, but also the 'soft or social systems' through which knowledge and ideas are spread and shared amongst people.

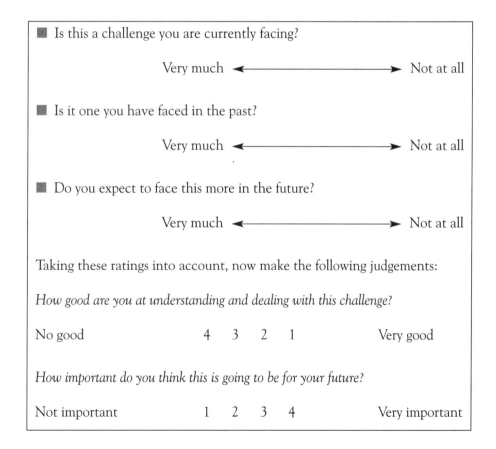

■ Is this a challenge you are currently facing?

Very much ◄————————► Not at all

■ Is it one you have faced in the past?

Very much ◄————————► Not at all

■ Do you expect to face this more in the future?

Very much ◄————————► Not at all

Taking these ratings into account, now make the following judgements:

How good are you at understanding and dealing with this challenge?

No good   4   3   2   1   Very good

How important do you think this is going to be for your future?

Not important   1   2   3   4   Very important

C12: Leading in networks

More and more work gets done by and through networks of individuals, groups or organizations. 'Networking' is both a personal activity of making, keeping and using contacts and also an organizational task of leading across networks to achieve collective work with different groups and agencies. The notion of the value chain shifts the focus from the individual company to the network of firms in a market and contemporary practices of subcontracting and partnerships reveal this interorganizational collaboration and connectedness. Networks provide the means to work outside and across the formal organizational and professional boundaries.

These practices call forth a new skills set for leadership that involve working with influence and complex patterns of power and interest. It places a premium on diplomacy, negotiation, brokering and personal networking. This calls for a certain kind of leadership that gets productive work done with particularly complex, and often changing, arrangements.

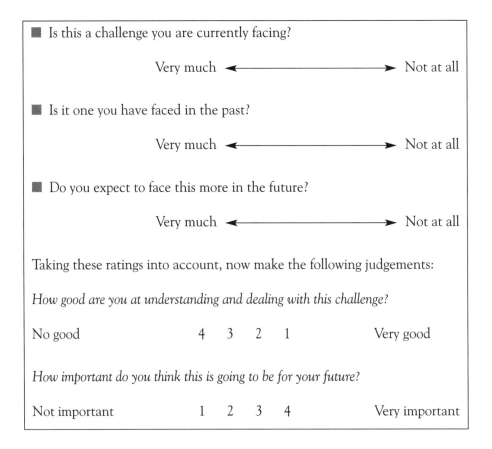

C13: Managing mergers

Bringing together separate organizations and projects into unified wholes is a new leadership art. Experience and evidence show that many mergers do not live up to the expectations and business cases for attempting them. They very often turn out to be more difficult, time consuming and expensive than they were initially expected to be.

Merger and acquisition processes tend to focus on business fit and commercial advantage and neglect the human and social 'capital' built up in these organizations. Merger processes also tend to be handed over to the rational project planners. However, pulling off the value-adding merger requires a considerable effort to involve and integrate the people who will run the new business. Bringing about mergers poses a particular leadership challenge involving a combination of logistics and project planning, together with an affinity for handling personal relationships and coping with cultural differences and sensitivities.

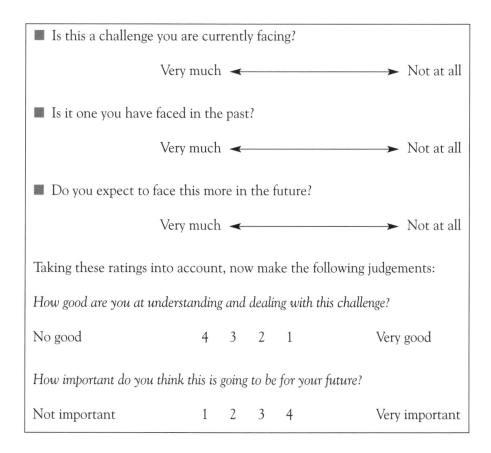

■ Is this a challenge you are currently facing?

Very much ◄——————————► Not at all

■ Is it one you have faced in the past?

Very much ◄——————————► Not at all

■ Do you expect to face this more in the future?

Very much ◄——————————► Not at all

Taking these ratings into account, now make the following judgements:

How good are you at understanding and dealing with this challenge?

No good   4   3   2   1   Very good

How important do you think this is going to be for your future?

Not important   1   2   3   4   Very important

C14: Making major change

Managing major change is a preoccupation that can take up a great deal of leadership time. Successfully handling change is a defining aspect of leadership. Change is increasingly continuous rather than one-off, and although some aspects of it can be planned, much of it is emergent. Change leadership involves dealing with situations that arise in the course of the process in addition to those which can be predicted in advance.

Major change usually involves large numbers of people, and there are usually many agendas present concerning what the change should be, what it is for and how it should be achieved. Listening to and balancing these views and concerns whilst continuing to move forward is one of the hallmarks of good leadership.

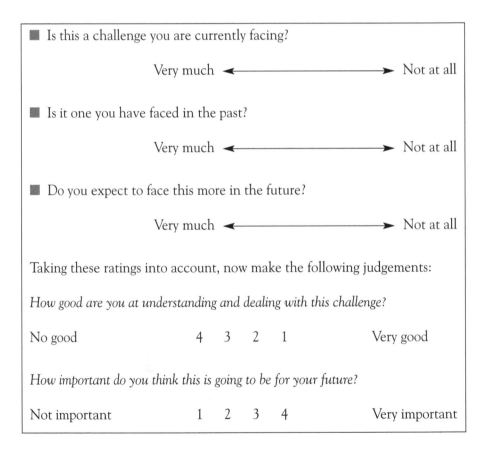

■ Is this a challenge you are currently facing?

Very much ◄————————► Not at all

■ Is it one you have faced in the past?

Very much ◄————————► Not at all

■ Do you expect to face this more in the future?

Very much ◄————————► Not at all

Taking these ratings into account, now make the following judgements:

How good are you at understanding and dealing with this challenge?

No good   4   3   2   1   Very good

How important do you think this is going to be for your future?

Not important   1   2   3   4   Very important

Prioritizing your leadership challenges

Now that you have worked through each of the *14 Key Leadership Challenges*, transfer your ratings for each of these into Table 2.1. Put your ratings of your capability with, and the importance of, each of these challenges in columns 1 and 2 and then multiply them together to give the priority ranking in column 3.

Table 2.1   Your priority leadership challenges

Challenge	Column 1: Your rating on how good you are with each one: from 4 to 1	Column 2: Your rating on how important each one will be: from 1 to 4	Column 3: Your priority for development: multiply columns 1 and 2
Developing direction and strategy			
Creating a learning organization			
New organizational structures			
Powerful teams			
Crafting cultures of innovation			
Fostering diversity and inclusion			
Promoting partnerships			
Improving work processes			
Streamlining			
Encouraging social responsibility			
Mobilizing knowledge			
Leading in networks			
Managing mergers			
Making major change			

Notes on the scoring

You will have noticed that the scoring numbers for capability and importance on each of the challenges run in opposite directions. The logic behind this is that it is the combination of your capability and the importance of the challenge that creates the priority.

If you feel that you are not good at a particular challenge (and therefore give it a 4 or a 3), and if the challenge is likely to be important (and so you give that a 3 or a 4), then multiplying these together gives an overall high score, which suggests a priority area.

If, on the other hand, you rate a challenge as less important (say as 1 or 2), then however good you are at it (1, 2, 3 or 4), this combination will produce a lower score and priority.

Having the numbers run in different directions creates a wider spread of scores than would be the case if they ran in parallel. Without this device, the scores for capability and importance would tend to cancel each other out.

To get full benefit in your personal leadership development, the higher priority scores indicate the challenges to which you might pay most attention in using this book. Of course, these are just indicators and, as with any metric that you apply to yourself or your situation, you should test these results against commonsense. Does this priority ranking make sense to you? Would your mentor or a close colleague agree with it? Use your own judgement in considering your priorities, and change them if you see a reason for so doing.

Part B

Assessing your leadership practice capabilities

Practices are those things that you are capable of doing, sometimes on your own but often with other people. You are likely to use a combination of the leadership practices when dealing with the kinds of challenges that you have already explored. When being assessed for your abilities, or being considered for a promotion or a new job, it is often your perceived capability in these practices that swings the judgement.

The first of the *7 Core Leadership Practices* chapters – *Leading Yourself* – follows as Chapter 3. It comes first and is included in Part 1 of the book because we consider it to be an essential practice and 'first amongst equals'. It serves to preface Part 2 of the book that contains the other six core practices of leadership. It is therefore excluded from this analysis.

The assessment process for the other six core leadership practices is more qualitative than for the key challenges. Because a practice is both personal and professional, both part of who you are and a recognizable service in the world, it is important to establish just what it means for you. Each of us has different interpretations of these practices – how they apply to us and how we do them – out of our own unique qualities and being.

Make notes on what each practice means to you. Next, jot down some ideas of what evidence you could give – probably on the basis of past achievements – of your ability to practise in this field. Finally, make an estimate of how good you think you are at this practice.

P2: On purpose

Being 'on purpose' is about making things happen. It involves both the will and determination to make it happen, and knowing what to do to achieve this.

Purpose is about specific goals or aims and also about a deeper and more enduring *sense of purpose* rooted in values. It is this deeper sense of purpose that makes the risks of leadership worthwhile. Leaders do things 'on purpose'.

Like all other practices, the ability to find direction and purpose can be developed and refined. It is important to find and understand your own purpose, and to develop your own practice of being on purpose. It is also important to be able to achieve common purpose with others – which can be a very different matter.

What does purpose mean to you – what is it and why does it matter?

_____

_____

_____

_____

_____

What evidence would you give, for example in a job application or interview, of

your ability to be 'on purpose'?

_____

_____

_____

_____

_____

How good do you think you are at being purposeful?

Not at all ◄——————————————————► Very good

       4   3   2   1

P3: Power

Nothing happens without the use of some power, and power comes in many forms. Power is the ability to do or to act, to get work done, to make things happen. Power can be both damaging and constructive, and using it for its beneficial effects while avoiding its destructive potential is a subtle practice.

In the context of leadership, power is social and relational; it is power with, from, over, and through other people. The unequal distribution of formal power in work organizations gives rise to the development of many alternative sources of power, which are often mobilized in more or less hidden political processes.

Wise leadership requires a knowledge of power, its sources and forms and how these may be used. Studied throughout human history, power remains a subject of endless fascination. Although highly desirable, it is a dangerous thing, associated with high risk. Yet lack of power is a problem too; powerlessness is also corrupting and makes of us victims and slaves.

What does purpose mean to you – what is it and why does it matter?

_____

_____

_____

_____

_____

What evidence would you give, for example in a job application or interview, of your ability to be 'on purpose'?

_____

_____

_____

_____

_____

How good do you think you are at being purposeful?

Not at all ⟵————————————————⟶ Very good

| 4 | 3 | 2 | 1 |

P4: Living with risk

Risk is the possibility or probability of undesirable or even catastrophic happenings. Some forms of risk are relatively objective, such as mechanical or system breakdown or failure; others are more subjective, such as risk to reputation or self-esteem. The cost, damage or pain involved in taking risk is sometimes for you and sometimes for other people. The consequences of risks may be either long term or short term, and can limit the future possibilities for action.

Leadership involves risk, because leaders must sometimes take difficult decisions on the basis of inadequate information. In this territory, it is important to become familiar with risk, its nature and its effects. The fear may never be fully overcome, but the practice of living with risk can be developed. This involves the ability to estimate and plan for risk, but also the cultivation of personal habits and approaches to taking and living with risk.

What does purpose mean to you – what is it and why does it matter?

_____

_____

_____

_____

_____

What evidence would you give, for example in a job application or interview, of your ability to be 'on purpose'?

_____

_____

_____

_____

_____

How good do you think you are at being purposeful?

Not at all ◄————————————————► Very good

      4   3   2   1

P5: Challenging questions

Questioning is the key to creativity, action and learning – it is where fresh ideas come from. Through questioning, other people's opinions and views can be drawn out, tested and brought into the decision process. Developing this practice is a critical aspect of leadership capability, because it is through challenging questions that purpose and direction are found.

The practice of asking challenging questions involves querying existing beliefs and practices in a more profound way than is usual. Astute questioning can bring out hidden assumptions and surface values and beliefs that would otherwise remain hidden. Critical questioning needs to be constructive in addition to challenging, and if this is achieved it can lead on to powerful action and learning.

What does purpose mean to you – what is it and why does it matter?

_____

_____

_____

_____

_____

What evidence would you give, for example in a job application or interview, of your ability to be 'on purpose'?

_____

_____

_____

_____

_____

How good do you think you are at being purposeful?

Not at all $\longleftarrow$ $\longrightarrow$ Very good

      4   3   2   1

P6: Facilitation

Leadership is often about getting groups or teams to work together effectively, and is usually best done by helping people to do it for themselves. Facilitation literally means making something easier, and is a subtle form of influence.

The term 'facilitator' often means someone who manages meetings, but in the context of leadership facilitation is an essential operational practice to enable people to share perceptions of what needs to be done, to co-operate on tasks and to work collaboratively rather than in isolation. Effective facilitation is measured both by enabling or empowering individuals to act and to learn and also by collective performance – by how well people work together.

What does purpose mean to you – what is it and why does it matter?

_____

_____

_____

_____

_____

What evidence would you give, for example in a job application or interview, of your ability to be 'on purpose'?

_____

_____

_____

_____

_____

How good do you think you are at being purposeful?

Not at all ◄─────────────────────────────► Very good

       4   3   2   1

P7: Networking

Networking is the key to connection power, one of the most underrated forms of power. Influence, inspiration and informal authority are exercised through networks of informal relationships inside and outside organizations and professions. These 'invisible' informal networks are a vital source of knowledge, information and energy in any organization.

Building personal networks makes it easier to contact and access relevant people when we need help to assess situations and accomplish tasks. A wide network gives the ability to cross departmental, professional and organizational boundaries to get things done. Such networks also help to create power for the others in these relationships.

Getting out more and networking is a crucial leadership practice.

What does purpose mean to you – what is it and why does it matter?

_____

_____

_____

_____

_____

What evidence would you give, for example in a job application or interview, of

your ability to be 'on purpose'?

_____

_____

_____

_____

_____

How good do you think you are at being purposeful?

Not at all $\longleftarrow$ $\longrightarrow$ Very good

| 4 | 3 | 2 | 1 |

Prioritizing your core leadership practices

What are the leadership practices that matter most for you – now and in the future?

Imagine the kind of work that you will be doing in the future. This is likely to be a combination of what you would like to be doing and what you will have the opportunity to do if you can convince others of your capability.

Imagine writing a description of the abilities and capabilities required for this work, using the six core leadership practices that you have just considered. What are the most important practices for you?

Now give each of these six core practices of leadership a ranking for importance in column 1 of Table 2.2, from 1 (low) to 4 (high). In column 2, copy in the ratings you have given yourself for capability at each practice – this time from 4 (low) to 1 (high). Multiply your column 1 and 2 scores to give a priority score for each practice in column 3. These scores give you a measure of priority, from 1 (very low) to 16 (very high).

Table 2.2 Your priority leadership practices

Core leadership practice	Column 1: Importance for future work: from 1 to 4	Column 2: How good you think you are at it: from 4 to 1	Column 3: Your priority for development: multiply columns 1 and 2
On purpose			
Power			
Living with risk			
Challenging questions			
Facilitation			
Networking			

Notes on the scoring

As before, the scoring numbers for your capability and the importance of the practice run in opposite directions. Again, the logic is that it is the combination of your capability and the likely importance of the practice that creates the priority.

This is just one way of creating a priority list. It is those practices with the higher scores that you might benefit most from concentrating on as you use this book and continue your personal development. Yet this is just one indicator. Use your judgement in considering your priorities, consult valued colleagues and friends and change them if you see a reason for so doing.

Next steps

Mark in your priority leadership challenges and practices from Tables 2.1 and 2.2 on the *21 Challenges of Leadership* map in Figure 2.1. Use this map of your priorities to decide which chapters to dig into next. All the chapters in Parts 2 and 3 of this book offer you ideas, activities and suggestions for tackling the challenges and developing your leadership practices, but it is best to choose one or two, or a few at most, to be a focus for your development. What are your three or four top priorities for development?

The final chapter in Part 1 – *Leading Yourself* – will help you to think about what is most important for you. Leading yourself means developing your personal leadership practice to deal with the emerging challenges facing you in your organization or community. Although leadership is about much, much more than your personal attributes and capabilities, leading yourself is at the heart of the matter of your leadership development. It is an appropriate place to start the rest of the book.

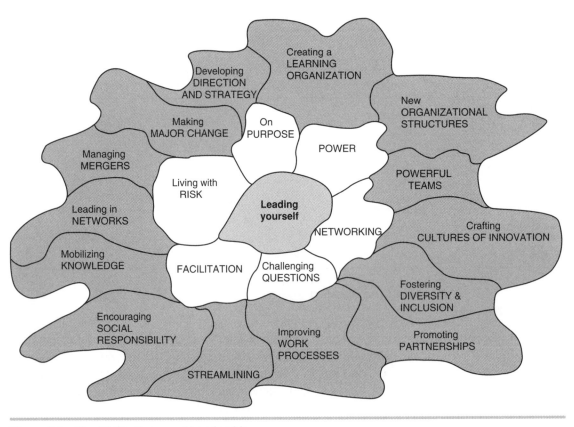

Figure 2.1   The 21 Challenges of Leadership

Practice 1: Leading Yourself

The process of becoming a leader is much the same as becoming an integrated human being
Bennis and Nanus (1997)

Introduction

Whether you are an aspiring or experienced manager, a new team member or a highly trained professional, you may be asking yourself questions such as:

- I'm good at what I do, but am I a leader?
- Leadership is clearly the future, but how can I contribute to it?
- Do I want any part in leadership?

Many people have an ambivalent attitude to leadership. We can see it is vital at certain times, and we notice when it is missing. At the same time, we have our doubts: we don't like to push ourselves forward; we don't want to become like 'them' or perhaps we have doubts about our own abilities – 'am I up to it?'

There is no one model for leadership, no single set of competencies. What you can bring to leadership depends upon who you are, the circumstances you find yourself in, with the colleagues you find there. Leadership is a deeply personal matter; you can only influence and offer it when you believe in what you are doing. What is it that you want for yourself and for other people? What you can offer depends upon who you are, what is important to you, how you see the world and how well you can learn.

This book defines leadership from the 'outside in'. We emphasize that it is the performance that counts; leadership is effective action in the face of the challenges facing organizations and communities. However, at the other end of these challenges – noticing them, choosing them, moving towards them or away from them – is the individual person in company with other fellow human beings. Some of these challenges are more personal and we call these practices – which are things that you do, usually in conjunction with other people. Practices are not the same as skills. Your own abilities, skills and qualities enable you to carry out these practices, but any leadership practice takes its specific form and importance from the collective context to which it contributes.

This chapter – the first of the *7 Core Leadership Practices* – is included in Part 1 of the book because this practice is essential and underpins the rest. However collaborative, leadership means personal commitment; the development of your practice requires 'the deployment of self' (Bennis and Nanus, 1997). Make your own choices from the other core practices, and develop other alternatives as you wish, but all leadership development is anchored in the practice of *Leading Yourself*.

You will have selected some challenges by using the *Leadership Prioritizer* in the previous chapter. By choosing a shortlist of priorities for your attention and commitment, you have already taken a first decisive step in leading yourself. This chapter adds to the *Prioritizer* data by suggesting that you seek the views and opinions of others about your leadership approach and capabilities.

In this chapter you will find:

- ideas about learning leadership and what it means to develop your leadership practice
- a do-it-yourself tool for self-awareness and feedback: 360° feedback
- further resources for exploration and developing yourself.

Learning leadership

Leading Yourself is about harnessing the transferable skills developed from working with any leadership challenge: it is about learning to fish for yourself, and not just accepting the gift of fish from others. As you develop your practice in contributing to current challenges, so you increase your abilities to face any new ones in the future. Working on and strengthening your practices will develop you as a person in your generic capability to contribute to leadership.

Learning a new leadership style

Helena fulfilled an important ambition when she was promoted to a senior management post at the age of 33. This was something she had worked for in the 12 years since leaving university. However, now that she had her top job, she experienced a new pressure to 'be corporate' that was difficult to reconcile with the informal style of leadership in which she had always prided herself. She found her boss's style unhelpful and irritating; although privately very frank, in public Graham always delivered the 'party line' without hesitation. He appeared to believe every word he said and showed no imagination or sympathy for those charged with implementing the new policies. Helena found this unacceptable as a model for her own behaviour, and she struggled to find a way of remaining true to her own values whilst being properly corporate.

Learning leadership involves adapting to new roles, tackling demanding tasks and using power in organizations; and it also means learning a lot about yourself. Helena needs to know who she is and to understand her values and purposes. She needs to know what she is good at and less good at, and how she can get better. It would help a lot if she knew how other people see her. How is she seen to be doing the job, say, compared with Graham? In order to lead in the way that she wants, she needs to know how to learn.

No one ever becomes a leadership expert, except in books, but everyone can improve their practice. The idea of *practice*, as discussed in Chapter 2, means that learning and improving are an integral part of working. This can only happen if you reflect on your practice. Like any other practice, learning leadership is a process of adaptation and improvisation on the basis of ongoing assessment: how did that sound?; where did that behaviour come from? Knowing yourself, listening to yourself, observing and listening to others, knowing enough about our own biases and preferences to make a balanced judgement are all vital on the practice front line. Reflective practice rests on the idea of 'using oneself as data' (Heifetz, 1994, p. 271).

Where should you look in using yourself as data? There are all sorts of possible directions for your personal and professional development. Here are just a few of the areas for exploration that may be useful in your leadership development:

- How you learn – your learning style, habits and preferences.
- Your purposes and values.
- Your personal preferences and constructs – your ways of seeing and interpreting the world.
- Self-awareness and how others see you.
- Looking after yourself – your health, fitness, work/life balance and emotional resilience.
- Managing your career and reputation.
- Deepening your leadership practice – the three levels of leadership: as doing things well, as doing things better and as doing better things.
- Exploring your understanding the wider world of social and economic trends.

You may already be familiar with some or all of these ways of looking at yourself and leadership. This depends largely upon the opportunities you have had for your own personal development thus far. If you are not familiar with any of these areas for personal exploration, some sources for development are listed for each of them in the Further resources section at the end of this chapter.

The next part of the chapter looks at a most important sources of data for *Leading Yourself* – how other people see you and your leadership. Getting this precious view may influence and complement the choices made in the previous chapter.

360° Feedback: with a little help from your friends...

The *Leadership Prioritizer* creates a shortlist of priorities for your leadership development based on which challenges you think are most important for you now and in the future. However, this is just your view; what do others think? If they were asked, what would those close to you say should be the things you should try to improve and develop?

The 360° Feedback activity is a process for eliciting feedback from a range of sources – colleagues, managers, your own staff, customers and clients. Done well, this generates views on your approach and performance from all angles. A simple questionnaire is sent out to a range of people who are asked to respond to certain questions. To protect the informants, the feedback forms are often sent anonymously to a third party, for example a Human Resources person, who processes and summarizes the data.

However, 360° Feedback need not be so formal; it is a useful technique that you can initiate yourself. If there is reasonable trust between you and those people you plan to ask to give you feedback, it does not need to be anonymous. Ask people if they are prepared to take part, then ask them to be as honest as they can be. If they are prepared to put their names to constructive advice then this creates the possibility for later and fruitful conversations in greater depth.

For leadership purposes, 360° Feedback is a more appropriate way of getting feedback than normal appraisal systems. It is less hierarchical, less connected to organizational control systems and much more appropriate to flatter structures and teamworking situations. In our DIY version, it is also self-managed, and you are much more likely to take advice when you have initiated and controlled the process than when you are subjected to it by others.

Activity: DIY 360° Feedback

1 First choose a range of people to ask to take part in this feedback activity. Choose people who interact with you from different perspectives, for example, your boss, someone who works for you, a colleague, a client, a business partner. You can include friends or family if you think this is appropriate. About six people is a good number.

2 Having chosen your people, ask each of them if they are willing to take part in a 360° Feedback activity to help you improve your leadership capabilities and performance.

3 Next send a simple questionnaire to the willing respondents and ask them to return it to you by a given date – say, by the end of the week.

The questionnaire can be based on any measures that you think are important. What are the aspects of leadership against which you would like to be rated?

You could brainstorm your own criteria with a colleague or two or ask around your professional network for possible criteria and formats. Alternatively, perhaps your organization has a model of leadership that is used to select and develop people?

When you have decided on your criteria, you need to format them into a questionnaire. There follows a sample questionnaire based on the criteria of the *7 Core Leadership Practices* as used in this book.

Dear Colleague

Please fill out this questionnaire on my leadership capabilities. The purpose of this is to help me improve in my performance, so please be as honest as you feel able to be in answering the questions. In return, I promise not to be thin-skinned. Your replies will be confidential to me and, with your permission, I may want to discuss them with you at a later date.

Please return this form to me by _____ (Date)
Many thanks for your help in this.
_____(Your name)

Scoring and analysing the feedback

Questionnaire Part A

Please rate me as you experience me on the following seven aspects of leadership.

1. *Leading Myself: my general ability in self-leadership, self-initiating and learning*
   How good am I at this?

   No good   1 2 3 4 5 6 7   Very good

   How important do you think this is for me in my leadership?

   Not important   1 2 3 4 5 6 7   Very important

2. *On Purpose: my ability to be focused and purposeful; to pursue goals but with a deeper sense of purpose and direction*
   How good am I at this?

   No good   1 2 3 4 5 6 7   Very good

   How important do you think this is for me in my leadership?

   Not important   1 2 3 4 5 6 7   Very important

3. *Power: my ability to use power in all its forms and in a positive way so that other people are not oppressed or victimized*
   How good am I at this?

   No good   1 2 3 4 5 6 7   Very good

   How important do you think this is for me in my leadership?

   Not important   1 2 3 4 5 6 7   Very important

4. *Living with Risk: my ability to estimate, manage and take appropriate risks to achieve important purposes*
   How good am I at this?

   No good   1 2 3 4 5 6 7   Very good

   How important do you think this is for me in my leadership?

   Not important   1 2 3 4 5 6 7   Very important

5. *Challenging Questions: my ability to ask good and critical questions which surface underlying issues and lead to creative outcomes*
   How good am I at this?

   No good   1 2 3 4 5 6 7   Very good

   How important do you think this is for me in my leadership?

   Not important   1 2 3 4 5 6 7   Very important

6. *Facilitation: my ability to help other people to get their work done – individually and in groups*
   How good am I at this?

   No good   1 2 3 4 5 6 7   Very good

   How important do you think this is for me in my leadership?

   Not important   1 2 3 4 5 6 7   Very important

7. *Networking: my ability to connect with other people to get access to information, resources and potential allies*
   How good am I at this?

   No good   1 2 3 4 5 6 7   Very good

   How important do you think this is for me in my leadership?

   Not important   1 2 3 4 5 6 7   Very important

Questionnaire Part B

Please complete the three sentences below:

(i) In your relationship with me, I find the following things that you do to be very helpful, so please continue to …

(ii) However, I would prefer it if you stopped or did less of …

(iii) And it would be good for me if you could start or do more of …

That's it. Thanks for this. Please send this form back to me at: _____ (*Address*)

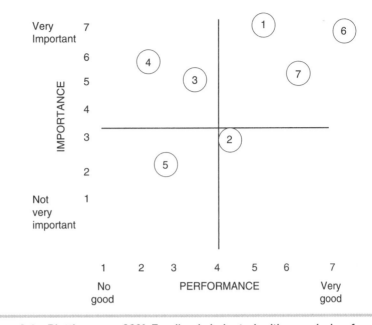

Figure 3.1 Plotting your 360° Feedback (adapted with permission from Boydell and Leary, 2004, p. 182)

When you receive the questionnaires back, they are likely to contain much useful information.

You can plot the scores from Part A on the grid shown in Figure 3.1

In the worked example given in Figure 3.1, the ratings from all respondents have been combined to give an overall score which combines importance and capability. In this example, the person being rated is seen as being very good at the important practices of *Leading Yourself, Facilitation* and *Networking* but much less good at the practices of *Power* and *Living with Risk* that are equally important for them at this time. These last two might therefore be the prime candidates for development for this person.

The more qualitative data from Part B cannot be analysed in the same way, but might provide the basis not only for some deeper insights into your leadership performance but also for improving your service to, and your relationships with, your respondents.

What are the three most critical insights to come from your 360° Feedback?

1

2

3

My leadership resolutions

Many leadership development programmes ask you to write a Personal Development Plan (PDP) with objectives and targets.

There are several formats for PDPs and there may be a standard one used in your organization. PDPs take the form of (i) identifying development needs, (ii) listing the activities, means and resources for meeting this needs and (iii) specifying targets – dates and/or performance standards – for review and evaluation, often with a mentor or other suitable person. If you do not have a ready-made PDP format to hand and you would like to have one, just use the recipe in three-column version shown in Table 3.1 to create your own.

We have some reservations about PDPs. They can become quite mechanical and concerned with box filling and ticking. They also depend a great deal on the person doing the reviewing and their motives. They can become a tool for performance management rather than for personal development. For example, in some professions, when people have been judged deficient in some aspects of their work, a PDP is often one of the required outcomes.

If you do not want a PDP, but do want to develop yourself and your leadership practice, then write instead some Leadership Resolutions. A leadership resolution (see Box 3.1) is *a statement of intent in the face of a challenge*, for example:

> I resolve to improve my use of power with my colleagues by being less timid and more assertive

or

> I resolve to get involved in the forthcoming merger of my department by volunteering to be part of the working party, with a view to learning about leadership in change management situations.

What are your resolutions for your own practice of leadership? In what directions do you want to develop and improve? What are the important challenges for you and how will you develop the strategies to deal with them? Do not create a long shopping list. Three or four of these leadership resolutions at any one time are plenty. When you have made your list, put it in your right-hand drawer where you will see it every time you look for your stapler or pen.

Better still, stick it above your desk, headed with a bold 'I RESOLVE...'. In this way you will invite discussion with those with whom you work. Who knows – it might help you recruit allies, or bring you useful feedback – and it may well contribute to the personal leadership development of others.

Table 3.1   Format for a personal development plan

Development need	How will this need be met?	Success criteria: how will I know when this has been achieved?	Target date
1.			
2.			
3.			
4.			
etc.			

Box 3.1   My leadership resolutions

My Leadership Resolutions

I RESOLVE…

These are my Leadership Resolutions. They are my statements of intent in the face of the challenges I see around me. Their purpose is to help me contribute to leadership around here and to develop my leadership practice.

I resolve to…

Signed: *Date:*

Conclusion

Leading Yourself means adopting a learning attitude to everything. For every action you take, you wonder what you will learn from it; from everything you see happening, you ask what lessons can be learnt; for every person you encounter, you consider what you can learn from them; for every problem or opportunity you meet, you think: how can I learn to do this better?

As the first of the seven *Core Leadership Practices*, *Leading Yourself* involves three interrelated strands:

- developing your leadership practice – by seeking out and contributing in challenge situations
- managing your own learning – by finding time, space and good companions to reflect on your actions and improve your capabilities
- knowing your own values – and relating these to the values of the other people involved in complex organizational challenges.

Without the first of these you will not be doing leadership at all; without the second you will not learn from what you do; and without the third, you will lack conviction when it really matters.

The suggestions for generating feedback and information about your approach and performance to leadership situations in this chapter will add to the priorities that have already emerged for you from the *Leadership Prioritizer* in Chapter 2. The next part of this book focuses on the other six *Core Leadership Practices* and these will also help you with your practice development requirements. If, as a result of working through this first part of this book, you have other needs and ideas about what you need to develop as leadership practices, use the generic framework of these chapters to devise your own plan for leadership practice development.

Adopting new leadership styles

A senior civil servant decided on a new personal leadership style for the final stage of his career. He has more or less stopped going to meetings or reading Email attachments. He has decided that he will only write six papers this year, and then of not more than two sides long, and that he will only wear a tie on 10 occasions. These are not just fancy gestures but part of what he calls 'undoing the hierarchy'.

How does he do this? 'By having constant conversations with people, by introducing people to other people, by finding out what people are doing and then trying to support them in what they are doing, by saying "we" and not "I".' He describes taking a new administrative secretary to an important meeting with ministers: 'I took her partly because I wanted to get to know her and the long train journey helped immeasurably with that, but also because I wanted to introduce her to people – people who are important in getting this work done. It is about giving authority away and trust and letting go and all that, but it is not about dumping it on people.'

Leading Yourself is a life-long preoccupation with personal and professional development. Why not start now?

Further resources

This aspect of leadership development is rich in resources. Below are some starting places for each of the eight areas for exploration listed earlier.

How you learn – your learning style, habits and preferences. Honey and Mumford have developed inventories for checking out your learning style based on David Kolb's learning cycle of Experience, Reflection, Ideas and Action. Peter Honey's website is *www.peterhoney.co.uk*.

Your purposes and values. The next chapter of this book, *On Purpose*, is devoted to this theme and also contains further resources on these aspects.

Your personal preferences and constructs – your ways of seeing and interpreting the world. Much of the work in this area stems from Carl Jung's theories of personality and George Kelly's Personal Construct Psychology (PCP). Of the many psychometric questionnaires and development activities available, one of the most widely used is Myers Briggs Type Indicator (MBTI) based on Jung's theories. This is only available to licensed practitioners but there are likely to be one or more of these in your organization. Jenny Rogers' *Sixteen Personality Types at Work in Organizations* (Management Futures, London, 1997) provides an excellent summary of the MBTI approach. Alternatively, you can get a do-it-yourself version via the Kiersey Temperaments Sorter from David Keirsey, *Please Understand Me II: Temperaments, Character, Intelligence* Prometheus Nemesis (Del Mar, CA, 1998), or at the URL *www.keirsey.com*. Sources on PCP are harder to find: *Tom Ravenette: Selected Papers – Personal Construct Psychology and the Practice of an Educational Psychologist* (EPCA Publications, Farnborough, 1997) is a good introduction.

Self-awareness and how others see you. Both MBTI and PCP work will help here together with the 360° feedback activity given in this chapter. See also Pedler and Boydell's *Managing Yourself*, mentioned below.

Looking after yourself – your health, fitness, work/life balance and emotional resilience. Mike Pedler and Tom Boydell's *Managing Yourself* (Lemos and Crane, London, 1999) will help with all these and generally with taking charge of yourself. A self-development group or a mentor is also indicated here – and for most of these areas for development. This is because many aspects of self-development are assisted by on-going support over time and are unlikely to be achieved by one-off efforts.

Managing your career and reputation. Managing your career involves understanding how organizations handle succession and development as well as your own aspirations. John Burgoyne's *Developing Yourself, Your Career and Your Organisation* (Lemos and Crane, London, 1999) will help you with all these aspects. These are also proper questions for your Human Resource Development department or adviser.

Deepening your leadership practice – the three levels of leadership. This is a whole theory of leadership in itself, and about learning at each of these three levels. It is available as an E-book, called *Doing Things Well, Doing Things Better, Doing Better Things* from Tom Boydell, who can be contacted at *tboydell@inter-logics.net*.

Exploring your understanding the wider world of social and economic trends. This can be pursued by cultivating reading, study and research habits. Taking one of the 'broadsheet' newspapers or the magazines specializing in such affairs is a good start. Searching on-line is a very good way of accessing this sort of information, which is often very specific to markets, industries or areas of concern. For example, an Amazon search under 'Trends' produces almost 6000 references ranging from Music and Asian Markets to British Social Trends.

References

Attwood, M., M. Pedler, S. Pritchard and W. Wilkinson (2003) *Leading Change: a guide to Whole Systems Working*, Policy Press, Bristol.

Bennis, W. and B. Nanus (1997) *Leaders: Strategies for Taking Change*, 2nd edn, Harper Business, New York.

Boydell, T. and M. Leary (2004) *Identifying Training Needs*, 2nd edn, Institute of Personnel and Development, London in press.

Heifetz, R. (1994) *Leadership Without Easy Answers*, Belknap Press, Cambridge, MA.

Part 2

Core Leadership Practices

Practice 2: On Purpose

4

... the first task of a leader is to define reality – that's another way of talking about purpose and direction ...
Bennis and Nanus (1997)

Introduction

Being clear about purpose lies at the heart of leadership. This is not merely about identifying a set of specific goals or aims – it is about a deeper and more enduring *sense of purpose*. This more profound sense of direction is rooted in what we value, and it is what makes the risks of leadership possible and worthwhile. Leaders do things 'on purpose'.

A sense of purpose runs deeper than the popular notion of vision. It builds on the foundation of established values and thereby honours the past in looking to future aspirations. A key element in purpose is the sheer force of will, the determination and persistence without which visions are mere dreams. A sense of purpose reminds us what we are for in addition to what we are against. Leadership is a performance art, demonstrated in facing up to and tackling the tough challenges. But without clarity of purpose – about what I/we are really here for – action can be chancy or erratic, driven by short-term, or even random, influences.

Finding direction and purpose is, therefore, one of the core practices of leadership and, like all other practices, it can be developed and refined. This chapter will help you find and understand your own purpose, and to develop your own practice of being 'on purpose'. In turn, this will help you contribute to leadership in challenging situations by achieving common purpose with others. This chapter addresses three related questions:

- What is a sense of purpose?
- How do I find my sense of purpose?
- How can I create common purpose with others?

It offers ideas and practical activities to help you and your colleagues get 'on purpose'.

What is purpose?

Over many years of consulting, David Casey, the international consultant and writer, has made the question of purpose central to his practice (Casey, 1993):

> *The speed of arriving at the answer to the question 'What is this group for?' varies enormously. Sometimes the answer is clear, universally agreed and forthcoming. Other times it is extremely obscure – every member of the group offering a different answer to the question and in the end the role of the group appears to be anything and everything from information exchange, decision-making, mutual support, strategy formulation, social chit-chat, monitoring performance, exacting revenge and nurturing habits, to providing a platform for the chief executive to ride his favourite hobby horse. In one organization I got on their nerves by persistently asking the question 'What is this group for?' over a period of nearly 8 months.*

Leadership creates meaning through connecting with purpose, and this is often as much about reconnecting with what is important as much as establishing new purpose. Purpose has three aspects:

- *The sense of purpose* that is the deep pulse within, the internal compass. It combines the elements of what are sometimes called mission and vision with the force of core values. It is closely connected with identity and underlies the will: what am I here for?; what is our work?
- *Direction* is the immediate intention, aim or goal, the desired objective in this situation. It embodies the desired vision for the future in specific circumstances. Direction gives point to purpose in particular situations: what do we intend to do?; what is the goal here?
- *Will* is the drive, determination, energy and effort to make things happen. It is the force that translates impulses and directions into practice. This element of purpose is often neglected in discussions of leadership that emphasise mission, vision or values but miss the importance of power, force and determination.

Goals alone are not enough. We live in an era when both organizations and governments are obsessed by target setting as a means of motivation and sometimes, especially in complex and confusing circumstances, it can be difficult to keep in touch with this deeper sense of purpose. The feeling becomes 'I know what the goal is, but what am I here for?' or, in the worst cases, 'I know what the goal is, but does it not conflict with what we are here for?'. It is important to hold on to the fundamental purpose of the work.

Finding a sense of purpose

This involves:

- finding your own sense of purpose
- working with other people – in groups, organizations and communities – to find common purpose.

Good leadership also involves meeting the purposes of others, often by bringing people with a common purpose together. In the fullest case then, a sense of purpose is:

For me, for us, for them.

Although we can work with other people's purposes without being aware of our own – indeed this might be one way of discovering your own sense of purpose – understanding *my* purpose is an essential part of doing things 'on purpose'.

Connecting with a sense of purpose

The quest for higher purpose is lifelong. As a core part of who we are, this impulse is often elusive, sometimes absent, at other times overwhelming, but in a way is always with us. Locating it in the midst of trying circumstances can be difficult.

A simple but effective activity, based on Personal Construct Theory, can put us in touch with our sense of purpose. George Kelly's Personal Construct Psychology (PCP) holds that each of us construes or understands the world via a set of unique personal constructs. Kelly took a 'critical realist' view that there is a real world out there, but that each of us perceives only certain aspects of that reality, and moreover perceives them differently, depending upon the constructs held. He devised several useful tools for illustrating his theory, one of which – laddering – helps locate the higher purpose in any situation.

Activity: my sense of purpose

This activity can be done alone but is better when two people do it together. In a pair, the person seeking to locate their sense of purpose can concentrate on responding and on recording their responses to the questions. The other person can help by asking the questions and keeping the process going until the possibilities have been exhausted. A skilled helper will vary the wording of the questions to match the nature of the responses, but their essential character remains the same.

Start this activity by eliciting a *personal construct* from three apparently mundane subjects, perhaps three people you know, or three items of your clothing. Personal constructs are bipolar in form, as in warm–remote, but are not simple opposites. Constructs may be described by single words or by short phrases, e.g. 'comfortable to wear'–'restricting'.

To help with this activity, a worked example is given below.

Kath's sense of purpose

[Kath's responses to the questions are in italics.]

Look at three pieces of furniture in the room.

   OK – curtains, rocking chair and table.

Name one way in which two are the same and one is different.

   Two of these are mobile; one is static.

Now, which do you prefer: mobile or static?

   Mobile.

So, what is it that is important about being mobile for you?

   More potential.

And, what for you is the opposite of more potential?

   Stuckness.

So, which of these two do you prefer: more potential or stuckness?

   More potential.

And what is it that is important for you about more potential?

   Because it is about hope and possibility.

And what for you is the opposite of hope and possibility?

   Despair.

That sounds like it – do you agree?

   Yes: this is me – I am always looking for hope and possibility.

You can tell when the sequence is finished when you begin to repeat words or synonyms and when there does not seem anywhere else to go. The effect of this process is to move you remarkably quickly from the concrete particulars of any situation to your personal core constructs and values. The effect of the laddering activity is to put you back in touch with what is important to you. In this example, Kath goes very quickly from inanimate objects to personal values. Some people may need to persevere longer than this.

In this simple personal example, Kath has clearly found a touchstone, something that can guide her in the situation she faces. Tackling the challenge will still not be easy of course, but she knows what she is for and what she wants to bring about. Now try it yourself, perhaps keeping in mind a current leadership challenge facing you: what are you trying to bring about here?

Eliciting a personal construct

1 Choose any three things or people that you know.
2 Describe a way in which two of these are the same and one is different.

Now you have a personal construct that can be used as the basis for the laddering activity. Work carefully though the questions below, writing down your responses to each before moving on.

Laddering questions

3 Which of these two words do you prefer?
4 What is it that is important for you about the preferred word?
5 And what for you is the opposite of that preferred word?
6 Then, which of these two words do you prefer?
7 Now, what is it that is important for you about the preferred word?

Continue to repeat the sequence as long as new material keeps emerging. This involves the repetition of the three questions:

- What for you is the *opposite* of that preferred word?
- Then, which of these two words do you *prefer*?
- Now, what is it that is *important* for you about the preferred word?

And so on.

Being committed

The power of commitment and will comes from this sense of being 'on purpose'. In many situations there is a need to align with and come together with other people in a collective will and purpose and this crucial leadership task is discussed later in this chapter. The laddering process will help you to understand and be in touch with your sense of purpose. You can use it with other people to help them think more deeply about their purpose in leading in any situation. Being 'on purpose' makes it clear what you are aiming to bring about in the world, and leadership implies such choices and commitments: which side are you on?; what do you stand for?; what is your work?; to what are you committed?

Keeping options open in the face of adaptive challenges and actually procrastinating can *look* like the same thing, but the difference is in how it *feels*. If a person is taking true responsibility for holding a question open, rather than just putting off the decision, they will experience the tension in that situation. It might be a huge relief just to drop it, but will this lead to acting in a way that is on purpose for them?

Acting on purpose

Brick laying

There was a traveller who, on arriving in a small town and coming across some bricklayers working on-site, asked each of them what he was doing:

> 'Laying bricks', said the first.
> 'Building a wall', said the second.
> 'Creating a cathedral', said the third.

But a fourth, who was working a little way off, said, 'serving God'.

This fable is a reminder of the different ways of interpreting purpose. The four bricklayers create a hierarchy of purpose, from the mundane to the sublime, from the notion of purpose as a target or goal to the deeper sense of purpose that provides the moral compass. Laying bricks only serves as a narrow purpose in this situation where there are bricks and mortar to hand; serving God can act as a direction finder in all aspects of life. To get an idea of your sense of purpose, try the following activity.

Activity: my purpose

1 Think of a recent experience in which you have been involved and influential. This could be a project at work where you have achieved some good results, or it could be a party or a trip that you organized.

   Now, thinking of your sense of purpose in that experience, consider the hierarchy in Table 4.1. Put an × in the third column of the hierarchy to represent the level at which you believe you were operating. To do this, you may need to translate bricks, wall, cathedral and God into your own situation – perhaps as follows:

   ■ personal 'brownie points'
   ■ good teamwork
   ■ enhancing the company's reputation
   ■ contributing to the wider society.

   Whatever labels you choose, the underlying hierarchy remains – we always have this choice of purpose.

2 Looking at where you have put your ×, and thinking generally about what motivates you, consider the following questions:

   ■ Would you say that the position marked is typical of you or not?
   ■ Does your sense of purpose move up and down the hierarchy depending on the particular situation or would you say that it was usually at this level?

Table 4.1 A hierarchy of purpose

Fable	Your translation	Your level of operation
Bricks		
Wall		
Cathedral		
God		

Most of us have multiple purposes – both lower, more specific ones, and higher, much broader ones. It is this higher sense of purpose that sustains us in complex and difficult leadership situations and over the longer run.

The how–why ladder

The hierarchy of purpose in Table 4.1 can be seen as a sort of ladder, and there are two types of questions that can be asked about any situation which move us up and down this ladder (Figure 4.1). First, there are 'how' questions, such as:

- How can I resolve this problem?
- How can I get help with this?
- How can I fit this into my busy schedule?

take us up the hierarchy or ladder, to a concern with action and implementation. Because most of us are employed to do things and to be active, we are culturally inclined to ask these 'how' questions. However, it is the 'why' questions that connect us to our deeper sense of purpose:

- Why should I resolve this problem?
- Why would anyone want to help me with this?
- Why should I change my busy schedule to focus on this?

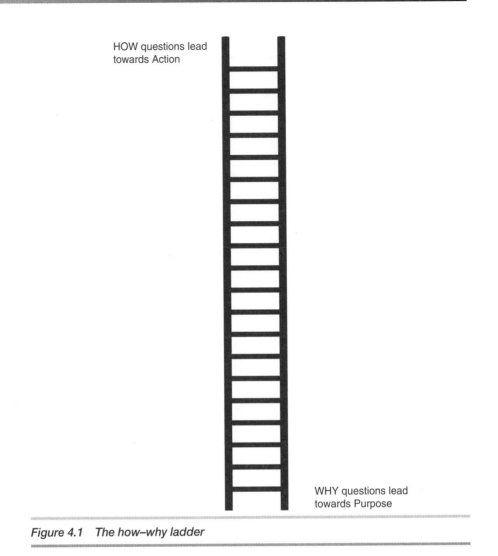

HOW questions lead
towards Action

WHY questions lead
towards Purpose

Figure 4.1   The how–why ladder

The rephrasing in these questions changes the whole direction of inquiry, taking us down the ladder to the bigger issues. These are the leadership questions.

It is often difficult to keep asking the 'why' questions in organizational situations. The pressure is always on to decide quickly and act without hesitation, which can result in behaviour of the 'ready, fire, aim' variety. In such situations it is especially important to be aware of the compass of higher purpose, for this is the key not just to good leadership but also to learning how to act differently.

Learning and purpose

The impulse is core to identity, an important part of who we are. Higher purpose emerges in response to such questions as:

- Am I doing my work?
- Am I doing the work I should be doing?
- What am I here for on this Earth?

Such questions are not easy to answer. This is partly because they present us with difficult moral choices about what to do and how to behave.

It's not cricket

As this is being written, there is an argument about whether English cricketers should play in Zimbabwe where the current government is seen as in breach of human rights conventions. In such circumstances, it is relatively easy to take a 'bricks' line and say 'I'm just here to play cricket. Politics have nothing to do with it'. Yet, for others, things are not so simple – they want to play cricket but also understand that their actions can be taken as supporting an undesirable government. How should they act?

In life it is often easier to take the 'laying bricks' line – but where is the leadership in that? Sometimes, by staying with the difficulty and confusion, we retain integrity as moral actors and keep the decision open. Leadership involves posing the difficult questions, or recognizing those questions which should remain open because they present challenges that need to be faced. These are the 'adaptive challenges' that Heifetz (1994, p. 2) makes the prime responsibility of leadership:

> … *Leadership that will challenges us to face problems for which there are no simple, painless solutions – problems that require us to learn new ways.*

There are plenty of these around us, from uncompetitive, inefficient or corrupt businesses to the endless problems of public health and welfare such as poverty, housing, drugs and child abuse. Tackling problems such as these demands not just novel solutions but changes in our own attitudes and behaviour. In short, such leadership requires us to question our own positions, reassess current practice and learn new ways. In facing up to and tackling the adaptive challenges in our situations, leadership and learning are never far apart.

Creating common purpose with others

> *The opposite of purpose is aimless drifting. But it can't be any old purpose that will animate, galvanize and energize the people. It has to have resonance, meaning …. Without a sense of alignment behind that common purpose, the company is in trouble.*
>
> (Bennis and Nanus, 1997)

The question of commitment is thrown into the sharpest relief when working with others on a common purpose. Common purpose is central to that close cousin of leadership – organizing. In this book, we talk less about leaders, who, after all, may have misled us as often as they have served us, and more about leadership as connecting with common purpose.

Common purpose is found in relationship and in a dialogue of those concerned. Individual purpose is as vital as ever, but individualism is increasingly dysfunctional in a connected and interactive era. As Hilaire Belloc said:

> *Decisive action in the hour of need*
> *Denotes the hero, but does not succeed!*

In the face of the challenges now coming our way, we need not so much heroic leaders as a more collective effort at leadership. The importance of 'collaborative advantage' (Kanter, 1989) is obvious when we see how clever and capable individuals can produce appalling inefficiency and incompetence through poor teamwork. This collective incompetence is no longer acceptable in our hospitals, government and businesses. However, the more compelling reason for a relational view of leadership is the need to share ideas, knowledge and learning as the basis of wealth and welfare creation. In a knowledge-based era, this sharing is badly done in hierarchies and best done in communities of peers.

The next activity will help with establishing a common sense of purpose in a community.

Activity: mine; ours and theirs

This activity (Table 4.2) uses the same hierarchy of purpose as in Table 4.1, but now with different columns.

1 Think of a current project in which you are involved. This could be a work project or one involving friends or family.

2 Thinking of your own sense of purpose for this project, put an ✕ in the Mine column of the hierarchy in Table 4.2 to represent the level where you wish to operate. Again, to do this, you may need to translate the terms in the hierarchy to fit this current project. In this situation what would be a good way to describe:

Table 4.2 A hierarchy of purposes

Fable	Translation	Mine	Ours	Theirs
God				
Cathedral				
Wall				
Brick				

- Bricks?
- Wall?
- Cathedral?
- Society?

3 Now, thinking of all the other people and colleagues involved with you in this project, put an × in the Ours column to represent where you think this group wishes to operate in terms of its collective sense of purpose.

4 Thinking of all those, not directly involved, who will be affected or impacted upon by the outcomes of this project, put an × in the Theirs column to represent what sense of purpose would best fit their aspirations.

5 Finally, looking at where you have put the preferences for the three different groups, consider the following questions:

- Are the various purposes clear?
- To what extent do we have common purpose?
- Are accountable are the people engaged on this project to the external stakeholders?

Conclusion

Our societies and organizations need the sort of leadership that tackles major challenges whilst being accountable to all concerned. The critical work of leadership includes welcoming the diversity of views within a community and negotiating common purpose for action and learning. Several other chapters in this book address this vital work.

The message of this chapter is: find your own sense of purpose, develop it and strengthen your practice or purpose. This is a philosophy for people who serve their purposes and not just their employers. It is important to find and build the communities that support you in your purpose, for with these others you are unlikely to achieve what you want to bring about.

We leave the question of purpose here for the moment. As a core leadership practice, it is never far away and returns whenever a key challenge appears. Practices are personal properties of individuals and simultaneously a collective means for tackling challenges in the world. Like the other core practices in this book, the practice of purpose is strengthened through action and learning; use the practice, and you will learn to do it better.

Further resources

Robert Quinn's book *Deep Change* (Jossey Bass, San Francisco, 1996) will help with the issues of working deeply with people on questions of purpose. The processes for finding common purpose amidst diversity are discussed in various chapters in this book, especially 14 (Crafting Cultures of Innovation) and 15 (Fostering Diversity and Inclusion). A book which contains useful tools and ideas for 'whole systems development' is M. Attwood, M. Pedler, S. Pritchard and D. Wilkinson's *Leading Change: a Guide to Whole Systems Working* (Policy Press, Bristol, 2003).

On the question of finding a personal sense of purpose, it is hard to know where to begin. All the great religious books that have ever been written address this issue, and their many more interpreters, such as John Bunyan with his *Pilgrim's Progress,* have guided whole generations of seekers. Those which have influenced us include Aldous Huxley's *The Perennial Philosophy* (HarperCollins, New York, 1990), Victor Frankl's *Man's Search for Meaning* (Washington Square Press, New York, 1990), Ken Wilber's *The Collected Works of Ken Wilber* (Shambhalla, Boston, 1999) and the iconoclastic *If You Meet the Bhudda on the Road: Kill Him!* Popular favourites include M. Scott Peck's *The Road Less Travelled* (Touchstone, New York, 1980), Paulo Coelho's *The Alchemist* (Harper, San Francisco, 1995) and even Pekka Himanen's *The Hacker Ethic* (Random House, New York, 2001). These books divide people: some of us find great inspiration in them, others find them meaningless or trite.

Instead of these books, why not start by asking your friends and colleagues what they are finding useful? In addition to providing you with more sources, this might get you into some very interesting conversations.

References

Bennis, W. and B. Nanus (1997) *Leaders: Strategies for Taking Charge*, 2nd edn, Harper Business, New York.

Casey, D. (1993) *Managing Learning in Organisations*, Open University Press, Milton Keynes, pp. 50–51.

Heifetz, R. (1994) *Leadership Without Easy Answers*, Belknap Press, Cambridge, MA.

Kanter, R. M. (1989) *When Giants Learn to Dance*, Simon and Schuster, New York.

5

Practice 3: Power

Powerlessness corrupts. Absolute powerlessness corrupts absolutely.
Rosabeth Kanter (1997)

Introduction

If the single word that sums up the external challenges of leadership is change, then the practice of power lies at the heart of its practice. The responsible use of power is perhaps the ultimate challenge of leadership.

Power has been written about and seriously studied through human history and remains a subject of endless fascination. We learn that it is both a highly desirable and also a dangerous thing, associated with high risks. Some of us are tempted by it and try to acquire it and monopolize it; others are wary of it and seek to deny it even when they hold positions of formal authority. Yet lack of power is worse. Powerlessness is corrupting too – it saps the will to live our lives and the ability to do our work; it makes of us victims and slaves.

> *... a monopoly on power means that only very few have this capacity, and they prevent the majority of others being able to act effectively. Thus the total amount of power – and total system effectiveness – is restricted, even though some people seem to have a lot of it.*

(Kanter, 1977, p. 166)

A core practice of leadership is to develop the total power of the organization, so that everyone who needs it has access to the tools for action:

> *... the meaning of power here is closer to 'mastery' or 'autonomy' than to domination or control over others. Empowering more people through generating more autonomy, more participation in decisions, and more access to resources increases the total capacity for effective action. The powerful are the ones who have access to tools for action.'*

(Kanter, 1977, p. 166)

Nothing gets done without power. Power is the ability to do or to act, to get work done, to make things happen. However, beyond this simple definition, power is hard to pin down; it has many aspects, effects and guises. Because it is omnipresent in human society, it is often coupled with other explanatory words:

- power and influence
- power and freedom
- power and control
- power and responsibility
- power and authority

- power and compliance
- power and resistance
- power and conflict
- power and corruption.

The first part of this short list reminds us why we want it, whereas the second part reveals the long shadow cast by power that prompts a proper wariness. Leadership should and must embrace power, but needs to do so wisely and responsibly. The aim of this chapter is to provide a starting point for that straight and narrow road.

This chapter contains:

- the power index for assessing your own sources and use of power
- a model of the sources of power in organizations
- the trap of oppressor and victim
- taking power positively
- further resources.

Power and its sources

Understanding and acknowledging the sources, uses and effects of power is a first step in this core practice of leadership. Power is a loaded term with many meanings and aspects. We associate it with 'organizational politics', which we do not like, and blame it for our misfortunes and for the failure of good ideas. Yet no good idea succeeds without the power to realize it. In the context of leadership, power is social and relational; it is power over, from, with and through other people.

In all social groups, certain types of power are unequally distributed. The deliberately unequal distribution of formal power in work organizations gives rise to particular ways in which this power is used, and also to the development of many alternative sources of power which are often mobilized in more or less hidden political processes. All of us need power in order to get things done. Wise leadership requires knowledge of the sources of power in a situation and how these may be used.

Using power

Are you a powerful person:

- in this group?
- in this company?

■ in this family?
■ in this community?

Each of the answers to these sparks off many more questions:

■ Do you have the power to make your decisions and advice stick?
■ What are the sources of this power?
■ Do you prefer to use some sorts of power rather than others?
■ Does your use of power result in an increase in the power available in the system or not?

The answers to some of these questions can be found by understanding how you use power with your work colleagues. The Power Index below will help you with this.

Activity: the Power Index

Think of a recent experience at work. Pick a particular situation to keep in mind as you answer the following questions. It could be a project you worked on over several months, or a particularly dramatic episode that sticks in your mind. It could also be a relationship that you have with some person or group of people. It does not matter which, provided that the experience is significant to you and is related to useful work outcomes.

Work through the following questions. For each question, choose one of these four options that seems to best describe your use of power in that situation:

■ little
■ sometimes
■ usually
■ always.

When you have decided which of these best describes your use of power in that situation, mark this with a ✕ in the appropriate column in Table 5.1.

Your preferred forms of power
You have now completed the Power Index on the basis of your behaviour in a recent experience, project or relationship. Now go back through the Index and think about how you would *ideally* like to act in any similar future situation. What is your preferred form of power?

To do this you need to use a different opening statement. Instead of 'In this situation, I influenced people and events by ...', use 'In future, I would prefer to influence people and events by ...' . This time, mark your choice in the appropriate column with a ✓.

Scoring the Power Index
The Power Index is based on six major sources of power and influence. In Table 5.2, these are listed together with the relevant Index item numbers.

Table 5.1 Use of power: in this situation, I influenced people and events by the items shown

Item	Little	Sometimes	Usually	Always
1 Using my formal power and position in the organization				
2 Warning of the consequences of certain courses of action that I do not like				
3 Praising people and recognizing their contributions				
4 Relying on my specialist knowledge and expertise				
5 Working well with people who I like				
6 Linking people to other sources of data and resources				
7 Being senior in the organization				
8 Suggesting that things could be difficult for them if I make an adverse report				
9 Offering people what they want in exchange for their co-operation				
10 My credibility and experience in the field				
11 Helping people to reflect and learn from my personal experiences				
12 Making suggestions for alliances and connections with other people and groups				

Table 5.2 The six sources of power and influence

Source of power[a]	Actual (×)	Preferred (✓)
Role and position [1 & 7]		
Coercion [2 & 8]		
Rewards [3 & 9]		
Expertise [4 & 10]		
Personal [5 & 11]		
Connections [6 & 12]		

[a] Numbers in brackets correspond to items in Table 5.1.

Assess your 'Actual' use of power by scoring each of your ×s, depending on where you put them:

Little = 1

Sometimes = 2

Usually = 3

Always = 4

So, for example, if you put your × for Item 1 in the 'Always' box and for Item 7 in the 'Usually' box in Table 5.1, you would score 7 for Role and position power.

When you have assessed your 'Actual' use of power, now add up your 'Preferred' scores in the same way.

The sources of power

So, what do these results mean? The Power Index is based on a model first suggested by French and Raven (1959). In broad terms, we can say that some sources of power derive from the *position* we hold in an organization whereas others are more do with us as *persons*. There are three types of *position* power:

- *Role power* derives from your role and status and the perception that you have the right to exercise influence because of this. This kind of power is linked to the hierarchical structure of an organization and defines the scope of your authority.
- *Coercive power* is based on the use of fear. It depends upon other people thinking that that you can punish them if they do not comply. Examples of this might include strong measures such as formal reprimands, the withdrawal of promotion or privileges, the allocation of unpleasant duties and even dismissal. However, there are many highly effective and subtler forms of coercion such as disapproval, withdrawal of friendship and exclusion from key meetings.
- *Reward power* is the twin of coercion – the carrot to go with the stick. *Reward power* is based on the perception that you have the ability and resources to reward the compliant. There are many ways to reward people, including praise, recognition, increased responsibilities and the granting of individual privileges. Pay or promotion or the allocation of desirable work are other possibilities.

There are also three types of *personal* power:

- *Expert power*, which is based on your competence or special knowledge in a given area. Expert power is based on credibility and the value attached to the particular field in which you can show competence.
- *Personal power* is based on the influence that comes from your personal attractiveness to others. It is the power which comes from your personal characteristics and charisma, your reputation and the respect of others or esteem in which you are held. Personal power is sometimes called referent power because it is based on the psychological identification of others with you.
- *Connection power* derives from networks and relationships. This kind of power can be used to build political knowledge, gather information, gain

personal support and feedback or build trusted alliances. Connection power was not in French and Raven's original list, but it has become increasingly important as a way of getting things done in a networked world.

The numerical scoring of the Power Index is a simple way of displaying difference. There are two main types of difference:

- the different sources or forms of power
- the difference between what you actually do and what you would prefer to do.

Using your power

It is helpful to discuss your Power Index results with a trusted friend or mentor. Which sources of power do you have access to in your organization? Are there sources of power that you are over-using? Are there sources which are available to you but which you are not currently using? How can you increase your power to bring about what you desire?

Now think about what you do with your power. Do you use it:

- to get things done?
- to enhance your own position?
- to enhance others?
- to …?

What do you want to use more or less of and why?

Power is easy to misuse and abuse, often hard to use wisely. Abuses of power that lead to bullying and oppression are all too common in the 'high-performance' culture so prevalent in many organizations. Beyond their often disastrous impact on individuals, people who resort to bullying to get their way – and which of us can say we do not from time to time? – also have a bad effect on the wider organization. *The more victims there are, the less power there is available to the organization to get things done.*

Oppressor and victim

A common problem in the use of power comes from our perception that it resides in individuals. We see people as powerful or less powerful, influential or ineffective. However, in fact, power is a relational phenomenon – it is generated and located in relationships, not in individual persons. This is not to discount those rare and desirable, inherited or learned, characteristics that we see in what we call charismatic or wise people, but to emphasize the social reality that these

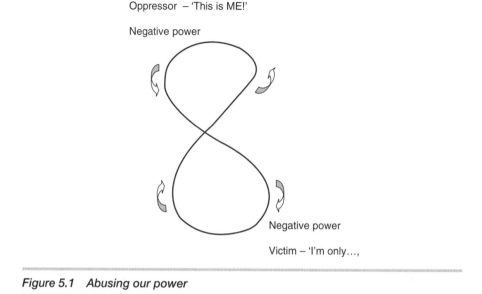

Oppressor – 'This is ME!'

Negative power

Negative power

Victim – 'I'm only…,

Figure 5.1   *Abusing our power*

people are only powerful because they influence *us*. If we are not impressed by the General's epaulettes, then he has no power over us, or with us.

To work well with power, we need to see this truth and to work with it. What sort of relationships actually generate power and which drain it away? How can we develop powerful relationships that result in good outcomes for all concerned? To answer these questions, it is important to consider the negative effects of misused power in relationships.

Activity: oppressor and victim

Figure 5.1 shows a model taught to us by a friend, Janet Atkinson. It shows a polarized relationship with oppressor at the top and victim at the bottom. Note how these two positions are chained together with a double loop. Try, for a moment, a journey around this double loop; start in any place and move round, pausing to remember when you felt like this: what does it feel like to be on top – *The Oppressor*? Perhaps childhood experiences come to mind as you think of how you dominated and threatened other children to get your way? When have you done this recently at work?

Now move down to the bottom – you are now *The Victim*. Is this familiar? How does it feel? What does it remind you of? Remember the times when you were weak and powerless – 'I'm only …'; 'If only …'; 'I can't …'.

The pattern of oppressor and victim is familiar to us all, from fairy stories and from life itself. Thinking about these things can sometimes be unsettling, reviving deep memories or throwing unwelcome light on certain aspects of life. However, unless they can find a way to break out, oppressor and victim are chained in a dance that

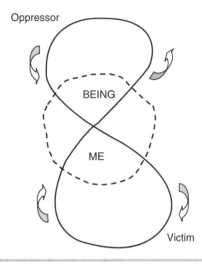

Figure 5.2   Using our power positively

they are condemned to continue. Breaking out and preventing this pattern from enslaving us is one of the fundamental aims of personal development. It is vital to the development of wise leadership.

The secret of using power positively is in the circle in the middle of the double loop in Figure 5.2. Work to enlarge that circle by being aware of the relationship with the other person or group; stay out of the territory at either end of the loops. Use your responsibilities to lead *with* others, feel on top only when others are feeling good and taking a positive view of themselves and what they can do.

Try for a moment a journey around this new double loop. Start in the middle and move round, but now with awareness, avoiding the outer parts of the loops beyond the centre circle.

What does it feel like to be in the middle – avoiding the traps of both oppressor and victim? Think of a relationship where you have this balance with another person or group; how does that feel? When have you done this at work recently?

The myth of empowerment

Kurt Lewin once said that 'Every generation needs to learn democracy anew'. The unequal distribution of formal power in organizations makes it easy for us to fall into the trap of oppressor and victim. Like chickens, perhaps we have some 'natural' tendency to form a hierarchical pecking order. Whatever the case, power relationships in organizations can damage people and seriously hamper performance, and it is the job of leadership to do something about it.

In recent times it has become popular to talk about 'empowerment', as in 'I empower you to …'. However, this sort of empowerment is a myth. When people say it, they usually do not mean it. This sort of empowerment does not alter position, pay or authority. If this affronts you and you disagree, try the following test:

Think of when you last 'empowered' someone: what power did you actually give them? And, if you did actually give them some actual power, did you take it back?

Empowerment is a confidence trick unless it comes with real power attached. There is a deeper truth here: the idea of empowerment is faulty because power is rarely given away and has to be taken. Enlightened leaders and monarchs can help, but democracy, fairness and justice have to be achieved.

Taking power positively

Bad experiences with power can cause the opposite of bullying – withdrawal. Wary of getting our fingers burned, we may prefer to avoid the risks of using power. Another friend told us a story of a Chief Executive who did not like to exercise her formal and legitimate power:

Make it so!

The Chief Executive was explaining a difficult situation to her personal consultant (coach). It concerned a recent team meeting where the decision under discussion was a difficult and controversial one. The Chief Executive was trying to give everyone their say and becoming irritated in particular with one person who was taking a strong position. After listening for some time, the consultant interrupted, and the following exchange took place:

Coach: 'It sounds to me as if you were trying to facilitate your team rather than lead it?'

CEO: 'Just what do you mean by that?'

Coach: 'It means that you were acting as a facilitator for a group and trying to bring about a consensus decision.'

CEO: 'And …?'

Coach: 'Well, in these circumstances, and if all the knowable information is available, you have to lead the team and make the decision.'

CEO: 'And how would I do that in this case?'

Coach: 'After a suitable length of discussion, you could stop the proceedings and ask each person in turn for their recommendation. Then you could say something like, "Thank you for your views – they are very useful. After listening carefully, I have decided to do it like this. I realize that some of you will not like this, but I think this is the best decision in the circumstances." End of conversation.'

CEO: 'Yes ....'

This conversation shows the coach suggesting that the CEO should acknowledge her legitimate position power and responsibility to make the decision. Facilitation might be a useful course of action in some circumstances, but here, where a decision is needed on the basis of what is known, leadership means taking the power and acting. Make it so!

The simple rule here is: 'Don't defer a decision ... unless there is an unknown that is knowable.'

In other words, if all the available knowledge is in your possession, why are you delaying?

Conclusion: the mirror and the window

Power is exercised most effectively by those with a strong will and determination to bring about what they believe should be done. As we saw in Chapter 4, the importance of will in leadership can hardly be overstressed. It is the combination of this will to see something happen with the power to bring it about that marks off the successful from the less successful.

Jim Collins and his colleagues studied US companies which had achieved the shift from good to great performance and kept this up over at least 15 years. Their 'Level 5 leaders' are characterized by an intriguing blend of just two qualities: intense professional will and personal humility.

The key to handling power lies in this combination of the personal with the professional. Adding the word 'professional' to will suggests an ambition which is not merely personal, but is in service to some wider or higher purpose; to use the great power of will in a responsible way requires a paradoxical but balancing, personal humility. Collins describes the actions of wise leadership, using the metaphors of the mirror and the window. When things go wrong, the Level 5 leader:

> *Looks in the mirror, not out of the window, to apportion responsibility for poor results, never blaming other people, external factors or bad luck.*

But when things go well, he or she:

> *Looks out of the window, not in the mirror, to apportion credit for the success of the company – to other people, external factors and good luck.*

> (Collins, 2001, p. 36)

The larger-than-life celebrity leaders who dominate the gossip columns of financial papers do not generally behave like this; rather the opposite, in fact. According to Collins' research, neither do they achieve great results for their organizations.

Further resources

As one of the main threads in the fabric of leadership, most books on this topic will devote some attention to power. However, much of this is not very imaginative. Ronald Heifetz usefully distinguishes between formal and informal authority and devotes Chapter 5 of his *Leadership Without Easy Answers* (Belnap Press, Cambridge, MA, 1994) to this. His whole book is suffused with sophisticated understandings of power and its working, especially in government and professional settings. Rosabeth Kanter has also said more useful things about power in organizations than most people, and Chapter 7 of her classic ethnographic study *Men and Women of the Corporation* (referenced below) is a masterly description of how things get done – or not.

In case you found this chapter a little naïve for your taste, Robert Greene is a modern Machiavelli and his *The 48 Laws of Power* (Profile Books, London, 1998) is a handsome book and a provocative read based on the view that 'power is a game of constant duplicity'. 'Never outshine the master' and 'Discover each man's thumbscrew' are indicative samples of the 48 Laws.

References

Collins, J. (2001) *Good to Great*, Random House, London.

French, J. and B. W. Raven (1959) 'The bases of social power', in *Studies in Social Power*, D. Cartwright (ed.), Institute for Social Research, Ann Arbor, MI.

Kanter, R. M. (1977) *Men and Women of the Corporation*, Basic Books, New York.

6

Practice 4: Living with Risk

*Leaders get attacked, dismissed, silenced and sometimes assassinated
because they come to represent loss*
Ronald Heifetz (1994)

Taking the heat

Leadership means taking risks, because it involves taking difficult decisions on the basis of inadequate information. Risk is the very essence of entrepreneurship – a valued quality in every organizational domain. At a personal level, risk-taking is associated with the characteristics of the creative person, along with imagination and the abilities to challenge the *status quo* and to tolerate ambiguity. It follows that, for leaders, it is better to ask for forgiveness than for permission.

So central is risk to leadership that the whole business is saturated with clichés and tales of the 'with one bound Jack was free' variety. Heroic theories of leadership continue to thrive on the fabled capacity of exceptional individuals to rise to this challenge. Despite the excesses of the celebrity CEO literature, the presence of risk does mean that leadership is often dangerous. To be in authority means being in the place where the difficult decisions are located. With any tough decision there will be losers, and the leadership must carry this risk.

However, the effect of this danger on those in charge is often anything but heroic:

> *With problems as tough as jobs, health and economic diversification, it is no wonder that everyone expects authority to make the decision. That seems our inclination – to look to someone or some agency to take the heat in choosing what to do. Ordinarily these expectations act as constraints on people in authority, inhibiting them from exercising leadership.*
>
> (Heifetz, 1994, p. 98)

We expect those in charge to resolve the intractable problems without pain or loss to ourselves. Authority figures are stuck with often impossible expectations – better services, but no more taxes; economize, but make no job cuts. It is these sorts of pressures that pressurize people into choosing safety first, and explains why authorities are often preoccupied with maintaining equilibrium and are seen as averse to change.

In situations of risk, the locations of leadership and authority may be very different. Because it is all too rarely exercised from high office, leadership must come from elsewhere, from those 'perceived as entrepreneurs and deviants, organizers and trouble-makers (to) provide the capacity within the system to see through the blind spots of the dominant viewpoint' (Heifetz, 1994, p. 183).

The adaptive challenges that demand learning and change in the ways things are currently done often first come to light through this sort of informal leadership. Some of the personal risks of leadership lie here: to safeguard my client or the public, do I risk unpopularity in speaking against the accepted view? Do I question the system and risk disfavour for the benefit of others?

Even those in authority cannot play safe for long. Take the decision and you risk unforeseen consequences; avoid it and you may be blamed for missing the opportunity. In the territory of leadership, it is important to become familiar with risk, its nature and its effects. The fear may never be fully overcome, but like the climber who tolerates exposure better through familiarity, the practice and performance can improve.

This chapter includes activities for estimating and planning for risk, together with proposals for taking and living with risk. It covers the following:

- assessing risk
- managing risk
- going public
- staying alive: action learning for leadership
- further resources.

Assessing risk

Given that risk is unavoidable, then how can it be assessed or calculated? As with all of the practices of leadership, the first step in living with risk is to know yourself, and how you respond to different situations.

Think of a risk you have taken recently. It need not be a very big one, but big enough that it made you stop and think and weigh the options. Perhaps you hesitated over it for a time, unwilling to commit. Now try the following activity.

Activity: a personal risk assessment activity

1 Why was this a risk for you?
2 What were the possible outcomes that you thought about in advance?

3 In making your decision, did you attempt to assess:
  ■ the likelihood of each outcome? – yes/no
  ■ the weighting or seriousness of the consequences of each outcome? – yes/no.

4 In the process of making the decision did you:
  ■ act impulsively in the face of the incalculable odds? – yes/no
  ■ haver in a fit of indecision for a long time, before deciding? – yes/no
  ■ avoid making a decision and let nature take its course – yes/no.

5 How did things turn out?
  ■ better than I could have expected
  ■ as I had hoped
  ■ not as I had hoped
  ■ disastrously.

6 Thinking back on this risk-taking situation, what was your main motive of your risk assessment or risk management thinking? Was it about:
  ■ *Discovering risk?* – looking to see what risks might exist.
  ■ *Managing risk?* – deciding how to deal with risks you knew were there.
  ■ *Avoiding risk?* – changing what you planned to avoid identified risks.
  ■ *Concealing risk?* – keeping the risk quiet rather than changing plans.
  ■ *Acknowledging risk?* – openly accepting that certain risks existed.

7 In general terms, where would you put yourself on the following seven-point scale?:

Risk Averse?	1	2	3	4	5	6	7	Risk Addicted?

Generally, we all set out to assess the risks of action and act on the basis of 'justifiable risk'. What justifies a risk varies from person to person, and from situation to situation: 'I am not afraid of heights but I hate to be seen to be failing'; 'you are happy to make a fool of yourself, but always avoid conflict'; and so on.

What did you learn from completing this personal risk assessment activity? Are you one who carefully thinks through the consequences of risk, systematically reviews the options and seeks to weigh the outcomes of each? Or do you prefer a more intuitive, action-oriented approach, relying on an ability to learn quickly from initial consequences? Do you generally imagine the worst possible outcomes? Or can you maintain an optimism that things will turn out well? The best decisions may require some of both.

Question 6 raises the important issue of risk management. What was your purpose here? Discovery and acknowledgement of risk are important in identifying and facing up to adaptive challenge. Do you see yourself as inclined to take risks in these sorts of situations or not? Are you are more cautious and risk-averse or do you see yourself as willing to take a fair measure of risk whenever opportunities present themselves?

Managing risk

The public practice of risk management is a big and growing business. It is key to the managerial control of safety, confidentiality, individual and professional accountability, competence, training and many other aspects of effective organization. Making sure that lines of accountability are clear, that safety systems are in place, that people are properly trained for what they are doing and so on are the very essence of good operations management. Running a hospital or a railway demands good-quality risk-management processes and procedures as a basis for day-to-day working.

The world of leadership overlaps with this, but is different. Here the issues and questions are less well defined, there are fewer relevant systems and procedures and interests form, re-form and shift about. Where organizing is rather fluid, with few clear authority lines or defined responsibilities, assessing and managing risk are a very different proposition. The systems may be available to deal with identified risks, but who decides what is a risk and what should be done about it? As an example, consider the crises in public health that now regularly erupt in a networked, mobile world.

SARS (severe acute respiratory syndrome)

At the time of writing in 2003, concerns about SARS are sweeping the globe, originating in China but causing the World Health Organization to warn travellers not to go to Toronto, where cases were found. SARS and other new illnesses create risks for many people and businesses. Take the Western universities, for example, who have been busy recruiting students from the East. When these students go home on holiday and come back a few weeks later to their international student residences, the ideal conditions for the incubation of a potential world pandemic may be created. What should the individual university authorities do? The current evidence is that they are each reacting very differently, and that there is, as yet, no best practice to follow.

It is these sorts of situations that define the need for leadership as distinct from management. There are no best practices to take the risk out of leadership on such matters of vital public import. Here leadership is often in the front line in this trade-off between safety and risk with some very difficult decisions to make: do we take this child from its family or run the risks of child abuse? Do we allow this elderly person to stay at home with the risks of falls and burns or do we take him or her into residential care and run the risks of the costs to personal independence and spirit? What looks like the safe option from one perspective may endanger life and liberty from another.

Managing this sort of risk and trade-off requires the balancing of both courage and caution. This is not a question of choosing either–or, but of handling the dilemma of choosing between two goods. The complementarity

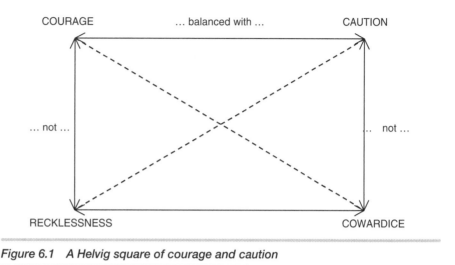

Figure 6.1 A Helvig square of courage and caution

of these equally desirable but apparently contradictory qualities can be illustrated by a Helvig square of values (Helvig, 1951) (Figure 6.1).

In a Helvig square, the two complementary qualities on the top line retain their value only when the tension between them is balanced. For courage to be increased, a complementary increase in caution is also required. When the balance on the top line is not maintained, these good values become debased and turn into the deteriorated forms on the bottom line. Courage becomes recklessness or foolhardiness without a balancing caution, and caution without a balancing boldness leads to avoidance and cowardice. The diagonal lines show the true opposites.

Examples of excessive courage and caution litter the organizational world. Survivors of the Enron scandal recall that the company had become so 'bold' that insiders had lost the power to discriminate between right and wrong. Enron was highly entrepreneurial, but lacked a proper caution, and so was lost. In other organizational worlds it is easy to find examples of excessive caution where the over-application of risk management, 'quality control' and concerns for probity smother any sparks of creativity or innovation.

Calculating risk

Faced by complexity, uncertainty and inadequate information, we may tend to freeze and become unable to act. In his book *Up the Organization*, Robert Townsend (1984) estimated that, as Managing Director of Avis, some 40% of the decisions he made were wrong. He stressed that the most important thing was that he made them and that this meant 60% of them were right – a good batting average, he reckoned. Not being able to act means that we cannot learn anything new about a difficult situation.

The calculation of risk involves the estimation of the possible consequences for any given action. This provides the basis for risk management where risks are either avoided altogether (the best option) or the unavoidable or unforeseen risks are handled by devising safety nets and inventing options to deal with these contingencies. The value of thinking about possible risks and seeking to calibrate them is that this activity might help us to stay mobile and proactive.

This is a very rational process. The alternative to this is to proceed on intuition, acting on hunches, staying alert and open to new information, because action creates information and information reduces uncertainty. In well-structured situations, rational planning can usefully precede action; in uncertain conditions, it is better to get into action, taking small steps and staying alert and receptive, because action generates information. Handling leadership risks often requires a combination of the intuitive and the rational approaches.

Here is a simple version of the rational approach. This is applied to a personal decision, but more sophisticated and organizational versions can be found in the books on risk management, some of which are listed in Further resources.

Activity: estimating risk and planning for contingencies

1 *Choose a decision facing you or your organization.* For practice purposes it can be any decision, however small, provided that it is surrounded by some uncertainty about the outcomes. It could be a purchase decision, a personal relationship or some aspect of organizational policy making.

2 On the basis of Murphy's Law ('If anything can go wrong, it will!'), *brainstorm and list all the possible outcomes,* good and bad.

3 Now, taking just the bad outcomes, *estimate the level of danger* of each of these risks, using the equation

$$R = P + S$$

where R = the *size* of the risk [Level 1 (low), Level 2 (medium) or Level 3 (high)], P = the *probability* of this happening (low/medium/high) and S = the *seriousness* of the situation, if it does happen (low/medium/high): (Two lows for P and S = a Level 1 R; a high P plus a medium S = a Level 3 R, and so on).

4 Now, just focus on the Level 3 risks. *What contingency plans can you put in place?* Again, brainstorm the options – what safety nets can you devise? What options can you invent for now?

It helps now to use some creativity techniques, draw the possible outcome or tell a story imagining that this has actually happened. Imagine how you feel in this disastrous situation. What can you do now?

This approach to thinking about risk will help whatever the outcomes. In uncertain situations, things are not likely to go to plan, but a bit of planning helps to prepare us for action and its consequences.

The incalculability of risk

There are several problems with the rational approach. Absence of evidence does not automatically mean that risk does not exist. If risks are not predictable, a rational approach may induce a sense of false security. In some instances the rationalization of risk through measuring the easily measurable and ignoring the unpredictable amounts to CYA (Covering Your Arse) or, at worse, 'technical concealment'.

According to Ulrich Beck (1992), the calculability of risk is one of our modern myths. In seeking to estimate the possible consequences of any action, by engaging in elaborate exercises of risk analysis, risk assessment, risk management and all the other controlling words coupled with risk in recent times, we are calculating the imagined effects of some probably scenarios, and not the actual risks of taking that action:

> *The studies of reactor safety restrict themselves to the estimation of certain quantifiable risks on the basis of probable accidents. The dimensions of the hazard are limited from the very beginning to technical manageability. In some circles it is said that risks which are not yet technically manageable do not exist – at least not in scientific calculation or jurisdictional judgement. These uncalculable threats add up to an unknown residual risk.*

(Beck, 1992, p. 29)

Yet, because so much has been invested in systems of risk management and we are easily impressed with science and number, we delude ourselves into thinking that these estimates are actual risk assessments. Indeed, the better we get at these estimates the worse we make it. Risk management at its best tells us something about the possible risks, and is the proper responsibility of good management. Where there are considerable 'unknown residual risks', this form of risk management can become an evasion of responsibility which abandons any future victims of unforeseen consequences. One courageous response to incalculable risk is to go public.

Going public

Cutting budget

Mark, a social services manager, was charged with cutting £400 000 from the £2 million budget for the transport system for disabled people. Such a large cut was not possible through incremental savings and demanded a radical approach – and it had to be done in this financial year.

This was a tough situation. In his analysis, Mark considered the various options open and also the possible risks, threats and consequences. Stopping the transport would have a severe social impact because people relied upon the system to get them from home to workplaces and day centres. Asking them to pay would hit the poorest and most vulnerable people in the city.

Mark decided to talk with the people who used the service. He held a meeting with some of them and put forward various options, including using existing public transport, charging for the service at a full rate or charging at a subsidized rate. What surprised him was the willingness of the service users to pay for the service – they were willing to pay the subsidized rate or in some cases even a higher rate. Either of these scenarios would make a significant contribution to meeting the savings required.

Another surprise was the source of the fiercest resistance. This came from two sources. First were the parents of children with learning difficulties. The parents were paid the transport allowance to allow them to run cars to provide transport for their children to the day centres. They used this allowance to run their cars even though many did not take their (now adult) children to the centres.

But the strongest opposition of all came from the minibus drivers and the attendants who accompanied them. Their concern was to maintain the *status quo* and they were reluctant to accept any additional duties such as collecting fares. The trades unions were swiftly mobilized. This dispute led to huge disagreements within the ruling political party, with the politicians responsible for the social services budget having stand-up rows with those responsible for transport – many of whom were sponsored by the drivers' trade union. This disagreement between two groups in the same party over which was most important – the drivers' conditions or the ability of social services to modernize and make savings – was the biggest issue in the whole process.

Without taking the risk of going public, Mark would not have learned those things which eventually led to the resolution of this situation. Sitting tight in his office and carrying out risk assessment and management procedures could not have produced this outcome. Once he had decided to take this risk, Mark met several surprises, some of them pleasant, that he had not considered in his planning and invention of options. Surprises, including unpleasant ones, are always likely to be part of leading in uncertain conditions. You cannot stay safe and still lead in these situations. In any case, so-called 'safe options' often turn out not to be safe after all.

So, take a risk, but share the risk by engaging allies and involving your users, clients or public. This may be as simple as telling some friends or colleagues about your situation. A special form of this move is action learning, a method devised to help people learn from very difficult problems through enrolling a few 'comrades in adversity' (see Chapter 7). Going public can also mean using stakeholder involvement processes and conferences, which are discussed in Chapter 15.

Because leadership is about taking risks and not playing it safe, people in leadership positions must find ways of sharing risk so that they are not left unsupported. Like other good ideas, 'risk sharing' has fallen victim to those seeking to evade the responsibilities of leadership and sometimes become yet another euphemism for job cuts, wage reductions and so on. True risk sharing (and risk management) involves leaders visibly sharing the costs and engaging in a process of learning learning.

Towards public learning

Two strategic leadership principles are:

- identifying the adaptive challenge – diagnosing the situation and suggesting what learning is needed to meet this
- giving the work back to the people – to the stakeholders and the people with the problem (Heifetz, 1994, p. 128).

Leadership '... requires an experimental mindset – the willingness to work by trial and error – where the community's reactions at each stage provide the basis for planning future actions' (Heifetz, 1994, p. 243). Giving the work back to the people who can learn and resolve the situation involves the risk of not controlling and of letting go. This is one of the most difficult risks for many people in leadership situations, and many such risks are covered up, avoided or suppressed. Initiating the processes of public or stakeholder engagement and learning is a high calling.

Heifetz (1994) gives the example of William Ruckelshaus, Head of the USA's Environmental Protection Agency, who was faced with a difficult decision over a copper plant at Tacoma, WA. Arsenic emissions from the copper ore used were a public safety hazard but the plant was the major employer in the town and an important part of the state economy. Ruckelshaus could have played safe and ruled on emission, yet he

> ... cut against the grain when he insisted that the public realize that the job of regulating pollutants was not simple a technical matter of setting safe thresholds of emission. Trade-offs would have to be made that involved value conflicts not amenable to scientific analysis. And if those trade-offs between jobs and health were to be faced, then perhaps new adaptations might be achieved in the face of loss.

(Heifetz, 1994, p. 98)

Only through dealing with such difficult situations can people begin to learn about living and working with this sort of risk. Once again, local people showed that they could share responsibility to managing this risk and that they could learn, in this case, for example, about the enormous costs of 'cleaning up' the environment. They were pushed by Ruckelshaus to face realities that required much change and adjustment. The learning spread beyond the locality as the Tacoma case became part of a wider national debate on managing environmental risks.

Risk sharing through public or stakeholder engagement and learning is no easy ride and, from a strategic standpoint, it may not be that easy to include everyone anyway. Sometimes parties must be excluded from the problem-solving process, because the disruption potential is just too great. In extremely difficult circumstances such as those in Northern Ireland or Palestine, delicate alliances have to be built before negotiations are even possible.

Staying alive: action learning for leadership

Leading in risky situations demands great emotional resilience. Keeping going forwards requires both an agility in learning and some personal survival skills:

> *Thus a leader stay alive not by 'playing it safe' but by taking deliberate risks based on his on-going assessment of the territory, knowing that corrective action will almost always be necessary. He takes the risk of challenging people, directly or indirectly, slow or fast, soft or hard, guided by his comprehension of and sensitivity to the changes people have to make in their lives as they take account of the questions he raises.*

(Heifetz, 1994, p. 243)

This sounds very masterful, and sometimes the adrenaline can more than compensate for the stress. Yet the costs in emotional energy can be very high. Drained by personal survival needs, the emotional intelligence available to the tasks in hand may be greatly reduced. The critical importance of emotional resilience suggests the need for personal support and allies.

For those risks which we can determine, we can establish systems of management. For those which we cannot, action learning is the vehicle and philosophy proposed by Revans for 'the posing of questions in conditions of ignorance, risk or confusion' (Revans, 1982, p. 567). The essence of action learning is to support people in the management of risk through examining the challenges besetting us and determining what to do next. In these circumstances, what guides us in escaping from our troubles or seizing our opportunities is as much our values as the methods and tools available to us. Revans notes that, as his managers matured in their judgements, the important injunctions were:

> *Never tell me what you don't mean.*
> *Never imply obliquely what you can't explain directly.*
> *Never make yourself believe what you know is untrue.*
> *Never invent the truth for other people.*

(Revans 1971, p. 132)

In risky situations, sound judgement is often a more useful quality than high intelligence. Any amount of intelligence will not tell us what to do. Action learning improves the quality of judgement in assessing, taking and learning from risk. More details on the action learning approach can be found in Chapter 7.

Conclusion

Risk and risk management are a major contemporary aspect of organizational life and constant companions of leadership. One of the pressures for alliances and interdependence amongst firms is the fact that global competition and market volatility can easily overwhelm the ability of any business to track and control risk. In government and public sector organizations, increasing service standards and targets, together with high visibility and threats of litigation, raise the pressure not only to manage risk but also to be seen to be doing so.

This raises the heat for the leadership of any organization. It makes essential systems for risk assessment and risk management, but it also means that risk avoidance and concealment are likely flourish, whilst entrepreneurial risk-taking may be imperiled. However, for good leadership, risk is not an option, but a *raison d'être* and the very ground of learning:

> ... the very origin of learning lies in the recognition of risk or ignorance, and management that believe they are already sufficiently well-informed to run their affairs properly will have no desire to learn; they will continue to make tomorrow's decisions as they made yesterday's, providing always that yesterday's still let them remain in business until today.
>
> (Revans, 1982, p. 590)

Further resources

There are dozens of books on risk, often specializing in, for example, finance or environmental issues. *The Book of Risk* by Dan Borge (Wiley, New York, 2001) comes from a financial perspective but is readable and seeks to apply systematic tools of risk management to your 'risk investment in life'. A simple and general book is Jacqueline Reynes' *Risk Management: 10 Principles* (Butterworth-Heinemann, London, 2001).

In more general terms and related specifically to leadership, Ronald Heifetz's *Leadership Without Easy Answers* (Belnap Press, Cambridge, MA, 1994) is in a different class to much of the leadership literature and continues to be a favourite. Reg Revans' *ABC of Action Learning* (Lemos and Crane, London, 1998) is his primer on action learning. It is brief, profound and full of insight for those leading in conditions of risk. Mike Pedler's *Action Learning for Managers* (Lemos and Crane, London, 1996) is a short action learning primer.

References

Beck, U. (1992) *Risk Society: Towards a New Modernity*, Sage, London.

Heifetz, R. (1994) *Leadership Without Easy Answers*, Belknap Press, Cambridge, MA.

Helvig, P. (1951) *Characterologie*. Ernst Klett Verlag, Stuttgart.

Revans, R.W. (1971) *Developing Effective Managers*, Praeger, New York.

Revans, R.W. (1982) *The Origins and Growth of Action Learning*, Chartwell-Bratt, Bromley.

Townsend, R. (1970) *Up the Organization, How to Stop the Corporation from Stifling People & Strangling Profits*, Coronet Books, London.

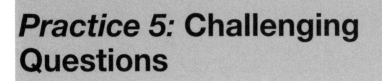

Practice 5: Challenging Questions

The essence of action learning is to pose increasingly insightful questions from an origin of ignorance, risk and confusion
Reg Revans (1998)

Introduction

The ability to pose increasingly insightful questions from an origin of ignorance, risk and confusion is a critical aspect of leadership.

> *An old training film shows a group of army officers poring over a map and engaged in an animated conversation. Each person makes different points and does not listen to the others very well. Suddenly, one voice silences the rest: 'Just a minute, where exactly are we trying to get to?'.*

The memory of this stagey old film still makes us laugh. It was actually making a rather heavy-handed point about the importance of setting objectives. The point here is that, in conditions of confusion and risk, a sense of direction is more likely to come from one good question than from an avalanche of proposals for action.

Questioning is the key to creativity, action and learning – it is where fresh ideas come from. Developing this practice is critical to leadership, because it is through critical questions that purpose and direction is found.

This chapter contains:

- an introduction to the power of questions and to questioning insight
- two models for thinking about how to pose challenging questions for action, leadership and learning – thinking, feeling and willing, and seven types of questions
- an activity for generating challenging questions
- further resources.

Developing questioning insight

Revans' complaint about traditional leadership education (Revans, 1998) is that it emphasizes the accumulated knowledge of the past (or P) rather than Q – the acquisition of questioning insight. In itself, knowledge is only a small part of what is needed for action and learning – more important is finding the right question. His point is that you only know what knowledge might be useful once you have the right question. There are three of these questions at the core of Revans' action learning philosophy:

- Who knows (about the problem, issue or opportunity)?
- Who cares (about this issue)?
- Who can (do anything about this matter)?

In turn, these deal with finding new knowledge, recruiting friends and allies and gaining access to the power and resources needed for achieving your purpose. These questions are so simple, that it is easy to miss how their profundity. Try their power for yourself.

Activity: Revans' essential questions

Think of a current issue or concern that you have and that you would like to do something about. This need not be a big thing, but something that has been on your mind or that you have been meaning to do and perhaps been putting off.

Now consider the following questions from Revans (1998, pp. 33–41). The questions are phrased for a shared issue in a team or group, but you can personalize them by changing 'we' to 'I', etc. You could tackle these questions in small sub-groups or, if you are doing this alone, make a few notes under each question before moving on to the next:

- What are we trying to do?
- What is stopping us from doing it?
- What can we do about this?
- Who else knows what we are trying to do?
- Who else cares about what we are trying to do?
- Who else can do anything to help?

However lost, confused or uncertain you are, these questions can be used to develop a way forward. Simply posing them and then attempting to answer them create a positive frame of mind. This is because these questions are intimately related to the three basic human processes of thinking, feeling and willing.

Thinking, feeling and willing

Figure 7.1 shows three fundamental human processes that correspond to who knows?; who cares?; and who can?

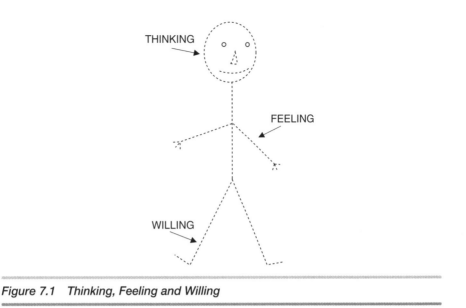

Figure 7.1 Thinking, Feeling and Willing

The processes of thinking, feeling and willing are all involved in taking action on any challenge. Although they are normally all mingled together, it can be useful to look at them as distinct processes that have different characteristics:

- *Thinking*, which may be said, literally and symbolically, to take place in the head, is about ideas, concepts, images, metaphors, theories and so on. It is also about reflections, assumptions, mental models and frames of reference that cause us to see situations in particular lights.
- *Feeling*, on the other hand, which we locate here symbolically in the body, is about emotions, sensations and energies, and also about atmosphere, ambience and vibrations.
- *Will* is about wishes, purpose, intentions and also about power and energy. As we note in Chapter 4, will provides the drive, determination and effort to make things happen. It is the force that translates impulses and directions into practice and is located metaphorically in the legs and feet.

There are many ways in which thinking, feeling and willing can be used. Here we are concerned with developing good questions to reveal insights for forward direction and action. Before the questions comes the listening; try the following activity:

Activity: listening for thoughts, feelings and will

Try this activity for listening silently and with attention – a surprisingly rare occurrence between people but an easy skill to learn. You can practice this in any meeting where someone is speaking about anything for a certain length of time, but it is probably better done on a one-to-one basis where you can discuss the outcome of your listening with a partner. An ideal situation is where someone wants to talk to you in private about something that is important to them – a coaching session or a conversation about a difficult decision. If this is not immediately available, you could simply asked a trusted colleague to tell you about an aspect of their work that they have been thinking about recently.

Listen to your colleagues for a decent length of time – say 10–15 minutes. Show your interest and attention by looking your partner in the face; pay attention, but try not to speak: you are there to listen, so sit out the pauses, and grunt if you must. This gives any speaker an unusual opportunity for an uninterrupted pursuit of a topic; a chance to explore a problem. In a surprisingly short piece of uninterrupted time, a person can explore their thoughts and feelings and desire for action. Through the agency of a silent listener, who by being there and restraining her or his own desire to talk, a vessel is created in which the speaker can sort out ideas, clarify feelings and recognize wishes.

If you listen carefully you may be able to pick out your partner's:

- *Thinking*. What is being said, the pattern of thoughts; is it logical? Detailed or general? In the past, present or future? Who is being talked about and who is not? What images and metaphors are being used? What assumptions are being made?
- *Feeling*. What is the speaker feeling? Notice the gestures, posture, tone of voice, way of breathing and the expression of the face, eye movement.
- *Willing*. What does the person want to do? What is just a wish and what is a definite intention to act?

If it is appropriate, when your colleague has finished speaking, play back your observations under the three headings of thinking, feeling and willing. How does this fit with the speaker's own perceptions?

Listening in this way may seem a bit unusual at first – because it is. But if you persevere and overcome the awkwardness of silences, you will find that this is an attainable skill, and a very valuable one. Good questioning usually comes with supportive listening because it is this which opens up the road to the useful questions.

Seven types of questions for leadership

After listening to problems or challenge to which there is no obvious answer, asking good questions is the most constructive response you can make. There is no need to bother with this process if the solution is straightforward or an answer is to hand. The importance of questions and questioning insight for leadership is because of the need to act and intervene in complex and difficult situations where there are no simple solutions.

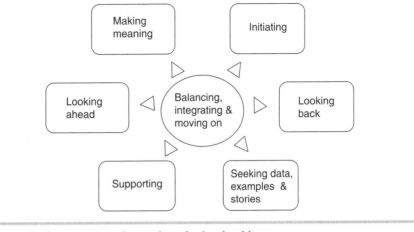

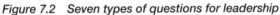

Figure 7.2   Seven types of questions for leadership

In such a situation there are some important and helpful questioning responses. Figure 7.2 shows that there are seven types of question that we can ask:

- questions to help find or make meaning
- questions about initiating action
- questions that cause people to think about the future and the consequences of action
- balancing, integrating, summarizing and moving on questions
- questions that cause others to reflect and learn from the past
- caring and supporting questions
- questions seeking examples or practical illustrations.

Examples of helpful questions under these seven headings are:

1. *Questions to help find or make meaning*
   - What does this mean to you?
   - What is this saying to you?
   - Can you see a pattern or a theme in all this?
2. *Questions that cause others to reflect and learn from the past*
   - Has this happened before?
   - Give me some examples of incidents like this in the past?
   - What have you learned from tackling similar situations?
3. *Caring and supporting questions*
   - I know you are good at … because I've seen you do it before; what is different about this situation?
   - How do you feel?
   - What would help you right now?

4. *Questions seeking examples or practical illustrations*
    - What sort of things are you talking about?
    - Can you give examples of other situations in which you feel this way?
    - Who else do you know who has had this issue?
    - What is generally seen to be good practice in this area?
5. *Questions that cause people to think about the future and the consequences of action*
    - What will be the consequences for yourself and all the others involved?
    - What blocks and obstacles are there?
    - What resources will this require?
    - Where do you want to be with regard to this in 6 months time?
6. *Questions about initiating action*
    - You seem to have several ideas for action, how do they fit together?
    - What alternatives and options do you have?
    - Of the various options, what is the best next step?
    - What do you want to do about this?
7. *Balancing, integrating, summarizing and moving on questions*
    - How is that point consistent with what you said earlier?
    - Can you see a clear trend linking the past, the present and the future?
    - So, what you seem to be saying is …?
    - Can you summarize the actions you are going to take?

You can use this list for ideas to start with, or to review your efforts afterwards. More important than 'getting it right' is the simple willingness to help the other person; commitment to your partner or partners is the first essential of the leadership relationship. Once you have this, then just get started and try some of these ideas, improving as you go.

Listening is often quoted as an important characteristic of the good manager or leader. And being listened to is indeed one of the best things that other people can do for us. When asked about those people who they saw as good managers, a group of staff said that they:

- were sympathetic and understanding
- showed interest in what I was saying
- respected me and my feelings
- still liked me even when I made mistakes or did stupid things
- sometimes challenged me and made me think
- told me how they saw me, but in a way that helped me to listen to them.

However, most good managers are not just listening, which, on its own, is rather a passive process. Questioning is much less often noticed than listening, but it is the vital other half of being supportive and responsive. It is the questions, based on the listening, that build the basis for constructive action on the challenges being faced.

Generating challenging questions

Getting to the route of the problem

In an action learning session, Sharon was asked what it was about her work that most concerned her and occupied her thoughts at the moment. After giving this some thought, she came up with:

I want to improve the relationships with a particular group of colleagues in order to work better with them.

After discussing this in the group, the other members came up with a long list of questions, including:

- How would you describe the relationship at present?
- What is your picture of a good relationship?
- What makes you think that you have a problem?
- What have you tried to do so far?
- Why do you want to do this?
- Do these colleagues want a better relationship with you?
- Who have you talked to about this issue?
- What would working better look like?
- Which colleagues are you thinking about?
- What feedback do you get from your colleagues?
- How do you think you can go about improving these relationships?
- How does this affect your work?
- What skills do you think you haven't got?
- How skilful are your colleagues?
- How might things be if you had better relationships?
- What would your best friend say to you about your working situation?

She was then asked to choose the three questions that most interested her. Especially, which were the most challenging, and had most impact as she heard them? After some thought she picked:

- Do these colleagues want a better relationship with you?
- What would working better look like?
- What would your best friend say to you about your working situation?

The three questions which she picked out as most interesting were those which had either not occurred to her before or had suddenly made her think. Each question led to a new train of thought. As she said about the first question:

When this was said, I thought it was outrageous, a stupid idea. Then I thought – this has never occurred to me! I had been preoccupied with my view of what I thought was the problem ... maybe there is no problem from their perspective?

A really good challenging question leads the other person to question themselves, and once this self-questioning starts, new avenues for action and discovery often follow. A good challenge is determined not just by the questioner, but by the quality of the relationship. If Sharon did not trust, and feel able to be open with, this group of people, then, however skilful the individuals present, there could be no such challenging questions.

Given that quality of relationship, any group of four or five or more can use this activity to generate challenging questions around any situation. Some groups will already do this sort of thing naturally as part of their routine. In a group where this is not normal, you may need some simple rules and facilitation to develop the method. The main thing is to follow the steps implied in Sharon's story in a rather deliberate and disciplined way, rather than jumping into a free-for-all of talk and advice. Get people to write down their questions once they have heard about the significant issue and then to read them out in turn, ensuring that the person with the issue listens to them and jots them down for future prompting, rather than trying to answer them on the spot.

Inquiring to learn

There is a shadow side to questions and questioning. Questions are powerful tools and can be used and abused. There is always the possibility of seduction and the unwary questioner can be lured by the power of questioning into pursuit, over-inquiry, cleverness and various other traps. All discussions of action in complex situations are ultimately bound up with values. Revans describes his experiences of working with managers:

> The greatest interest to them was that of a value system. What were the standards of integrity against which all final judgements were made by those with whom they worked – including themselves? ... [This] led them to define the most valuable question they had learned as 'What is an honest man, and what need I do to become one?'

> (Revans, 1998, p. 85)

The advice from the Harvard Negotiation Project is:

> ...inquire to learn. And only to learn. You can tell whether a question will help the conversation or hurt it by thinking about why you asked it. The only good answer is 'To learn'.

> (Stone et al., 2000, p. 172)

So, the touchstones are honesty in enquiry and asking yourself whether this is likely to lead to learning for the person concerned. Some of the traps around questioning that we have fallen victim to from time to time are:

■ *Giving advice disguised as questions.* Questions of the 'Have you thought of using a big hammer on it?' variety are often attempts to give advice or make a suggestions rather than making a genuine enquiry. It is far better to offer the advice openly, which makes it easier to accept or reject.

■ *Influence disguised as questions.* Questions of the 'Are you going to answer the telephone?' variety are actually attempts to get other people to do what you want. These questions do not really offer the freedom of movement that they appear to imply. Just ask for what you want – politely.

■ *Cross-examination.* When one question leads to another and you seem to be 'on to something', this trap can lead to a courtroom situation and put the other person in the dock. Questions that start with 'How do you explain … ?' may be on this road, and of course if you get to 'I put it to you that … ?' then the game is really up. It can be very helpful to lead someone down an avenue or enquiry, but the purpose is always to promote the action and the learning of the person with the problem or the dilemma, and not to prove anything. If you want to air a theory, then do so openly.

■ *Generating defensiveness.* What makes a challenging question depends upon both the questioner and receiver and their relationship. When we are pursued or cross-examined, a natural reaction is to close up and become defensive. This is death to any learning. Even apparently polite or innocent questions can have the effect of shutting people down, as can pressing people to answer. Although a challenging question repeated sometimes produces useful outcomes, the main rule is to invite people to respond to questions – and allow them always the right to refuse that invitation.

A good groundrule for any learning group is to encourage people to ask all the genuine questions that occur to them, however impolite, but also to enshrine the universal human right for the person being questioned of declining to answer.

Further resources

Douglas Stone, Bruce Patton and Sheila Heen's *Difficult Conversations: How to Discuss What Matters Most* (Penguin, Harmondsworth, 2000) from the Harvard Negotiation Project is a very clear, friendly and helpful guide to all aspects of difficult conversations, and has useful comments on the role of questions. Their picture of the three essential conversations ('What happened, Feelings and

Identity') has some overlap with our Thinking, Feeling, Willing model. This book will give you a great deal of clear guidance and advice for recognizing and negotiating these conversations.

Reg Revans placed questioning and enquiry at the very heart of his theory of action learning – a philosophy and approach that we believe is highly suited and apposite to leadership challenges and situations. His short *ABC of Action Learning* (referenced below) contains his essential wisdom about enquiry and much, much more.

Appreciative inquiry also works via questions. This is an alternative approach to action learning which shares many characteristics but is distin- guished by the stress placed upon emphasizing the positive and not to use the language of problems or deficits. A short and simple guide is David Cooperrider and Diana Whitney's *Appreciative Inquiry* (Berrett Koehler, San Franciso, 1999), which also gives many further sources and references.

References

Stone, D., B. Patton and S. Heen (2000) *Difficult Conversations: How to Discuss What Matters Most*, Penguin, Harmondsworth.

Revans, R. W. (1998) *ABC of Action Learning*, Lemos and Crane, London.

Practice 6: Facilitation

Facilitation is the right hand of leadership

Introduction

Facilitation has emerged strongly in recent years as an important leadership practice. With workplaces changing at unprecedented rates, the practice of facilitation can help individuals, groups, whole organizations and networks to get their work done more effectively. Work has 'intensified', the pace seems faster and more furious but, curiously, sometimes less seems to get done. Busyness and overload can lead to situations where we feel that we have enough on just to cope with our own work, and have little time to support or assist others. This helps to explain the common phenomenon that 'teams' are often anything but.

We define facilitation simply as 'helping people get their work done together'. Leadership as facilitation means encouraging people to share their perceptions of what needs to be done, to co-operate on tasks and to work collaboratively rather than in isolation. Effective facilitation is measured both by enabling or empowering people to act and to learn as individuals, and also by the collective performance – by how well people work together. The term facilitation is familiar in terms of 'managing' meetings. In the context of leadership, it becomes an essential operational practice that promotes the strategic aim of enabling people to do their work:

The strategic challenge is to give the work back to people without abandoning them. Overload them and they will avoid learning. Underload them and they will grow too dependent, or complacent.

(Heifetz, 1994)

Giving the work back to the people may be easier said than done. The best people to resolve a situation are usually the locals; yet these people may be split in their views and opinions. Leadership is frequently surrounded by different views and conflict about what should be done and not done. Facilitation means facing up to these differences, not avoiding them; it means providing a structure or framework within which people can progress their work in a productive way.

This chapter addresses four questions:

■ What is facilitation?
■ What is the process of facilitation?
■ Is help always helpful?
■ Where can I get further information and help?

It offers advice and practical guidance on how to develop the core leadership practice of facilitation.

What is facilitation?

Facilitation is very practical; essentially, it is about putting the fine words of leadership into action. Like the other core leadership practices, it is a daily activity, done here or there, as one encounters people in situations. The practice of facilitation is a good working habit, an everyday accomplishment, but, like all practices, it is more than just a habit, because it is always being revised and developed. Our practices comprise our most valuable skills and qualities but we also practise them in order to get better.

Table 8.1 shows some characteristic activities of leadership and some corresponding activities of facilitation. This table demonstrates that facilitation is the right hand of leadership. Leadership can be about a sense of direction or a sense of what is right and wrong, and not necessarily what is practical or convenient. Skilful facilitation can help here. When leadership reflects the difficult question or challenge to which there is no obvious solution, this can plunge us into self-doubt and even despair. In the face of this, facilitation is irredeemably cheerful, always optimistic, always looking for a practical way to move forwards.

Being facilitative

There are twin aspects to this job. As a process that helps people to get their work done, it is both about accomplishing tasks and about helping individuals work well together. In destabilizing situations such as organizational change or restructuring, leaders acting as facilitators can help a great deal. With the ground shifting under your feet, it is hard to feel secure or confident, but facilitation can bring a settling and calming influence. In the face of uncertainties, helping groups of people clarify their goals and choose practical ways forward is good and useful work. It helps us to be more positive about the situations in which we may find ourselves.

Table 8.1   Leadership and facilitation

Leadership is ...	Facilitation is ...
Taking a long term view	Helping people to find their own views of the future
Concerned with values and moral purposes	Concerned with clarifying different values and creating common purpose
Pointing out the adaptive challenge to be faced	Asking people what sense they make of their situations and how this challenge affects them
Articulating vision	Encouraging people to understand their own hopes and dreams and enabling self-expression
Focused on the future, on innovation and change	Helping people to make sense of the new, to understand the implications of alternative futures and to ask 'what does this mean for me?'
Seeking collaboration and commitment	Exploring opinions, positions and commitment; clarifying the options and seeking common ground
Giving the work back	Helping people get their work done together
Listening to the hard questions	Protecting the 'critical friends' who raise hard questions and challenge common assumptions
Moving towards, and not against, conflict and difference	Reassuring people that conflict is normal in challenging situations and helping people get things in perspective and to resolve internal conflicts
Seeking to serve and to improve service to others	Focusing people on the practical issues and tasks and on what they can do to improve the service they offer

The new team

In the aftermath of a major shake-up following a merger, restructuring and some redundancies, the regional director of a large utility found that she had an almost completely new team. Instead of just managing engineers, she now had a cross-functional team comprising engineers, customer service people, information managers and administrators. This marked a major change for everyone, including the regional director herself. She knew from personal experience how unsettling it was and she had little idea herself how best to proceed in setting up the new team.

Still in this state of mind, she convened a first meeting of the dozen or so most senior and experienced people. 'Much of this meeting was taken up with people meeting each other and then with discussing the recent changes. Some people were angry and frustrated about what had happened without consultation, others were wary and uncertain about what might be coming next. It was hardly a good situation for being positive', yet the regional director went along with this tone and shared some of her own feelings. After a couple of hours the best she could think of was to suggest that they called it a day for now, fixed another meeting for a week's time and asked everyone to come back with some proposals for reorganizing the service configurations in the region.

Most of the time at the second meeting was taken up with people learning from each other about the different aspects of the business, much of which was unfamiliar.

Despite this slow pace, the regional director was beginning to get a sense of progress. In the last half hour of the meeting she posed the questions 'what are we trying to accomplish in this region?' and 'how will we know when we are getting there?'. She had not really planned these questions, although they were in her mind and this seemed to be the right time. 'Of course it would take more meetings to agree the common ground and create a plan that could then be taken out to the wider workforce, but people were listening to each other, they were interested in each other – that felt like a good start.'

Had she read a good book on facilitation skills, the regional director might have felt that she should have helped the group to:

- agree its purpose and direction
- clarify its objectives
- define the roles of members
- plan tasks
- map processes
- make decisions and agreements
- air and resolve conflicts.

However, whilst these are all important aspects of helping people get their work done together, they were not the most important things to do at this time. In the face of anxiety, distress and novelty, what actually happened – and which she allowed or helped to happen – was more useful:

- getting together
- meeting and getting to know everyone
- encouraging the sharing of views from everyone
- listening to each other
- accepting different opinions and feelings
- posing useful questions for progress at the right time.

Facilitation is rarely rocket science. Helping this group of people get on with the job together meant helping them move from anger and distress to a more positive frame of mind. Although we usually make out that work is rational, the people who do it are certainly not, at least not all of the time, and certainly not after a big shake-up.

The process of facilitation

That said, many aspects of the facilitation process are straightforward. The fundamental human processes of meeting, greeting and expressing feelings and opinions need to be given time and space; then, and only then, can the logical sequence of the tasks in the first list above be followed. However, before sketching out this generic process, what would you say is your basic approach to running a meeting?

Below are the three key activities for any meeting; look at this list and, given a 2-hour meeting, what would you say was the right order and about the right amount of time to spend on each of them?

- tackling the business agenda
- meeting and greeting
- exchanging information.

A common error in facilitating meetings is to try and get to the agenda and the decision-making too early. It is very easy under time pressure to underestimate the importance of the fundamental human processes displayed in the utilities case. By contrast, one colleague follows this pattern:

- meeting and greeting   50 minutes
- exchanging information   40 minutes
- tackling the business agenda 30 minutes.

Her meetings can be a bit frustrating for those not used to them; they seem to ramble about and go off at all sorts of tangents. But they do seem to come to good decisions, and quickly, right at the end. Her rationale is something like this: 'People come to meetings glad to see each other and interested to meet any new people. They naturally want to exchange news and gossip before becoming more disciplined about what information they need. By the time we get round to the actual agenda and the decisions, people have already been giving thought, consciously or unconsciously, to these issues and have already worked out their positions. The decision process is usually quick because it is mainly about checking exactly the details of the mandate – what is wanted, and by when. It is all so much easier when people volunteer to take on bits of the agenda – and so much more enjoyable.'

Compare this with some 'businesslike' meetings, which can be more predictable, but also drawn out and lacking commitment on decisions. They may be strongly chaired without much opportunity for those present to find their voices and exchange news and information; consequently, people have to 'warm up' and work out what all the agendas are under the guise of progressing the business decisions – all, actually, very inefficient and unsatisfying.

Facilitators focus on tasks

Having said this, the rational route is often the best way to go. For a group of people in some turmoil or split over which way to go, following an orderly process is healing in itself. In these circumstances, spending too long on the sharing of grief can makes things worse; better to get on and do something. A generic process for facilitation is presented in Table 8.2.

Table 8.2 Facilitating aims and objectives

Step	Action	Key questions
1 Generate aims	Ask each person to write their aims on Post-its, then post up and brainstorm in whole group for any which have been missed	What needs doing in this situation? What do we need to do to fulfil our function and purpose? What could we do that would be useful? Have we missed any important aims?
2 Sort aims	Ask a few volunteers to cluster the Post-its. Then check the meaning of the clusters with the group	Have we got all the possible objectives? What are the main clusters and what are they about?
3 Agree priorities	Ask pairs to agree the top 3 or 4 priorities and then compare lists in the whole group	What are the top priority aims for us? Are we agreed amongst ourselves? Are our priorities the same as those of our key stakeholder, client or customer?
4 Action plan	Ask the group to form into sub-groups – one for each aim – and draft action plans	If we are not agreed on our key priorities, how will we resolve this? How will these aims be accomplished? What needs to be done, by when, etc.?
5 Mandate actions	For each of the action plans, ask the group to allocate roles and responsibilities	Who will do what, by when, etc.? How will we know when an aims is accomplished? How and when will we review progress?

This particular example focuses on creating agreed aims or goals but this process can be applied to any task facing any group working together – generating innovative ideas, planning change, mapping pathways and work processes, resolving conflicts, making decisions and agreements, and so on. In effect, Table 8.2 is a map of the process to follow to complete the task.

Activity: facilitation process

How do you develop this map of facilitation process for any of these tasks? Start by listing the steps in the left-hand column of Table 8.2: what are the logical stages you have to go through to get to the desired end-point? If you were seeking to resolve a conflict for example, the list of stages might look like this:

- Acknowledging the conflict: getting agreement on the problem.
- Expressing differences: getting all the opinions and positions on the table.
- Clarifying differences: what are the dimensions of difference.
- Establishing common ground: what do we agree on?
- Negotiation on areas of non-agreement.
- Agreement or decision.

Obviously, actually resolving a conflict is not as simple as this might imply – but at least it gives you an idea of where you are heading and, crucially, it might encourage you to tackle a conflict rather than avoid it.

The second step in creating a map of the facilitation process is to list the questions in the right-hand column of Table 8.2: what are the key questions which must be answered at each stage? In the example above, this list might start with these questions for stage 1:

■ What is the nature of this conflict?
■ Does everyone know about it?
■ How important is it?
■ Are we agreed that we should try to sort it out?

And so on down the list of stages, until you have listed all the critical questions to be answered before moving on. These questions are as vital as the stages because they tell us exactly what is involved and when it is time to move on.

The third and final step in this process is to fill in, in the middle column, the Actions you will take as facilitator. The middle column is about involving everyone and bringing about good collective agreements and decisions. Here are some general principles to aid thinking about this column:

■ Ask people to write down their initial thoughts on paper before discussion.
   [This ensures that (i) everybody gets a chance to think and (ii) everyone has something to say.]
■ Use pairs, threes or small groups to generate diversity of views or ideas.
   [People warm up better in small groupings, tend to generate more ideas quickly and are less likely to take up strong public stands that are difficult to retreat from.]
■ Use the whole group to make decisions and agreements.
   [Ideally, democracy generates commitment and a fair allocation of responsibilities.]
■ As facilitator, try to limit your contributions to the content of the discussion especially when it comes to making decisions.
   [You should be (i) focusing on the process and (ii) on getting decisions agreed by the group.]

This is the time when the experience of a professional facilitator comes in handy, because it involves understanding the best ways to involve people and to work with the group to accomplish the task. You might find it helpful to talk this column over with someone else.

With a facilitation plan you now have a roadmap of where you want to go. So now you can get on with it; practice makes perfect.

Is help helpful?
(attributed to Jack Gibb)

It is useful to remember that the best judges of helpful facilitation are those whose work has been in some way facilitated. Human beings and their relationships are complicated and helping is not always easy or straightforward. Sometimes our wanting to help gets in the way; sometimes people look as though they need help but actually don't want it. Help may indeed not actually be helpful. As a humorous postcard once indicated: 'If things don't improve soon, I shall have to ask you to stop helping me!'.

Help sometimes appears as a tough challenge, along the lines of the old saying 'Blessed are those with friends willing to act as enemies'. The main thing about acting as a critical friend is to be sure that you *are* actually acting as a friend and not as a bully on a power trip, or possibly more likely, satisfying a personal need to feel helpful. All relationships involve power, without power nothing gets done, but power in relationships can be healthy – each of us is aware of who is trying to influence who to do what; and making their own decisions about what to do next; or unhealthy – I feel I have the right to tell you what to do; you do as I say because you defer to me. Here is a story of critical friendship from personal experience.

Critical friendship

When I was trying to make up my mind whether to leave my secure, if no longer challenging, employment in the Business School, I was helped greatly by David, a friend who made what appeared to be two unkind remarks. I had been in full employment for over 20 years, and my children were leaving home – I pondered lengthily on whether it was time to make a move. On one occasion, he said to me that if I were to be cut through the middle, then around the outside of the cross-section, as on a stick of rock, would be seen running all through the legend 'Sheffield City Polytechnic' (as it then was). On another occasion, listening to me rehearsing my plans for the umpteenth time, he said, 'you have more safety nets than Billy Smart's Circus!'. Both of these remarks were eventually helpful to me, although I hated them at the time. I did not like the thought of being branded for life and I bridled at the idea that I could not take a risk. It took another year to make the move, but like small stones in a shoe, these comments eventually did their work.

Most of the time, being facilitative is about being more conventionally encouraging. Critical friend-type help should be used sparingly and then carefully. It can easily misfire, but when done skilfully in a good relationship, it can be the best sort of help. Being able to be helpful in this way is about more than being skilful, it also requires good heart and good intentions. Mistakes made in good heart at least are easier to forgive.

Further resources

As the right hand of leadership, facilitation crops up all over this book and there are useful examples, activities and tools that can be used to facilitate various different tasks in all of the chapters.

A most useful book which has influenced this chapter and which deals with the nuts and bolts of facilitation on many practical tasks at work is Richard Weaver and John Farrell's *Managers as Facilitators: a Practical Guide to Getting Work Done in a Changing* Workplace (Berrett Koehler, San Francisco, 1999). This hands-on book provides detailed guidance on how to facilitate such tasks as developing purpose statements, prioritizing goals, making decisions, preparing budgets, resolving conflicts and so on. It contains useful information and tools for use in groups such as process mapping, parking lot, multi-voting, affinity and cause–effect diagrams and debriefing. Whereas Weaver and Farrell focus largely on face-to-face groups, Margaret Attwood, Mike Pedler, Sue Pritchard and David Wilkinson provide ideas and illustrations for promoting and facilitating change in large groups and whole systems in their *Leading Change: a Guide to Whole Systems Working* (Policy Press, Bristol, 2003).

If you are interested in going more deeply into the skills of facilitation, there is a small industry to be found here. A good basic guide is F. Bee and R. Bee's *Facilitation Skills* (Chartered Institute of Personnel and Development, London, 1998), and Roger Schwartz's *The Skilled Facilitator: a Comprehensive Resource for Consultants, Facilitators, Managers, Trainers and Coaches* (Jossey Bass Wiley, New York, 2003) is almost all it claims to be.

Reference

Heifetz, R. (1994) *Leadership Without Easy Answers*, Belknap Press, Cambridge, MA.

Practice 7: Networking

I don't know, but I know someone who does ...

Introduction

Leaders live in networks. Influence, inspiration and informal authority are exercised through relationships with other people who may be bosses or subordinates, colleagues or external consultants, peers or business partners. These networks of relationships are the lifeblood and energy source of any organization.

Peers are a most valuable source of information about what is happening: they can offer advice or counsel, give feedback on your behaviour and help you think through options for action – all on the basis of equality without fear of grace and favour. Networks are key to *connection power* – one of the most underrated forms of power and one that has grown in importance in the information age.

Developing connection power means building personal networks that also help create power for the others in these relationships. They make it easy to contact and access relevant people when we need help to accomplish tasks. A wide network provides the wherewithal to cross departmental boundaries and other disputed territories, including even hierarchies, to get things done. Through connecting as peers we can access people in authority structures, both more and less powerful than ourselves. If you know your boss only as a boss, and not also as a fellow member of a project or the local branch of your professional association, your 'bandwidth' with that person remains much narrower than it might. And the same is true of people who work for you. The narrower the bandwidth, the fewer are the sources of information, power and influence.

Networks also aid innovation; better-connected doctors, for example, are more likely to adopt practice innovations than those who are relatively isolated (Rogers, 1995, p. 301). In knowledge-based work, a person's effectiveness rests increasingly on the richness of their personal networks. In his study of general managers, Kotter (1982) found that those most likely to be successful in their careers are those who develop the most effective lateral relationships.

Personal networks vary greatly in shape and extent. As individuals, we have personal characteristics that make some of us more natural networkers from the nursery onwards. A first step is to become aware of our own preferences and how these affect your actions and those around you. A second step is, from whatever base, to build your networks and connection power as an essential element in your leadership.

This chapter contains:

- ■ an introduction to personal networks
- ■ a network mapping activity
- ■ ideas for organizing to help others network more
- ■ further resources.

Personal networks

The inaugural lecture

Recently, I attended the inaugural lecture of a friend and colleague of some 30 years. The hall was filled with an excited community, many of whom had never met before. They were family and friends, academic colleagues, clients and business acquaintances; they were old students, some now retired, and new postgraduates. Also present were some local dignitaries from the University and the city.

I reflected on the diverse nature of this network. Previously invisible, it would soon disappear again and forever. Although virtual and transient, it was over 30 years old, enduring and continuing. How much effort David must have put in to creating and maintaining it – but then he was always a network wizard, enjoying the company of many kinds of people and delighting in moving in different worlds.

On leaving, I met another old colleague, also due to deliver his inaugural lecture. I commented on the size and liveliness of the congregation. 'Yes', he said, 'isn't it terrifying, I only want half a dozen at mine.'

Personal networks are unique, available only to or through the person who composes and maintains them. They come in all sizes and express personal preferences and ways of working. They can be seen as a personal extension of the person who animates them. The queen of network wizards is Carole Stone (2000), who claims 14 000 entries in her electronic address book; but then she does little else – giving rise to an old joke about notworking.

But 'knot-working' is the order of the day in complex environments involving multiple partners. As a Health Service manager said, in the light of the imminent disappearance of her organization, 'I'm not too worried, I'm sure I will find a berth … my main value to any organization is my contacts and networks'. In all these contexts, as extensions of people, personal networks are vital to organizations.

Networks are like string bags: any one knot is only connected to four others, but those four are connected to four more, so that the original knot or node or person is only one step away from 12 new people and only two steps removed from a further 36. Faced with a problem to which we don't know the answer, we call the person most likely to know, if he/she doesn't know, he/she probably knows someone who does, … .

Think about your personal network.

Activity: my personal network

My contacts: Write down the names of the people you consult and talk to on each of the following questions: who can I …

	Inside work	Outside work
… go to for general sharing and catching up?		
… ask about specialist information in my field of work?		
… ask about solutions to business issues and problems?		
… get help from with thinking through a particularly difficult work issue or question?		
… get approval and validation for a course of action I am thinking of taking?		
… ask for advice about a tricky moral or political issue?		
… tell good news to?		
… tell bad news to?		
… share a secret with?		
… take a risk with?		
… just say 'hello' to and keep in touch from time to time?		

What do you notice about your collection of names? For example:

- Are you a person who has lots of contacts, say 20 plus, or a person who prefers a small, enduring network, say six or so?
- Are you relying on the same person or persons for many different types of advice or help?
- Are you better connected at work or outside work?

Strong ties and weak ties

A further step in the analysis of your network is to look at your strong and weak ties. The difference between these two types of relationships lies at the heart of the magic of networking.

To think about strong and weak ties, map your contacts as in Figure 9.1, putting yourself at the middle of the web and connecting yourself to all the other people by lines. Put frequent contacts, and people with whom you are close, nearer to you and join them with thick lines – your strong ties; put less frequent contacts, and people you are less close to, further away and connected by thin or dotted lines – your weaker ties.

In the example given in Figure 9.1, the central person has strong ties with Chris, Pete, Hans and especially Sophie. They may work closely with these people, perhaps in the same work group, and consult them often, probably relying on them for personal support. It is the strong ties that provide the bonding and resilience in a network.

The group of people joined by broken lines are weaker ties; these are people consulted less often and perhaps on specialist issues.

It is these weak ties that constitute one of the most important qualities of networks – their ability to bridge across organizational and other boundaries to bring in new knowledge and innovation. If you rely upon a small, tight network, you may find that you are short on weak ties.

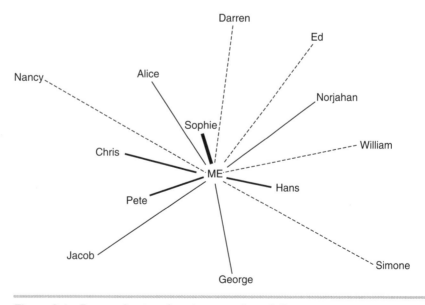

Figure 9.1   Personal networks: strong and weak ties

Bridging and bonding

In social network analysis there are two main dimensions – bridging and bonding. Bridging measures the reach of a network – how far does it extend geographically, occupationally, socially, by interest group or knowledge area? Bonding measures the strength of ties in a network – strong ties are personal relationships renewed on a regular basis; weak ties are remote links made through other people, of the 'I don't know but I know someone who does ...' type.

Obviously these are very different types of relationships. Weak ties are not really relationships at all, but contacts from whom you can get valuable information or help on a one-off or very occasional basis. For example, once, during a national rail strike, when I had to get to Dover to catch a boat and train to Milan, I was able to call a person who belonged to the same professional association. This person worked for the Harbour Board and very kindly agreed to let me park there for 2 weeks, even sending a key through the post. I had never met this man before and, apart from saying thanks and sending the key back, have never been in contact since.

It is this 'strength of weak ties' which marks a critical aspect of all networks. Although we think of our regular contacts and personal relationships as 'our network', in fact they are only part of the picture. The real power of your network lies in who you can reach through your existing ties. With the people you know, you already have a trusting relationships in which you readily give and take. However, the willingness of strangers to help in this way is a most remarkable thing. This reciprocity can extend much further than the more usual helping the friend of a friend. Professional membership, for example, often brings with it an obligation to engage in 'loose reciprocity' – a willingness to give something to someone from whom you are not likely to get anything back directly. This is not just a matter of altruism, as you never know when you will need a parking place or something equally useful, but it does demonstrate the high level of trust which is one of the most attractive aspects of networks.

Are your strengths in bonding or bridging (Figure 9.2)? 'Hubbers' are the network wizards, proficient and committed to networking as a lifestyle. 'Butterflies' have many, many contacts but do not linger for long and may lack the strong ties to deliver on tasks. Lots of us are 'Local Heroes' and not a few professionals are 'Loners' by formation and preference. If leadership is thrust upon such people, then the challenge is to overcome long-held habits and actively seek to widen the network.

Robert Cross (2000) has demonstrated the power of weak ties to show how far people reach outside the firm in search of useful knowledge. In his research on management consultants, his respondents relied more heavily on weak ties with people outside their own units to find the actual ideas to resolve work problems, whilst using their strong internal ties to help validate possible solutions.

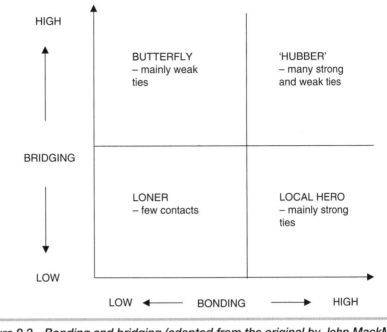

Figure 9.2   Bonding and bridging (adapted from the original by John MackMersh)

Extending your reach

Depending on your strengths, you will probably benefit from extended networks, both through building up strong ties around particular tasks or projects and by increasing your reach in search of new knowledge. In a classical experiment amongst doctors, Coleman and his colleagues found that innovativeness in adopting the drug tetracycline was associated with seven measures of network interconnectedness:

- affiliation with the hospital as a regular staff member
- more frequent attendance at hospitals staff meetings
- sharing an office with one or more doctors
- being named as a source of information and advice by other doctors
- being named by other doctors as someone with whom they discussed their patients
- being named as a friend by other doctors
- reciprocating the same links reported by other doctors who choose the respondent as a discussion partner.

These seven factors of interconnectedness were a better predictor of innovativeness than any personal characteristics; in other words, what happens between people is more important for innovation than what is within individuals (Rogers, 1995, pp. 299–303).

The prescription for extending your network in terms of strong ties is contained in Coleman's seven measures of interconnectedness. Just translate these into your context and get on with it.

To extend your reach to bridge beyond your colleagues and your organization, you need to get out more. There are many, many ways of doing this, including some very obvious ones such as going to conferences or courses. Whatever the quality of the presentations at such events, top rankings in evaluations are nearly always given to meeting new people and 'corridor conversations'. The formal programme just gives you an excuse to go and meet people.

A friend, who had spent most of his life in a particular industry, joined a local 'Common Purpose' programme with people from different worlds – commercial companies, local government, charities, voluntary associations and the professions. Despite his senior position, he managed to make all the monthly attendances for a year. He hit it off with someone from a charitable organization and, a year or so later, this changed the course of his career. Getting out creates the chance for chance to happen.

Organizing for networking

The benefits of reaching out are not just personally important, they are also vital for your colleagues and for your organization. If personal networking is one of first responsible practices of leadership, then thinking about how to organize in order to encourage your colleagues to increase their reach and connectedness comes a close second. This can be approached at several different levels. For example:

On a one-to-one basis: you can encourage your colleagues to read this chapter and do the activities for themselves and become aware of their own personal networking practice and preferences. Ask them to think about the opportunities they have for increasing their reach through:

- working parties
- special project groups
- professional associations
- communities of interest and practice
- alumni groupings
- Internet communities.

or even by setting up special interest groups of their own. A striking aspect of the history of science is how two or more researchers were approaching the same idea at the same time but in different locations, unaware of each other. This is less likely to happen in big science these days, but it is very likely to be happening more locally. Who else is interested in what you are doing? How can you get in touch with them? What could happen if you started talking about it?

In groups and meetings: any regular and routine business meeting can be transformed by very simple changes to promote discussion and exchange. Under pressure from agendas, many of these meetings begin too abruptly with Business Item One. Instead of doing this, start with a 'Round Robin' (going round the group to hear from each person in turn without interruption), on, for example, 'What's new in widget design this month?'.

This creates possibilities for people to contact each other later and to talk one to one, but it may also help with the business in hand. In many meetings, this sort of listening and communicating time at the outset will do wonders for later business-focused discussions, because everyone has been involved and refreshed by the ideas.

Designing working space: some workplaces are actually designed to promoting meeting and networking. Although communicating and talking to other people is a major part of work, many offices and workplaces are built apparently to isolate people as much as possible. Narrow corridors maximize personal space whilst reducing conversation space.

Some visionary architects have tried to do different things. The Ark is a building that looks like an ocean liner near the Hammersmith flyover in London. It was designed to be more like a theatre than a conventional office, with a multipurpose auditorium, for conferences, lectures, sales meetings and artistic performances, which opens out into a small square with an atrium and bar. The entrance floor has a large meeting point to encourage meeting and experience sharing and has 'world information' shown on large screens. The designer's brochure describes it as 'An escape from the traditional, centrally governed business into a network-oriented one ... An open concept, designed for people to communicate, to help ideas flow, to make information come alive. You might even say, to give chance a chance. The Ark is designed to make it easy for people to meet, to relax, to discuss, to exchange ideas ... a town under a roof' (Hastings, 1993, pp. 93–94).

Failing your own Ark, you can think about meeting and conversation space and how to use it. How can you maximize the space for 'corridor conversations' to give chance a chance? Decide where to hold meetings. Have this one at your house? Even making small physical changes to your usual room can have a major effect on conversation. Round tables are better than rectangular ones for sharing views. Dispensing with the table is a more dramatic intervention.

Get out more

According to some observers, networks are the organizational form for the 21st century. Chapter 21 focuses upon these organizational aspects. Although it is clear that organizational networks are very different creatures from personal networks, what is not always noticed is that the two are closely linked. Organizational networks need much more than alliance agreements and electronic connectedness to make them work. It is the practice of personal networking that supports organizational efforts to link across the value chain.

The idea of industrial clusters – firms in the same trade or industry which gather together in the same geographical area – has been around for centuries. In these clusters, firms do not go in for vertical integration with every function in-house, but become very specialized, taking on just a small sliver of a product or service according to their core competence. This is only possible because of the dense network of suppliers and business partners to add in the other parts and complete the service to the customer. Such clusters are often remarkably successful:

> ... one town (Salkot) in Pakistan plays a dominant role in the world market for specialist surgical instruments made of stainless steel. From a core group of 300 small firms, supported by 1500 even smaller suppliers, 90 per cent of production (1996) was exported and took a 20 per cent share of the world market, second only to Germany. In another case, the Sinos valley in Brazil contains around 500 small-firm manufacturers of specialist high-quality leather shoes. Between 1970 and 1990 their share of the world market rose from 0.3 to 12.5 per cent and they now export some 70 per cent of total production. In each case the gains are seen as resulting from close interdependence in a co-operative network.
>
> (Bessant and Tsekouras, 2000)

Researchers argue as to whether it is the learning and the exchange of know-how that plays the central part in this sort of business development or whether firms simply gather like this to take advantage of local and specialized labour markets. Wherever the truth lies, it is not electronic networking but human contact that is making these formal and informal organizational collaborations tick. Reports from Silicon Valley in California show that, despite virtualization, these hi-tech firms like to be close together and work in each other's backyards. The managers in these firms get out a lot. They are visiting each other's facilities and in each other's offices on a regular basis. It is this intricate and regularly renewed web of personal contacts that lays the foundation for the organizational networks which are essential to this mode of production.

The message for leaders is obvious: get out more, particularly with those people, partners, competitors, consultants and commentators who share your interests. The more contact you have with them, the more you extend your personal reach and your grasp, and the more you create the chances of making successful arrangements for clustering and network organizing.

Further resources

There are lots of books on personal networking and you will find a selection on most station and airport bookstalls. Most of them say very similar things but they might be useful to spark off ideas. Carole Stone's book (referenced below) is one of these.

The Complete Idiots Guide to Knowledge Management by Melissie Clemmens Rumizen (CWL Publishing Enterprises, Madison, WI, 2002) has some very simple advice on how to improve your knowledge networking. If this sort of book appeals to you, it does make the welcome point that knowledge management is done by people and not by computer networks.

References

Bessant, J. and G. Tsekouras (2000) *Developing Learning Networks*, AI & Soc 15:1–1, Springer-Verlag, London.

Cross, R. (2000) 'More than an answer: how seeking information through people facilitates knowledge creation and use', *Organizational Communication and Information Systems*, submitted.

Hastings, C. (1993) *The New Organisation: Growing the Culture of Organisational Networking*, McGraw-Hill, Maidenhead.

Kotter, J. P. (1982) *The General Managers*, Free Press, New York.

Rogers, E. M. (1995) *Diffusion of Innovations*, 4th edn, Free Press, New York.

Stone, C. (2000) *Networking: the Art of Making Friends*, Vermillion, London.

Part 3

Key Leadership Challenges

Challenge 1: Developing Direction and Strategy

Leadership is the collective capacity to create something of value
Peter Senge

Introduction

'Forward-looking and inspiring', or 'strategic and innovative' or 'direction and commitment'? Choose any of the many books on leadership and it is likely to have a list of leadership attributes such as these. All these lists are likely to include the core characteristic of giving direction, setting strategy or pointing the way to the future. This is one of the constants of leadership.

Setting direction can be a complex task in uncertain conditions. However difficult, choosing strategic direction in a rapidly changing world is not an option, but a requirement. A future orientation is part of staying with the game, and a key to learning.

This core characteristic is sometimes called vision:

> *To choose a direction, a leader must first have developed a mental image of a possible and desirable future state for the organization. This image, which we call a vision, may be as vague as a dream or as precise as a goal or mission statement. The critical point is that a vision articulates a view of a realistic, credible, attractive future for the organisation, a condition that is better in some important ways than what now exists.*
>
> (Bennis and Nanus, 1985, p. 89)

This is helpful because it emphasizes the need to look to the future. However, we have mixed feelings about this notion of vision. We prefer the notion of purpose and of being on purpose (see Chapter 5), which we see as a stronger and more enduring driver. Visions are often ephemeral things, fleeting and fantastic, which can blind as much as they can inspire. A sense of purpose includes the future vision but binds this to core values and the will and energy necessary to make a difference. Without a clear sense of purpose and where we are coming from, it is easy to feel directionless, however fast we are moving.

We are also unhappy with Bennis and Nanus's implication that vision is the property and inspiration of the single heroic leader. Leadership and management, strategy and operations are not just activities or functions. They carry status in organizations. To be strategic is to be important; to be operational is to be lower placed. With this logic, strategy is obviously a job for top people:

> *Our senior management used to be very hands-on and involved in everything. Then we had an inspection in which they were told that they were not sufficiently strategic. Since then we haven't set eyes on any of them.*
>
> (Further Education College lecturer, 2002)

And this is all too common. Not only does this separate strategy from implementation – one of the critical problems of our time – but it leaves those charged with running the business in the dark:

> *They might call it strategy, but it feels like chaos to us.*
>
> (Un-named prison officer quoted at the time of a major reorganization of the prison system)

We believe that leadership is about collective purposes achieved by people working in concert. Whatever the future we strive for, it has to be our vision. This means that those taking responsibility for leadership need to develop processes of involvement for creating desirable pictures of the future, to ensure that the 'we' is more than just window dressing. This is closer to the spirit that Heifetz invokes when he says that leadership is not a position but an *activity* that generates socially useful outcomes. It is:

> *the activity of a citizen from any walk of life mobilising people to do something*
>
> (Heifetz, 1994, p. 20)

The starting point for a collective approach to direction and strategy is found in the actual work and the challenges faced there. What are we trying to do? What is stopping us? How can we move forward? These are the everyday questions in every working practice, in every workplace. Here is a group of citizens trying to do something useful.

Community midwives

A group of community midwives began meeting informally to improve the care in their city for women and babies with HIV/AIDS. They came together as a result of a two of them meeting over coffee to talk about their work. This led to a meeting, which attracted most of the other midwives and which went well. The meetings continued on a regular basis. By creating a forum for a conversation that had not been happening before, the group became more widely influential. Having come together voluntarily to improve their practice, they have become a useful part of the public health system. The Strategic Health Authority has asked the group for advice on policy and also for help in implementation. Not all the group are keen on this idea. Is this the sort of group we should be? Will this help women and their babies?

In this example, direction comes from being clear about your purpose, from finding collective purpose and then by acting on this to bring about something useful. In the rest of this chapter we provide models and tools for helping you to get started on finding collective direction and for generating strategies that engage all those concerned to move purposefully into the future. The rest of this chapter contains:

■ a model of the eight elements of a learning approach to strategy together with a questionnaire for assessing yourself and your colleagues
■ a tool for creating common direction in your organization through scenario thinking
■ further resources.

A learning approach to strategy

Traditionally strategy work and direction finding involve such activities as:

■ analysing the organization's environment and planning to take an advantageous position in it
■ forecasting the future and creating rational strategic plans to fit
■ understanding 'internal' resources: the core competencies, of an organization and organizing to make best use of them
■ identifying the big decisions that matter and getting them right.

These activities all have their place but they do not deal well with the question of learning. More recent ideas make a learning approach to strategy more overt: setting a direction of travel but hanging loose in order to react swiftly and creatively to new situations and to take advantage of any new opportunities. Recent ideas about this approach stress both vision and dialogue:

■ *Transformational* thinking seeks to develop 'stretching' directions which inspire people to work towards them, developing themselves as they do so. Because the new vision is beyond where we are now, energy is released by our joint efforts to achieve it. It becomes modified it as we go along, with individuals innovating and stretching themselves to discover new ways and to do things they have not done before.

Box 10.1 The eight elements of a learning approach to strategy

Space:	giving individuals space for learning and responsible experimentation
A Big Picture:	explaining the strategic context of work and plans
Feedback:	seeking and passing on comments on strategies in the light of implementation experience
Participation:	facilitating participation while ensuring decisiveness
Holding Framework:	creating a climate where existing working methods can be challenged and changed in a co-ordinated manner
Experiment:	enabling responsible experimentation and sharing of learning
Learning:	encouraging a 'solve and learn' rather than a 'blame and punish' approach to problem solving
Personal Example:	personally and visibly modelling a learning attitude and approach.

■ *Dialogical* ideas encourage leaders to orchestrate discussions that lead to shared understandings and commitments. The dialogue involves open discussion of the organization's purpose and project and what is being learnt about how to progress it in action. The leadership's contribution is to set up the frameworks and structures for dialogue to take place and to encourage everyone to take part in it.

From this perspective, strategic leadership develops around a collective conversation about the future, and the concerted action learning that is stimulated by this. Leadership means supporting space for individual learning and the sharing of this intelligence with others whilst at the same time encouraging everyone's participation in strategy improvement and review. This releases the power of individual learning and links it to organizational learning. The vision is one of people as partners in strategy implementation, with everyone networked to provide a powerful collective intelligence.

There are eight elements of this learning approach to strategy (Box 10.1).

Activity: questionnaire – a learning approach to strategy

Here is a questionnaire to check your or your team's standing on the eight elements of a learning approach to strategy listed in Box 10.1. You can use it either as a self-rating questionnaire for individuals and teams or as a more general survey of the style of strategic leadership in an organization. You can do it here and now for your own benefit, but the best results come from talking over the results with other people. It takes only a few minutes for each person to complete and score the questionnaire, but considerably longer to discuss the findings and implications.

For each of the following 24 questions, rate yourself on the five-point scale:

I rarely or never do this = 1 – 2 – 3 – 4 – 5 = *I always or regularly do this*

Try to avoid using 3.

1	I encourage others to undertake new projects to widen their experience	1 – 2 – 3 – 4 – 5
2	I always explain the big picture behind current projects	1 – 2 – 3 – 4 – 5
3	I ask for feedback from stakeholders on the strategies we are following	1 – 2 – 3 – 4 – 5
4	We try to involve everyone in arriving at decisions	1 – 2 – 3 – 4 – 5
5	I encourage all team members to question our ways of working	1 – 2 – 3 – 4 – 5
6	People are encouraged to work in small groups for learning purposes	1 – 2 – 3 – 4 – 5
7	We treat crises and problems as opportunities for experiment and learning	1 – 2 – 3 – 4 – 5
8	I publish my own personal development plans to my team	1 – 2 – 3 – 4 – 5
9	All our people are expected to have plans for their personal development	1 – 2 – 3 – 4 – 5
10	We take time out to take a 'helicopter view' of what we are doing	1 – 2 – 3 – 4 – 5
11	I always want to hear how strategies are working in practice	1 – 2 – 3 – 4 – 5
12	As much as possible, I involve all those people concerned with a problem in arriving at a solution	1 – 2 – 3 – 4 – 5
13	Anyone who wants to change the way we do things can give it a go	1 – 2 – 3 – 4 – 5
14	When people try things out which work – or don't work – we all want to know about them	1 – 2 – 3 – 4 – 5
15	When someone makes a mistake, we know it will start a good discussion	1 – 2 – 3 – 4 – 5
16	In team meetings, I make it plain what I am learning from what we are doing	1 – 2 – 3 – 4 – 5
17	When I meet with colleagues I always check on what they have been learning recently	1 – 2 – 3 – 4 – 5
18	I have a strong sense of strategic direction and communicate this	1 – 2 – 3 – 4 – 5
19	My team is keen to pass on to our bosses how well they think implementation programmes are going	1 – 2 – 3 – 4 – 5
20	Up to the deadline, everyone around here can have their say	1 – 2 – 3 – 4 – 5

21	People consciously think about how they are working on a regular basis	1 – 2 – 3 – 4 – 5
22	We make time for the regular transfer of knowledge across teams	1 – 2 – 3 – 4 – 5
23	When a problem crops up, there is competition for who gets to work on it	1 – 2 – 3 – 4 – 5
24	I maintain the space for my own learning in spite of the pressures	1 – 2 – 3 – 4 – 5

Scoring

Add the scores from the 24 questions in the eight vertical columns:

QUESTIONS:	1	2	3	4	5	6	7	8
	9	10	11	12	13	14	15	16
	17	18	19	20	21	22	23	24
TOTALS:	[ ]	[ ]	[ ]	[ ]	[ ]	[ ]	[ ]	[ ]
	1	2	3	4	5	6	7	8

This Learning Approach to Strategy Questionnaire assesses you against the model of eight elements above, that is:

1 Space
2 A Big Picture
3 Feedback
4 Participation
5 Holding Framework
6 Experiment
7 Learning
8 Personal Example.

What this means to you in the context of your organization is a matter for reflection and discussion – there are no right and wrong answers. However, if you think that this is a good way to work, then scores of 7 or less on any element might indicate that you need to make greater efforts here, whereas a score of less than 4 would indicate considerable grounds for concern. On the other hand, a score of more than 9 on any element shows that you are making good progress here, and a score of more than 12 indicates that you are setting a fine example for others to model.

Review

Before moving on, you might like to take some time to reflect on the findings from the Learning Approach to Strategy Questionnaire. Here are some review questions to ponder on or to discuss with colleagues:

■ What are your strengths as a strategic leader?
■ How do your responses to this activity compare with those of your colleagues?

- What *one* thing could you do to develop yourself in this context?
- What would you say are the strengths and weaknesses of your organization as a whole?
- How could you encourage the development of your organization along these lines?

Creating common direction

The fish rots from the head. (Old Chinese saying.)

(Bob Garratt)

In many organizations, setting strategy and direction remains the province of great men or top teams – and their consultants. As the college lecturer and prison officer quoted above show, this lamentable state of affairs can lead to strategies that ignore the knowledge and intelligence of the rest of the staff and of the organization's stakeholders. At best those charged with implementation are told which direction to march in; at worst, as the old joke goes, they are kept in the dark and fed on manure.

The way to move out of this pernicious trap is to start by creating a common direction with a much larger group of people. There are various ways to do this, and the tool offered in this chapter helps you to build some alternative scenarios for the future in collaboration with others.

'Collaborative advantage' has been a goal for many organizations since Rosabeth Kanter's suggestion that this was the key to business success in a new, interconnected world (Kanter, 1994, pp. 96–108). Yet it remains true that this is easier said than done.

Collaborative advantage

A management consultant was reflecting on a long experience of working with senior teams on strategy questions. 'I seem to spend a lot of my time trying to encourage them to collaborate ... because they spend so much of their time using their strategic abilities to compete with each other.' 'However', he continued, 'I often wonder if I'm right in this because they live in such a competitive world and I suppose they do need to hone their competitive skills. The problem is that they can't give it up when they get in there. This means that they can't listen to each other in the right way and they can't learn from each other.'

This inability to learn is a great threat to any organization. We may not – indeed we are unlikely to – get the direction right first time, but if we are confident in our abilities to learn, individually and collectively, then we can adjust, flex, move quickly to change. Scenario thinking helps groups of people – from small teams to large stakeholder conferences – to start thinking about the future directions for the organization. It differs from strategic planning in making the process more important than the outcome. Out of these discussions can come not only some valuable options, but even more significantly, perhaps, a general readiness for the future and an understanding that this will involve change and learning.

Scenario thinking

If something can go wrong, it will – Murphy's Law.

Scenario thinking is about sharpening our collective appreciation of the key challenges that could face us under different conditions. The trap of prediction and plans can be avoided by looking at long term possibilities and proposing alternatives which express uncertainty in structured ways. This is strategic thinking rather than strategic planning.

In the simplest form of scenario thinking there are three basic scenario (Figure 10.1):

1   Middle ground: 'the future will be much like the present'.
2   Best case: environmental conditions favour us.
3   Worst case: environmental conditions work against us.

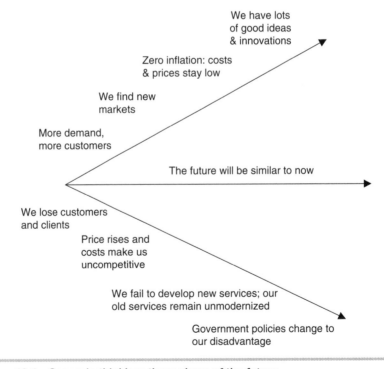

Figure 10.1   Scenario thinking: three views of the future

There can be many variations on these basic scenarios, and larger groups in particular can generate multiple options, all of which will add to the richness of the future picture. In the example given below, the simple design is followed. Sources for more complex versions can be found at the end of the chapter.

Activity: brief for scenario thinking

Divide the group into three, perhaps to represent the whole or perhaps to maximize diversity of views and scenarios. If you want to follow the basic three scenarios sketched in Figure 10.1, then ask the group to self-select or allocate them to the three teams and ask them to think in those terms. If you want to encourage diversity and maximize the options, then divide the group into as many teams as possible (a minimum of three or four per group is probably necessary to get good creative thinking).

Set the date for 5 or 7 years into the future. The trick is to get people to think *as if the future had already happened.*

1 Brief everyone as follows:
   'It is 20__ [5 or 7 years from now], how are we leading strategic change and its implementation in this organization?
   ◼ What has changed for our:
      — clients or customers and their level of service & satisfaction?
      — staff and their commitment & motivation?
      — business partners & the relationship we have had with them?
      — other stakeholders, including the communities we work in?
   ◼ What have been the critical issues since 20__ [today]?'
   NB. Put yourselves into the future, work from the perspective of 20__ [5 or 7 years from now]; talk about now in the past tense; use 'we' and not 'they', you are still here directing the organization.
2 The groups should then disperse to a private space equipped with whatever materials they might find useful: flipcharts, coloured pens, collage materials, modelling clay, etc.
   Fix a time for them to come back with their findings and ask them to present these in whatever way they think will have most impact.
3 At the appointed time, have the teams present their scenarios. Encourage the other teams to support rather than compete (although you may have to bow to the inevitable at times) by asking questions only for clarification.
4 When all the teams have presented their scenarios, facilitate a whole group discussion around the question:

> *What are the strategic themes and issues that we should be pursuing now in order to maximize our chances of getting to where we want to be?*

Conclusion

Scenario planning is not complicated and the brief given in this chapter is enough to get you and your colleagues started on the process. However, this sort of thinking is well written up, and if you are keen to develop a deeper perspective then the sources below will help.

The value of scenario thinking is that it demonstrates that different futures create different challenges, and this is very helpful in terms of mental preparation for alternatives and contingencies. It helps to develop the 'mental muscles' in individuals and organizations for finding direction in complex circumstances. Above all, it shows the importance of the ability to learn from experience, which is the best guarantee for future success.

Further resources

Bill Weinstein's 'The use of scenario thinking: can a scenario a day keep the doctor away?' in B. Garratt (ed.), *Developing Strategic Thought: Rediscovering the Art of Direction* (McGraw-Hill, Maidenhead, 1995) is a straightforward guide to this process. Other chapters in this book are also helpful, as are Garratt's other books which focus on the difference between directing and managing in organizations and on the role of directors in creating the learning organization. A more recent book is Kees Van den Heijden's *The Sixth Sense: Accelerating Organisational Learning with Scenarios* (Wiley, Chichester, 2002), which builds on the author's previous work and the famous scenario development work done at Shell.

Leading Change: A Guide to Whole Systems Working by Margaret Attwood, Mike Pedler, Sue Pritchard and David Wilkinson (Policy Press, Bristol, 2003) gives a whole systems thinking perspective on developing strategy and leadership, and will help particularly in working with big groups and conferences.

References

Bennis, W. and B. Nanus (1985) *The Strategies for Taking Charge*, Harper and Row, New York.

Heifetz, R. (1994) *Leadership Without Easy Answers*, Belknap Press, Cambridge, MA.

Kanter, R. M. (1994) 'Collaborative advantage: the art of alliances', *Harvard Business Review*, July–August, 96–108.

11

Challenge 2: Creating a Learning Organization

The people in here know the answers and can do it
Chief Inspector, Transport Police

Introduction

Leadership and learning are closely connected. Following new paths leads to exploration, discovery and learning. In the learning organization, leadership can be defined as learning on behalf of the organization.

Organizations start as ideas in the heads of people. Many of these are stillborn. Of those brought into life, many do not survive infancy. The 40–50 per cent that do make it are busy, active places, full of learning taking place naturally. The dangers to learning lie beyond this pioneer stage. As the company grows older, as the original market declines or as the influence of the founders weakens, the initial working and learning energy gets lost. Learning companies make conscious efforts to retain this energy.

> A *learning company is an organization that facilitates the learning of all its members and consciously transforms itself and its context.*
> (Pedler, Burgoyne and Boydell, 1996, p. 3)

In this definition, individual and organizational learning are linked together. Action in such an organization is designed not only to solve the immediate problem, but also to learn from this experience and to spread that learning to wherever it might be most useful. Companies are made up of individuals but often the whole knows less than the sum of the parts. People learn all the time but often the organization does not learn from its own people. This basic fact is well understood by the manager who provided the quote to start this chapter. The learning organization has a value and a faith in learning for all its people and understands that transformation – unlike change – comes from within.

Reg Revans's ecological equation:

$$L \geqslant C$$

holds that learning (L) – in any organism, animal, human, organization – must equal or exceed the rate of change (C), otherwise that person or organization will be in decline, falling behind the times. The demand for high-quality leadership is because of this need to deal with high levels of environmental change whilst delivering demanding performance goals. In the flatter network form now evolving in many organizational settings, these qualities are necessary in more and more of the people concerned. The learning organization aspires to a performance culture that is also a learning culture. Here people are encouraged to pursue results energetically and also to learn from their experience by continuous open and critical review. To meet the targets and goals, leadership must facilitate, rather than impose, learning and transformation for all.

This chapter contains:

- proposition X: maximizing performance and learning
- what does learning organization look like?: stories and glimpses of the idea practice
- how to sustain excellence and learning
- a tool based on the EFQM's Excellence Model for assessing the learning organization in any company of people
- further resources.

Proposition X: maximizing performance and learning

The learning organization is of particular interest because it promises to unlock a potential that has not been achieved by command and control. This is not an airy-fairy proposition but a deliberate strategy to generate better performance through learning. However, the pressures and seductions of position power are such that managers find themselves demanding performance and this means that, much of the time, short-term targets drive out the longer cycle of learning.

In his research with management accountants and their firms, Alan Coad has proposed two fundamental orientations producing two very different patterns of behaviour. Individuals (and firms) with a 'performance goal orientation' are concerned with *achieving positive evaluations* (and avoiding negative ones), whereas those with a 'learning goal orientation' are concerned with *increasing their competence* (Coad, 1999, pp. 110–111). The danger of getting performance management out of balance is the effect that it has on staff morale and levels of trust. In Chapter 23 we note the 'Mad Management Virus'

(MMV) that seems to grip organizations that get stuck in setting more and more targets policed by inspection and control systems employing negative feedback. A dehumanizing system cannot be a learning system. To learn, people need to feel good about themselves, feel confident in their capabilities and feel able to take the risk to try something new in order to change. Note how much this is to do with feelings. MMV is the explanation for why the powerfully liberating ideas of total quality and learning organization are so often turned into bureaucratic exercises.

If the wisdom to fix the problem resides within, this can only emerge by encouraging people to question how things are done. Reg Revans, the practical philosopher of action learning, proposed the shortest definition of the learning organization as 'the upward communication of doubt' because 'doubt ascending speeds wisdom from above'. Fresh questions allow a wise leadership to reflect, learn and perhaps change course; the lack of these leaves senior people without good intelligence from the front. How to strike the balance?

Can the two be done at once (Figure 11.1)? The philosophy of the NHS Trent Region could be summed up as 'Meeting your targets gives headroom for development'.

Proposition X holds that you can be both top-down and directive whilst also being facilitative and supportive. These two pressures are often assumed to be contradictory rather than complementary. Proposition X is thus a tough challenge. Yes, it was said that Trent was successful in meeting Government targets and also regarded as very developmental compared with other Regions. Successive Regional Directors pursued a local tradition of strong performance management whilst impressing the expectation of development for all people from the Chief Executives down.

Proposition X was given added impetus by the Government's modernization agenda and its array of performance targets. The aspiration of public service modernization amounts to a massive cultural change, particularly in terms of making (in reality rationed) services more 'client or user focused'. This is an Olympian task unlikely to be achieved by performance management alone. Trent sought the long-term development of people and organizations in the face of these targets, through a combination of leadership development programmes

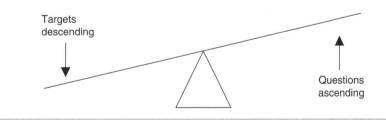

Figure 11.1 The see-saw of performance and learning

and support for displaced Chief Executives and Directors. One interesting innovation was the forming of local leadership development cells. These cells were development spaces to encourage local leaders in each health community, and for once, they were not filled from above.

What does a learning organization look like?

Later in this chapter we develop a model of the learning organization and describe the significant characteristics. Before that, however – on the principle that 'the wisdom to fix this business resides within' – it is important to think about the internal vision in any organization. What does this idea means to you? We have found in our travels that different people and organizations interpret this idea in marvellously diverse ways – all of which help them to achieve what they are seeking.

Here are some stories, in response to the question 'How is your business a learning organization?'.

Learning organizations

'We decided to do 360° feedback in our organization in a way which is truly about learning and not about funnelling or challenging. Most 360° feedbacks are anonymous – which does not fit with our open values – so we designed our own system. Appraisees have the choice of whether they want to share their feedback … It's a making sense process, a conversation; it's about learning.'

'I am the Medical Director in a University Hospital. The hospital is full of different professional groups – doctors, nurses, therapists, researchers, technicians of many varieties – this can be bad for patients. We started a disease management programme and all the professionals learned to define this process together. This is a seed for a new learning culture.'

'For 10 years I was the manager in a publishing company, I then left to become a wife and mother at home. After some time I got in touch with a local organization that helps people to learn to deal with themselves and others in a development process. Now, with seven others whom I met, we are going back to work in profit and non-profit organizations. We always work in pairs to evaluate our work. We have four meetings a year to share and help each other.'

'In this company we have declared that we are going to be a learning organization. Not only this but that we are going to be a world class learning organization! We have a "learning table" at lunchtimes – where you can have a free lunch but you have to talk about learning in some way to the other people you find there.'

'To us being a learning organization means sustainability. A manager I know wanted to develop his people but had little money. So he made his poor performers redundant and made a considerable investment in training the others. Customer satisfaction went from 60 to 90 per cent – but how do you sustain this?'

'One good shot. Do you play golf? One good shot keeps you playing the game. I became Head of Human Resources in a company that was in survival mode. I wasn't told this when I joined. It was a time when they were most closed to learning, but in a way most open. I read books and we transformed the company over 3 years – it was a Camelot experience – by pulling teams together we saved millions, and saved the company. We had a very hierarchical, paternalistic boss, but we managed to involve everyone up to him. But after survival the old organization came back, not straight away, it took about 18 months. We have been doing it hierarchically for 3000 years – why do we think we can do it in 10 or 20 years? For 3½ years we had a great time. Nine or ten of the top twelve players have left the organization now; they couldn't stay.'

These short stories give some glimpses into the realities faced by different people seeking to bring about the learning company idea. Some of the actions are straightforward – learning tables, 360° feedback, multi-professional process redesign teams – but however simple and singular, they can have a powerful effect literally and symbolically. It depends on *how* you do them.

Other stories concern system-wide efforts at development and raise the key question of sustainability. One encouraging story shows how the practices of learning together are not to be confined within the boundaries of existing work organizations. Others raise questions of values and contexts. Would you make some of your people redundant in order to invest in others? Could you? Should you? What does it take to sustain the learning?

Discovering difference and sustaining learning

Many, if not most, organizations are natural learning environments when they first start, but later in the organizational life cycle learning can come through crisis – as in the Human Resources Director's story. This company was stuck and very closed, but it was also open for anything that might save it. This was an opportunity to do something different, and discovering difference is the starting point for learning.

Some organizations are able to sustain a sort of 'continuous revolution' in thinking and learning. Rob is the owner-manager of an engineering company that employs almost 100 people making and servicing air conditioning systems. Founded in 1975, Welbeck Resources was then largely supplying the coal industry, but had to move smartly and diversify as its host industry gradually disappeared. Rob describes a regular learning cycle occurring approximately every 3 years:

Learning cycle

We've managed to stay just profitable enough to keep it going. We've never hit the jackpot financially but that is because we are more growth oriented than results oriented. If we just stabilized, the results would improve dramatically because we wouldn't be putting time, effort and money into growth projects – like the export one which is absorbing a lot at the moment. But if we don't make the effort now, in 5 years time we'll be the poorer for it.

We have a 5-year plan and we know where each department is going in quite a lot of detail. We monitor monthly and check the strategy annually, but every 3 years we have to sit back and ask ourselves are we where we said we would be. We're doing it now, as we did 3 years ago. We didn't plan this, it just happens in this business; 3 years into a 5-year plan you find that things have changed. Our 5-year plans tend to take us 8 years anyway, but that's not important; what's important is that we've done our thinking about where we want to go. So every 3 years we do something different to look at what we're doing.

All these initiative that we get involved in such as quality, investors in people, strategic analysis, leadership training and so on, only replicate what we did as a matter of common sense when we were a very small company. We didn't think about it then, we were small, close-knit and communications was 100 per cent. You never needed prompting. During the middle years, when the business issues began to take over, we lost that. It's taken conscious effort and thought to bring that back into what is now a larger business. It's ironic that so much effort has to go into doing something that we once found easy!

Assessing the learning organization in your business

As can be seen from the experiences of Rob and the other storytellers in this chapter, the learning organization can take many forms. How this idea develops depends upon the type of business concerned, the context and the situation, and above all the people in that organization – their skills, values, beliefs and aspirations. Having said this, there are some models of learning organizations that might be helpful in plotting your own course.

Modelling the effective organization is a traditional pursuit in business schools and consultancies. Various strands of thinking have contributed to the making of the concept of the learning organization. Systems thinking and total quality management (TQM), especially in the teachings of W. Edwards Deming, have been strong influences. So has the idea of excellence, famously introduced in the bestseller *In Search of Excellence* (1982), and which has become an enduring focus for many organizational improvement schemes ever since.

However, the problem with excellence is sustaining it. Even a few years after the publication of Peters and Waterman's book, researchers were gleefully pointing out how many of their sample of companies no longer met the original criteria. They had, in various ways, fallen from grace. Recent organizational models have addressed the sustainability problem by using the idea of organizational learning to help companies stay forever young (and excellent). The European Foundation for Quality Management's Excellence Model (EFQM) is one of these. We use it here because it combines the wisdom of TQM with the ideas of excellence and learning, and also adds the element of corporate social responsibility which is a theme of increasing interest.

In essence, the EFQM's Excellence Model (Figure 11.2) is a simple one (albeit much complicated by the paraphernalia surrounding its self-assessment and points-awarding processes so loved by those of the 'bean-counting' tendency).

The problem with all such models – especially when they are made up of the lines, boxes and linearity of the wiring diagram or engineering blueprint – is that they encourage people to believe that they are true. 'Leaders devise clear visions', 'systems produce quality', 'enablers' lead to results, and so on. Such simple nostrums totter in the face of the recent insights of complexity

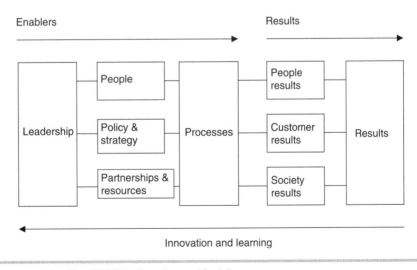

Figure 11.2   *The EFQM's Excellence Model*

theory and of the old knowledge about the effects of power and politics in influencing what actually happens in organizations. Yet some people still seem to believe that by following the map that they will actually enter into the promised land. Even worse than this, some seem to believe, having collected lots of data, statistics and pieces of paper about the boxes and lines, that this activity in itself has brought the organization to a state of sustained excellence.

However, even if such maps are sometimes dangerous, that does not mean that they should not be used. These are treasure maps to encourage excitement, exploration, discovery and learning and not plans for installing central heating systems. The EFQM's Excellence Model and all other models, including our own 'The Eleven Characteristics of the Learning Company' (Pedler, Burgoyne and Boydell, 1996, pp. 15–18), should not be treated literally, but metaphorically. Their purpose is to help you start, to help generate ideas amongst those trying to bring about this vision in their own territory. Once this is accomplished, they should be discarded in favour of the local live agenda before they become oppressive.

The personal and organizational challenge of learning

The metaphor of the learning organization poses two major challenges for organizational leaders:

- the personal challenge of leading and behaving differently to stimulate learning – in yourself and in those around you
- the organizational challenge of mobilizing change and learning on a more systematic basis throughout the enterprise.

The first of these challenges involves leading by example and making learning a central value and aspect of how you do things. Do you ...

- have a mentor, personal consultant or learning set?
- put time aside in advance for learning activities?
- build learning reviews into projects and meetings?
- seek feedback on your actions and make it easy for people to give this?
- make learning and development a key aspect of appraisals – both of your own and those you conduct with others?
- acknowledge your own learning in public – especially when you have been wrong?

All of these signal the importance of learning as a value and as a daily activity in your working life. We take our examples and role models from our seniors, and the higher up in an organization you are, the more important it is to manifest these and other learning behaviours. They will be noticed and imitated. They are contagious and will spread to others. An absence of these will be equally effective in driving out learning for other people and from the organization.

The second challenge demands a more systemic and systematic approach; personal example is not enough to bring about a transformation of the whole. This can only be done by the cultivation of processes and practices that enshrine learning throughout the corporation. This is a tough challenge and one which takes 3–5 years to progress, but it can be done by embedding the sort of values implied in the personal list above. This challenge involves tackling such questions as:

- How can we create development opportunities for everyone in this organization – no matter how humble their position?
- How can we create feedback loops based on performance as a matter of daily business practice?
- How can performance management systems teach people how to use finance and other resources more effectively?
- How can we set up learning partnerships with our key business partners?
- How can we ensure that what is learned in one part of the organization is available to other parts as and when it is needed?

One global company that we worked with added 'action learning' to the balanced scorecard for all its teams. Most teams complied and used the available facilitators to explore the idea for one afternoon and then ticked the box. This is not what was intended and it certainly did not bring about the learning organization. This vision takes a bit more effort and sophistication.

Activity: applying the ideas: a treasure map

As noted earlier, one of the most useful aspects of the EFQM's Excellence Model is the way in which it combines several streams of thinking from excellence, total quality and learning organization. This produces a set of fundamental elements around which the more formal model is constructed. Going back to these essential elements provides us with the basis for a 'treasure map' rather than a wiring diagram. Figure 11.3 provides a simple tool based on these underlying elements to help you check how your department or company measures up to the learning organization idea. This map has eight blocks of indicators, one for each of the fundamental elements around which the formal EFQM's Excellence Model is constructed.

Score your unit, department or organization by looking at each block in turn and reading all the indicators about that element. How does your unit measure up to these aspirations? Taking all these indicators into account – and any others that you can think of which are relevant to you – and give yourself an overall score for that element, from 1 (very poor at this or non-existent) to 10 (very good at this or fully achieved).

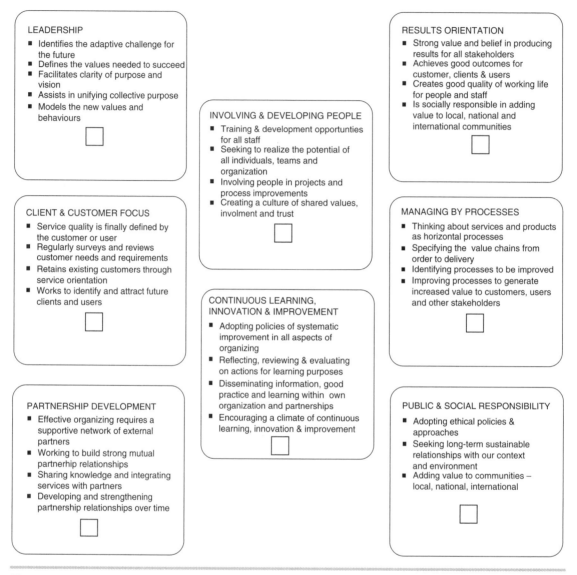

LEADERSHIP
- Identifies the adaptive challenge for the future
- Defines the values needed to succeed
- Facilitates clarity of purpose and vision
- Assists in unifying collective purpose
- Models the new values and behaviours

RESULTS ORIENTATION
- Strong value and belief in producing results for all stakeholders
- Achieves good outcomes for customer, clients & users
- Creates good quality of working life for people and staff
- Is socially responsible in adding value to local, national and international communities

INVOLVING & DEVELOPING PEOPLE
- Training & development opportunties for all staff
- Seeking to realize the potential of all individuals, teams and organization
- Involving people in projects and process improvements
- Creating a culture of shared values, involment and trust

CLIENT & CUSTOMER FOCUS
- Service quality is finally defined by the customer or user
- Regularly surveys and reviews customer needs and requirements
- Retains existing customers through service orientation
- Works to identify and attract future clients and users

MANAGING BY PROCESSES
- Thinking about services and products as horizontal processes
- Specifying the value chains from order to delivery
- Identifying processes to be improved
- Improving processes to generate increased value to customers, users and other stakeholders

CONTINUOUS LEARNING, INNOVATION & IMPROVEMENT
- Adopting policies of systematic improvement in all aspects of organizing
- Reflecting, reviewing & evaluating on actions for learning purposes
- Disseminating information, good practice and learning within own organization and partnerships
- Encouraging a climate of continuous learning, innovation & improvement

PARTNERSHIP DEVELOPMENT
- Effective organizing requires a supportive network of external partners
- Working to build strong mutual partnerhip relationships
- Sharing knowledge and integrating services with partners
- Developing and strengthening partnership relationships over time

PUBLIC & SOCIAL RESPONSIBILITY
- Adopting ethical policies & approaches
- Seeking long-term sustainable relationships with our context and environment
- Adding value to communities – local, national, international

Figure 11.3   Learning organization treasure map

You can do this by yourself, but it is far better done in a team or in a conference meeting. Using this simple tool in small groups, large numbers of people can deliver a quick assessment of where they see the strengths and weaknesses of the organization.

Next, decide what you want to do with these results. Here is a series of questions to consider, depending upon your purposes:

- What do these results mean?
- Is this an adequate measure for our purposes?

- Which areas of organizing do we most want to improve?
- What actions shall we take?
- How will we evaluate and learn from these actions

We call this a 'treasure map' to encourage you to go for gold without believing that a slavish following of this route will actually get you there. A treasure map is more help than a rainbow, but it is still only a map. Use it to get your bearings and to ask questions about how you are doing things. If you wish, you can turn it into a more traditional questionnaire, by taking the individual items out of the eight blocks and making them into questions with scaled 1–5 answer options. It can then be distributed to larger numbers of people. Experiment, innovate and, above all, use the treasure map to learn; that is where the true gold lies.

Conclusion

There are no magic potions or formulae for bringing about the learning organization. Any action, taken after due deliberation and with intent to change something, will lead to learning. The learning organization will want to harness this learning and knowledge and spread it to those places where it can best be used. It will try to get the best into all its parts and to exchange what works with its business partners. What you do is not particularly critical – as long as it fits the situation – it is *how* you do it that is crucial.

Learning is a fragile plant when young. In harsh conditions, buffeted by the north-easterlies of top-down performance management, it is easily discouraged. Learning from practice, passing it on, questioning the actions of others when they do not make sense (however high up) are all perfectly sensible and natural things to do, but in organizational settings they frequently take courage and determination in addition to intelligence. It is the critical responsibility of leadership to ensure that the climate exists to grow the seeds and shoots of learning into strong plants that flourish and disseminate their wisdom throughout the business.

Further resources

The source book for the EFQM's Excellence Model is *Guide to the Business Excellence Model: Defining World Class* (British Quality Foundation, London, 1998). However, there are many books and articles that use and develop this model in specific contexts such as healthcare or manufacturing. A good place to start would be to look over the back issues of the journal *Total Quality Management*, which has papers on this in almost every other issue.

Our own book, *The Learning Company: a Strategy for Sustainable Development*, referenced below, provides an alternative to the EFQM model. It is strong on models and tools and the *Energy Flow* of the learning company in particular overcomes the restrictions of linear models. The main framework is 'The Eleven Characteristics of the Learning Company', which comes with a questionnaire to use in assessment and development.

The bestseller on the learning organizations remains Peter Senge's *The Fifth Discipline: the Art and Practice of the Learning Organization* (Harper and Row, New York, 1990). Senge is particularly good on the systems thinking that underlies this idea.

Reference

Coad, A. (1999) 'Some survey evidence on the learning and performance orientations of management accountants' *Management Accounting Research* 10, 109–135.

Pedler, M., J. Burgoyne and T. Boydell (1996) *The Learning Company: a Strategy for Sustainable Development*, McGraw-Hill, Maidenhead.

12

Challenge 3: New Organizational Structures

Structure follows strategy
Alfred Chandler

Introduction

Many years ago, Alfred Chandler taught that form should follow function. Any new organizational structure should be based on the new strategy to be followed: what are the new purposes, aims, objectives and business processes? And what structures will best enable these?

A form that delivers the function must somehow pull together the myriad complications of product and service streams, market and user demands and the proliferating specialisms, units and departments found in a large enterprise. Ordering the taxonomies of organizational roles and specifying the responsibilities and relationships of units is no easy matter to get right first time, or indeed to get right for long.

However, there is no area of leadership where the satirical 'ready, fire, aim!' applies more aptly than to the question of new organizational structures. For many newly appointed Chief Executives, there is a great pressure to change things from the outset. And for many such people, organizational change equates with creating new structures.

The three envelopes

There is a joke about a new Chief Executive, who on being appointed, seeks out the old Chief for advice. The deposed leader is wary, unwilling to proffer advice. 'Please', urges the new man, 'there must be something that you can pass on to help me?' 'OK', says the old leader at last, handing over three numbered envelopes, 'At times of difficulty, open these in order and follow the instructions'.

The new leader thanks him and leaves. After 6 months in post, and as the honeymoon begins to wear off, questions arise about the state of the organization. As these get louder, the new Chief decides he must act, and opens the first envelope. Inside is a slip of paper bearing the words 'Blame your predecessor'. 'Hmmm', thinks the Chief Executive, 'Good idea'. Accordingly, he puts it about that the problems of the present are due to the ideas of the old leader and this has the desired effect. A few months later, however, the unrest returns, now with increased volume. After a few sleepless nights, the new leader opens the second envelope, to find a slip that says 'Restructure'. 'Excellent!', he thinks, immediately announcing a major reorganization, and stipulating a complex process of working groups.

As people becomes busily engaged on organizational redesign, all energies previously devoted to questioning and complaining are channelled into the crafting of new models and the debating of their relative merits and demerits. Everyone is busy and happy, up to and beyond the point of the installation of the new structure. This structure is better in some ways, but there are also several unanticipated problems. Soon, the questioning and muttering return with even greater force – 'Is our leader really up to the job?' After seeking to weather this storm for a few months, the Chief Executive turns to his last envelope. The slip now reads : 'Prepare three envelopes ...'.

Developing an effective organizational structure is a testing challenge and, as the joke suggests, the new leader may feel the need to act precipitately rather than wisely. If restructuring is treated as a chance for a new appointee to make his or her mark, or as a technical task to which there is a best solution, there are likely to be problems. This chapter contains the following:

- a short history of organizational structures
- organizations as structured networks: a design framework
- enabling structures: helping people work better together
- collaborative structure: an appreciative inquiry tool
- further resources.

From hierarchies to networks

'From hierarchies to networks' (Morgan, 1989, p. 66) is the shortest way of describing the history of organizational development. As the oldest form of organization, the hierarchy can be traced back in military and church practices for thousands of years. In the late 19th century, as an antidote to the arbitrary nature of German family firms, the sociologist Max Weber specified bureaucracy as an ideal type for the command and control of business. Whilst this notion of a hierarchically ordered structure was not new, Weber's ideal type marks the start of the idea that organizations need to be designed.

It was not until the second half of the 20th century that this classical model began to be seriously challenged. By this time, the rigidities and limitations of bureaucratic structures were becoming obvious, especially in terms of their ability to adapt and learn in the face of increasing rates of change and turbulent markets. Design efforts now sought to loosen up the bureaucracy, for example through the matrix organization. This seeks to balance the power of the vertical and functional silos of finance, production, R&D, etc., with cross-cutting project teams and task forces focusing on the lateral value chains of products and services to customers. This dual focus has proved hard to manage; the 'pay and rations' silos have shown a remarkable capacity to wrest back the power and resources from the more locally responsive projects and business teams.

The current design favourite is the managed network (see also Chapter 21). This aims at a loosely coupled organization guided from a core which sets strategic direction and manages performance against targets and contracts. The dilemmas in this type of structure are over how to devolve and subcontract as much as possible and what to hold tight. The ideal firm is now more of a cluster or system of interacting units rather than a single, bounded entity.

Rabobank

A Netherlands bank, Rabobank, has built upon its cooperative history to transform itself by establishing three levels of internal networks. The Chief Executive explains, 'The hierarchical, pyramidal structure, with its tendency to uniformity, belongs to the past. The present era demands differentiation and specification, and with that, units with a large degree of autonomy.'

This new organizing model aims to serve market and client needs by the better use of the knowledge and expertise of all employees, especially front-line service staff. This knowledge is so widely distributed that '…it has become impossible and unnecessary to manage organizations from the top. Hence it is better to think in terms of *the network concept*. … Central to [this] is that all cells, call them expertise centres, in the network have their own responsibility. One cannot speak of subordination, but of mutual service rendering based on equivalence. It is a living organism, in which every cell performs its own function, without getting formalized instructions. The core notions of a network are "working together" and "environmental awareness". Only by realizing that your behaviour affects other cells in the system, will you make good choices' (Pettigrew and Fenton, 2000, p. 60).

Organizations as structured networks

In their ideal form, networks are flat, freeform, self-animating structures. In seeking to harness some of these qualities, the challenge is to add some degree of structure and management in order to control and direct them. Networks excel in sharing know-how and delivering locally at low cost, but they are notoriously difficult to steer or to hold accountable. Goold and Campbell (2002) offer a complex but well thought through template for designing organizations as 'structured networks'. Their framework comprises four 'drivers' of organizational fit that set the constraints for the designer:

■ Product/market strategies – how will the organization succeed in its various chosen fields of operation?
■ Corporate strategy – what are the priorities for the organization as a whole?
■ People – what are the skills and preferences of the available people?
■ Constraints – what are the external, environmental and other internal factors that limit the design possibilities?

These straightforward drivers are complemented by five design principles for the configuration of subunits and their interrelationships:

■ Specialization – are the unit boundaries defined so as to maximize the benefits of specialization?
■ Co-ordination – are all the activities that need to be most co-ordinated included within single units?
■ Knowledge and competence – does responsibility devolve to those with the best available knowledge and competence?
■ Commitment and control – does the design facilitate low-cost co-ordination with high commitment?
■ Innovation and adaptation – will the structure promote innovation and adaptation as circumstances change?

These design principles will inevitably pose a variety of dilemmas and difficulties in being implemented in any organization. Nonetheless, the drivers and principles provide a useful checklist against which to weigh any organizational design proposals. Measuring against the drivers should indicate whether form will indeed follow function. It will also highlight two critical tests for any proposal which seeks to harness the desirable qualities of the network within a corporate control structure:

> *What are proposals for 'corporate parenting' in the network? And will these add value to the operating units, or merely add redundant hierarchy?*
> *Do we have the people and the skills to operate the proposed structure?*

The advantages claimed for the network organization are flexibility and freedom of action at local level together with speedy learning and knowledge sharing. This depends a great deal on the sophistication of the design being proposed. Of particular interest here are the following questions:

> *Do creative people and specialist units have enough autonomy, freedom and protection from the parent organization?*
> *Have we specified clearly enough the coordinating links between units: both the strong links of accountability and the weak links of knowledge sharing and learning?*

All these questions point to the limitations of organizational design: we can and should do the best possible in terms of a good design, but so much depends upon *how this design is interpreted and enacted by the people who inhabit it*. Network organization poses a considerable leadership challenge for people who have grown up in more formal structures. Bureaucracies are designed for rational management and control, but networks run on leadership. Ricardo Semler asserts that *not* controlling is so difficult for people in senior positions that this is the very factor that gives Semco its competitive advantage. In this well-publicised Brazilian manufacturing company, 'no-one is in control. If you don't even know where people are, you can't possibly keep an eye on them. All that's left to judge on is performance' (Semler, 2003).

Goold and Campbell's framework for the design of structured networks will be of great help to anyone seeking to test this model for organizational design. Nevertheless, their conclusion is a bold one:

> For those managers uncertain over how much attention to give to the soft issues, our rule of thumb is 'Get the design right first and worry about the additional soft issues during implementation'.
>
> (Goold and Campbell, 2002, p. 247)

This impulse feels familiar, but it should be resisted. If the 'hard wiring' of the organisation does not enable the 'software' to work well together, a new architectural folly is in the making. To meet the leadership challenge, networks have to be carefully designed, but even more skilfully led.

Is there one right structure for the organization?

There are a number of limitations to the strong case for organizational design. A strong design brings clarity and stability, a framework for decisions and authority that can make organizational life simpler and less stressful. However, the stronger the design, the more resistant it is to change in the face of the inevitable decay. It is said by designers that their structures will last for 5–6 years, but this may be an optimistic assumption. Can organizations be designed to allow for emergence and for an incremental restructuring on the basis of learning from experience?

One way of managing this is to think in terms of alternative structures and not to rely on one to do everything. Organizations contain many possible structures. To test this notion in a simple way, take the organization chart or organigram showing the formal lines of communication and accountability in your organization. Now, using some coloured pens, draw some of the informal links that you know about to create your own picture of how things really happen around here. Who has a relationship with whom? Who really talks to whom? Who has the ear of whom? Who do you know who can get things done for you?

The invisible organization

In a learning set, a hospital doctor told the story of his being invited by a colleague to join the local Masonic Lodge. During the time he was thinking about this, he found that various people were seeking him out and giving him words of advice and encouragement. What surprised him was that these were usually people he did not know at all or those who would not normally stop and talk with him. He also noticed that people who were quite junior in the organization could be quite senior in the Masons. When he decided not to join, these encounters immediately stopped and the people melted away. But for a while he had seen a completely different organization.

The organizational chart has a value as a 'Who's who?' and a 'Who's where?', but learning how to get things done around the place is to do with knowing who really has influence and power, and understanding the appropriate cultural rules. Accepting the organigram as a true map of how things happen would be the managerial equivalent of going to the stores in search of a left-handed screwdriver.

The lines and boxes of the organizational chart are but a skeleton brought to life by those humans who inhabit them. From a social constructionist standpoint, organizational structure is produced and re-produced on a daily basis by people, by their values and their cultures, in their everyday actions and relationships. The vitality of this human construction is facilitated or blocked, encouraged or inhibited, by the shaping effects of formal structure.

Perhaps the single formal structure is a myth or a ceremonial applying only in certain situations. The soldier who says, 'I will do that only if you command me' and the inspector of police who says, 'This is an order, *sergeant*', emphasizing the lower rank of the person being addressed, are everyday recognitions both of the specific function of formal structure and of its wide operational limitations. It is a first or last resort that shows how things should be done, but it is not how most of business is done.

The organizational iceberg (Figure 12.1) conceals most of its bulk below the surface. Above the waves are the visible and formal structures of the organization. These are the rational aspects upon which managers concentrate their managing efforts. These are also the aspects of the organization that get changed. However, much of what you bump into when you are trying to do things is concealed below this level. These invisible, less acknowledged aspects are less available to scrutiny, rational analysis and change but they constitute the energy sources for a lot of the organizational action.

There are many existing alternatives to the formal structure of the organization. Of particular current interest is the structure of knowledge in a

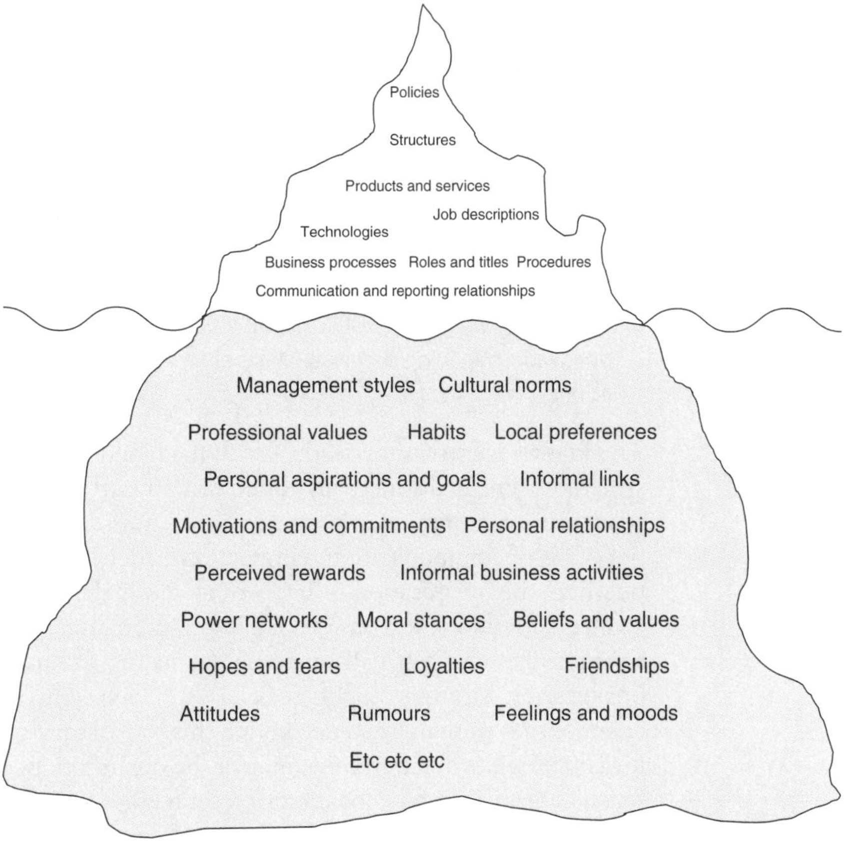

Figure 12.1   The organizational iceberg, (after Plant, 1987, pp. 128–129)

company. The following is a new way of mapping the organization as an overlapping set of communities of practice, knowledge and interest.

Big Company plc

The information specialists in a large multinational company have identified four types of 'knowledge communities' that could be supported from their central resources. Although this classification does not cover the full complexity of who knows what in this global business employing some 40 000 people in more than 40 countries, it provides the basis for their information and knowledge management strategy:

■ FUNCTIONAL COMMUNITIES – hierarchically organized and part of the main organizational structure, e.g. Human Resources, finance.
  Support priority: Essential

■ INITIATIVE NETWORKS – project based or problem-focused groups of people collaborating worldwide on specific tasks in short hierarchies with a project manager, e.g. procurement, business strategy.
  Support priority: High: key to added value
■ COMMUNITIES OF PRACTICE (COPs) – practice-based groups of people worldwide with some hierarchy and corporate responsibility, for example, for producing 'best practice' guidelines, e.g. maintenance engineers, supply chains, human resources, remuneration and benefits.
  Support priority: Medium
■ INTEREST or KNOWLEDGE COMMUNITIES – interest-based groups of people worldwide, including professional, academic and leisure interests; no hierarchy.
  Support priority: Low

This knowledge structure overlaps with the functional, business and hierarchical structures, but is distinctively different. For certain purposes this alternative structure might be an important part of the design. These more informal networks of communication, connections, friendships and alliances may well be where the organization is 'happening' most; they are likely to be the source of much flexibility, learning capability and creative potential. Currently, the functions get the first call on resources in Big Company plc, but a learning organization strategy might seek to influence this. Obviously, all these communities were in existence before this way of seeing came along. This new lexicon provides an alternative map of the organization, giving a different basis for the organizing and allocation of resources.

Enabling structures: working better together

In contrast to the architectural view of 'Getting the design right first and worrying about the soft stuff later', it is these so-called 'soft' issues that actually constitute the toughest challenge. Finding a way of helping people work better together should underpin the entire structural strategy:

> *The new structure is a hard demonstration of your seriousness around the softer issues. Because you are taking charge and deliberately constructing the organization to fit your purpose, this is mistaken for centralization ... but it is not centralization but integration ... people won't put up with centralization ... decisions are not centralized but allocated to particular locations. There are three main locations: corporate, regions or functions and business processes. Decisions are integrated through crossover membership of the various teams, with functional people in the regions and business teams and a majority of people from the businesses in the process teams. So the centre does not make the*

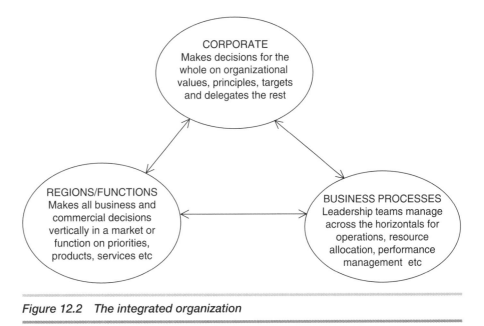

Figure 12.2   The integrated organization

decisions – they are made in a federal network with clear accountabilities. This is the way we want to work.

(Plc Human Resources Director)

This illustrates the effort needed to ensure that the structure and the behaviours of people and teams are intimately connected and interdependent. This federal network structure only works through a careful crossover of people between functions, businesses and processes, which, taken together, creates the overview and integration of the complexities which make up the organization (Figure 12.2). Equally, the architecture should enable the people and communities within and around a business to work together better. And, as markets shift, businesses change and functions move in importance, it should retain an air of provisionality and lend itself to easy adaptation.

To close this chapter, the following is a tool based on the practice of appreciative inquiry that can be used to generate ideas for a new structure in collaboration with all those who must make it work.

Activity generating a collaborative structure: an appreciative inquiry tool

Appreciative inquiry accentuates the positive and aims to help groups and communities to bring about change through generating new thoughts, images and possibilities. In the example given below, a group or team works with one of its members or a small subgroup who 'hold' the change issue. The aim is to help this person or subgroup realize a more positive future, grounded first in what is good about their experience, then powered by images of what would be ideal for them.

The rules of the game are for everyone is to Be Positive! All questions, all responses must emphasize the positive.

Step 1: Good stories

Start by asking people to tell stories about ways in which their current organization works really well. To help people tell their stories, prompt them with such appreciative questions as:

- When do you feel most positive and engaged about the way things work around here?
- Please describe a high spot in your experience of the organization – when did you feel good about working here?
- What aspects of organizing do we do really well?
- What have we got right in terms of organizational design?

… and so on.

Step 2: Positive futures

After generating some good stories and positive images of the current organization, the next step is to develop some ideas about possible futures. For each person who told a story, now ask:

- What would help you to achieve more?
- If we redesigned the organization, what would really delight and benefit your customers and clients?
- How could we improve on the way performance is managed?
- Who would you like to link up with and have a connection with?
- How could you learn more from people in the organization?
- What would your work look like if it was designed around the things you truly value?

… and so on.

Step 3: Constructive next steps

When all the stories and ideas about possible futures have been aired, the whole group then summarizes and records the ideas for organizational redesign. This might take the form of some redesign proposals or some next steps for further research, such as:

- What might be done next which does not involve any redesign?
- What further work or research do we need to do to clarify our ideas?
- What redesign proposals shall we put to the Board?

You must end by agreeing at least one positive next step towards a more desirable future

Three groundrules

1 The main rule for working in this way is to be determinedly positive. (There are plenty of other forums to talk about problems and negativities.)
2 The redesign issue affects and involves everyone. You will need to recruit enough of these other people to help you with this appreciative inquiry. Choose positive people, including supportive colleagues and friendly clients or business partners.
3 Do not use a facilitator but do it yourself. You might feel silly around the rule of only being positive at first, but it requires everyone to put themselves in that frame of mind for a short time. Try it: it might even work!

Conclusion: overmanaged but underled?

The distinction between managing and leading has been reinforced in recent years by a growing sense that many organizations are overmanaged but underled. Although managing and leading are both essential and overlap in practice, they do denote different patterns of behaviour and action. The two dimensions that emerged from early leadership research saw managing as being more about 'concern for the task' and leadership as more about 'concern for people'. Devising new organizational structures is part of the impulse for good managing and effort put in here weights that side of the balance.

Structure and culture are as complementary as managing and leading. New organizational structures are one part of rebuilding and redirecting an organization or a business. They are part of a rich blend that goes to make up an integrated organization of key functions, core business processes, technologies and people in all their teams and communities. They can help by contributing to new ways of working. Any organizational design is only as good as the willingness and ability of its inhabitants to animate it, but sometimes people need to be persuaded that different roles, unit boundaries and relationships will work better if only they give it a go.

Is your organization in danger of being overmanaged and underled?

Further resources

Michael Goold and Andrew Campbell's *Designing Effective Organisations: How to Create Structured Networks*, referenced below, is the best current text on this topic. This is a sophisticated but practical design primer that goes into considerable detail and is well illustrated with case examples.

Andrew Pettigrew and Evelyn Fenton's edited volume *The Innovating Organisation*, also referenced below, is a more academic book based on a collaborative effort by an international consortium of researchers. It is notable for its in-depth case studies of network organizations and for the Editors' topping and tailing chapters that synthesize a wide range of studies in describing 'the organizational form for the 21st century'.

References

Goold, M. and A. Campbell (2002) *Designing Effective Organizations: How to Create Structured Networks*, Jossey Bass, San Francisco.
Morgan, G. (1989) *Creative Organisation Theory*, Sage, London.
Pettigrew, A. and E. Fenton (eds) (2000) *The Innovating Organisation*, Sage, London.
Plant, R. (1987) *Managing Change and Making it Stick*, Fontana, London.
Semler, R. (2003) *The Seven Day Weekend*, Century, New York.

13

Challenge 4: Powerful Teams

How can a team of committed individuals with individual IQs above 120 have a collective IQ of 63?
Peter Senge

Introduction

The organization of golden dreams is made up of cohesive teams in which people pool their skills, talents and knowledge to tackle complex problems and come up with groundbreaking solutions. Suffused with spirit, these teams have no barriers, no factions and produce consistently high quality, constantly improving their outputs.

Dream on. In reality, teams that present a public face of cohesion often fall apart at the seams under pressure, they may be unsupportive to members or riven by internal conflicts and 'turf wars' and talented individuals do not always make good team players.

Despite the concerns, the stock of the team concept remains very high indeed. As a basis for organizing people and tasks, it has few peers in human resource development thinking. The ability to work in teams is prized as a valuable organizational asset. As standards have risen, competition increased and clients and customers become more demanding, the individual worker needs team support to deliver a good service. Cohesive teams are largely self-managing, enabling them to make the best local decisions and the effective organization is made up of a coalition of such teams.

The notion of team-working goes further still. A distinction can be made between teams as small groups of people collaborating to achieve a common purpose and team-working which describes an organizational culture of trust, support, interdependence and collaboration.

As work has increased in complexity and unpredictability, the notions of both teams and teamworking have become very widely accepted and promoted – often uncritically. Basic questions such as:

■   Why do we want teams?
■   Is a team needed for this work?

are rarely put. Advice for 'team building' – as if this were a matter of putting blocks in place – is usually rather standardized and rarely explores the complexity of the different types and situations to be found. It is relatively easy to set up a new team with good working habits, harder to rescue an established but dysfunctional team and a much bigger job to develop a teamworking culture.

The quest to develop powerful teams will encounter these widely different situations. In this chapter, you will find advice on

■   helping people decide whether they need to be a team or a group
■   forming a new team
■   working with established and dysfunctional teams
■   developing an averagely performing team to help them do better
■   creating an organization-wide culture of team-working.

This chapter will sharpen your view on these topics, enable you to make a diagnosis and provide the tools to make a start on helping bring about more powerful teams and team-working.

But first of all, do we really need a team for the work in question?

Does this job really need a team?

Not all jobs do. There are many tasks that can be done either through good allocation of work to individuals or carried out by a group working more or less co-operatively. As David Casey puts it, a surprisingly useful question with which to begin is: 'Why should you work better as a team?' (Casey, 1993, p. 34).

What determines the need for a team more than anything else are the

■   degree of complexity of the work
■   extent to which a group is required to work co-operatively.

Getting together to exchange information, share out work, update each other on progress and make simple operational decisions does not require the full interdependent collaborative working of true team-work. For all these purposes, a degree of co-operation is all that is required amongst a group of people (Figure 13.1).

On the other hand, teams are definitely needed for the difficult or uncertain work of managing a complex system, developing an organizational strategy or sharing learning from a dynamic and emerging situation. These circumstances

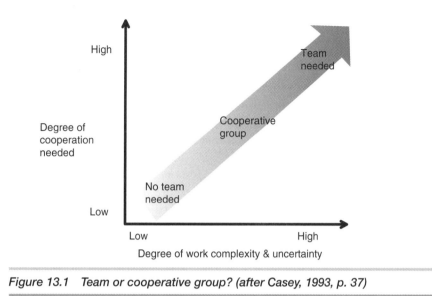

Figure 13.1   Team or cooperative group? (after Casey, 1993, p. 37)

require a high degree of collaboration and interdependence, where it is not enough just to meet, agree a course of action and go off to implement it as individuals. Here, to bring about a good collective result, it is essential to persevere together with openness, trust, commitment and a degree of selflessness.

Casey (1993) points out that it is a mistake to try and drag groups up to the top right-hand quadrant of Figure 13.1, first because they may not need to go there but also because they may not want it. It may be too difficult to work as a team for all sorts of reasons; it may require the sort of commitment to work together to which people will not sign up. An obvious example here is where there is mistrust between a group and a leader, or perhaps where there is fear and uncertainty about the intentions of senior managers. In these circumstances it will be difficult, and perhaps unwise, to persuade people to make this commitment.

Creating powerful teams

Once the need has been established, and there is a basic willingness to develop the team, there are many helpful measures available. In the rest of this chapter, we offer guidance for each of the team situations presented in the Introduction starting with the new team and then dealing with the various types of established groups before commenting on the ambition to create an organization-wide culture of team-working.

New teams

More has been written on this than almost any other aspect. Teams were the great discovery of the organization development movement of the 1960s and 1970s when much attention was given to group behaviour, group development, inter-group conflict resolution and the like. Teams and groups still retain a great hold on the managerial imagination because of their self-organizing capability; a good team removes the need for the first-line supervision previously seen as a key linchpin in the chain of command.

Consequently, there is more advice on setting up new teams than on most other topics. Some of these are listed in the Further resources section at the end of the chapter, and other sources of help can be found in Chapters 7 and 8 on Questions and Facilitation. Because this is a 'greenfield' situation, new teams can be set up largely without historical baggage – this is a new start and we can set the working processes and groundrules as we want them. The script for developing new teams is straightforward and includes:

- clarifying the purpose and tasks of the team
- establishing team roles
- creating working processes and groundrules
- running productive meetings
- making good decisions
- building the capacity of the team
- practising action learning (see Chapter 8)
- keeping all of these processes under review.

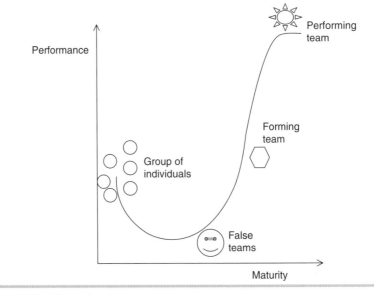

Figure 13.2   Team development curve

A famous model of team development suggests that groups go through the stages of forming, storming, norming and performing (Tuckman, 1965) and illustrates the basic truth that it usually takes time to develop maturity (Figure 13.2).

However, in organizations and especially when introducing quality or other new initiatives, teams are sometimes thrown together and assumed to be fully operational. A new management system decrees the need and there is a rush to setting up teams – on paper – without any attention to their development. Consequently, many of these new, so-called 'teams' are merely aggregations of individuals or false teams.

The team-based organization

With the help of consultants, a large multinational set up 'autonomous working groups' in its R&D Division. On a given day the old departments and units were dissolved and the new teams were 'installed'. Various new rules and 'Team Charters' had to be observed, for example, teams were to have no formal leaders but different members would be accountable for delivering different items on the team's 'Balanced Scorecard'. Over the next few months the new teams spent a great deal of their time trying to understand and also circumventing these rules. Team performance across the Division was patchy. Many teams found it hard to establish their new common purpose and worked individually or in partnership with one or two others.

These sorts of problems with new teams can be avoided, but only by giving proper attention to the forming and development process.

Established work groups

Existing teams can be crudely categorized in three ways:

- high-performing teams
- OK teams
- struggling teams.

High-performing teams

These may not need much attention beyond recognition and resourcing because they have developed their own good habits for action and learning. These teams are often the most self-critical and open to learning, so they probably have their own arrangements for both personal and team development. They might even have a regular consultant who has been part of their development, but they are not dependent upon such outside assistance. Reward these teams but watch for complacency, exclusivity, competitiveness, customer condescension and all the other trappings of success.

OK teams

The first question to ask about these teams is whether there is a need to do anything. Are they OK enough to continue or are there serious questions or complaints about their performance? Also, does the team want to do anything differently? If there are doubts about performance, or a desire to improve, what will help them build better performance? In the case of the following OK Team, there was evidence of both.

The OK Team

The OK Team were encouraged by their leader to look at customer evaluations of their main project. She pointed out words like 'adequate', 'satisfactory' and 'provided us with a 75 per cent solution' and asked the team how they felt about these comments. It emerged that the project brief had not been entirely clear and that communications with this customer had been minimal. It was also clear that some team members thought they could do better. Following this discussion, the customer was invited to a full-day meeting. The team prepared the questions they wanted to ask and sent a note to the customer explaining this and suggesting that it might be good preparation for them too.

The customer was pleased to be involved and responded enthusiastically to the questions. What surprised the team members most was that although the customer was critical about some aspects of their performance, he was 'on their side' and clearly wanted to help them do better. The OK Team had not seen the customer in this light before.

Averagely performing teams may stick to tried and tested methods because they do not feel safe or confident enough to venture further. In action learning, a distinction is made between *puzzles* – which, however difficult, have right answers or best practice solutions – and *problems*, which do not. Installing equipment, constructing a building, writing a partnership agreement are all puzzles, with an expert source to be found somewhere that can provide right answers. However, motivating someone, building a team or actually creating a partnership are all problems; there are no right answers here, however many books are written about them. No team can tackle these sorts of problems unless they have confidence in each other and in their collective and collaborative ability.

Puzzles where both the problem and the solution are readily understood will be found in Box 4 in Figure 13.3.

Averagely performing teams may lack confidence and prefer stay on the safe ground of Box 1 or Box 2 situations. Getting into Box 3 and especially Box 4 – inventing tomorrow's problems (and their solutions) – is important in making significant contributions that really make a difference. These uncharted and ambiguous areas require moves beyond the comfort zone, territory open only to teams confident enough in their own collective abilities to face any challenge.

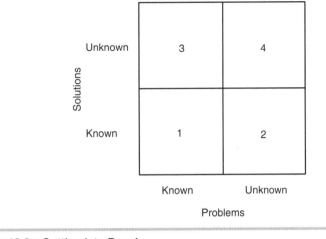

Figure 13.3   *Getting into Box 4*

Struggling teams

Struggling teams pose the biggest challenge of all established groups. These may be teams in name only, consisting of isolated individuals or subgroups, divided by various dis-integrating issues:

- fighting for 'turf' within the team
- individuals avoiding anything that will make them look bad
- avoiding disagreement and plain speaking
- going along with 'consensus' decisions that nobody wants
- quality of leadership
- poor personal relationships
- unresolved conflicts.

What can be done here? To improve things in any team, these difficult and entrenched issues will need to be flushed out as a start to developing healthier relationships and more productive working practices.

However, there is no guarantee of success. Surprisingly, perhaps, not all teams are committed to working together, and it is not sensible to make this assumption. Acknowledging this simple truth can help avoid some of the obvious errors. Teams not committed to working together are highly unlikely to want to learn together. The Media Design team below is a classic case.

The Media Design team

The Media Design team is a talented bunch of folk. These 11 people work to a properly structured and focused agenda, but they lack the collective desire to manage it well. The relationships between members are fractious and cliquey and behaviour is poor; team members commonly

- make political statements
- manoeuvre for positions
- self-market themselves at the expense of others
- show off and generally try to impress
- put other people down
- show distrust and even dislike of colleagues
- openly compete for work with clients.

Because of the difficulties experienced in reaching consensus, the Media Design team has started to vote on issues. However, people tend to vote for their allies irrespective of technical know-how and professional arguments, and there are lots of poor decisions. Customers complain but are fobbed off or ignored.

The Media Design team is far from unique. In teams like this, $2 + 2 = 3$ or even less, and the collective output is actually worse than that which the individuals working alone could achieve. This team has frequent experiences of the Abilene paradox – where we take decisions that nobody really wants.

The Abilene paradox

Jerry Harvey (1974) tells the tale of a Texas family who take a nightmare trip on a hot summer afternoon. With nothing to do and nowhere to go, people are listless and bored, and someone suggests that they goes to Abilene for an ice cream. This turns out to be a dire experience for which everyone blames each other. It subsequently turns out that no-one really wanted to go – including the person who made the suggestion. How does this happen? Why have …

'four reasonably sensible people, of our own volition, just taken a 106-mile trip across a Godforsaken desert in a furnace-like temperature, through a cloud-like dust storm to eat unpalatable food at a hole-in-the-wall cafeteria in Abilene, *when none of us had really wanted to go*?'

Harvey suggests that teams often take actions in contradiction to what they really want and thereby defeat the very purposes they are trying to achieve. Individuals privately agree on what they want to do, but do not communicate this and, on the basis of misperceptions and invalid information take decisions which no-one really wants. Not surprisingly, people are fed up about this and tend to blame each other and especially any leaders.

Teams such as the Media Design group may be trapped in this sort of pattern unless the fundamental issues can be grasped. This may be slow and difficult work and, before committing the considerable resources likely to be needed, it is always worth considering structural solutions, including the question of whether there is a problem of the wider organizational design that is blamed on this team. The structural solutions include:

- Do they really need to be a team?
- Could they be managed better?
- Can the work be redesigned?
- Is it this team that is the problem or is the organization designed to direct problems here?
- Should this team be broken up and re-formed?

Support and challenge for high performance

The ability to face challenges on the outside comes from inner strength. High-performing teams develop a high balance of challenge and support. These twin team qualities build together: to develop internal challenge actually requires a high level of support to the give security and confidence for risk taking. In teams with high challenge but low support, it feels unsafe and risky really to take risks – the consequences of getting it wrong are too great, you are out on a limb with no back-up.

As Figure 13.4 shows, some teams may appear to be highly supportive but are low on challenge. Such teams apparently feel safe and secure, but this is not a true security because it is never tested and, when it is, it will probably turn out to be illusory. This is not a powerful team.

There are many ways to build support and challenge. Nothing supports people more than being listened to; nothing challenges more than opening

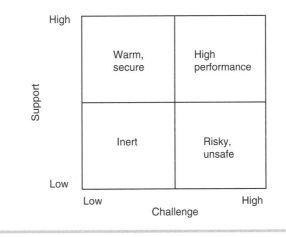

Figure 13.4   *Building support and challenge*

yourself to a good question which makes you think about what you're trying to do and why. These are simple solutions, easily available to the team that can ask for help. Power in a team can also be built by practising action learning – if this is what members want to do. You can read more about how to do this in Chapter 8. Advice on facilitation can also be found in this chapter and Chapter 7.

Another simple tool to build the power of any team is the Customer Survey.

Activity: a customer survey

In any team, first agree that you are all 'up for this' and then follow these steps:

1 List all the customers, clients or end users served by this team. You may divide them into internal and external to the organization – whatever classification makes sense to you.
2 Now rank order the clients or customers by importance to this team.
3 Divide into pairs and choose two customers off the list. Ensure that the team as a whole is covering the most important clients.
4 The next step is to go off and make an appointment to see the customer and interview them. However, before you finish this meeting, fix a time to meet back again to compare results.
5 Interview your clients in pairs. Ensure that you cover the following questions:
   - How much do they know about you (your team)?
   - What do they want and expect from you?
   - What do they think of what they are getting now?
   - How would they like to see their service improved?
6 Meet again to share your learning. Take it in turns to go round the pairs and hear their stories. When all have been heard, classify the findings of your combined research under the questions as in 5 above.
7 Finally, and importantly, decide:
   - What have we learned about ourselves?
   - What are the implications for this team?
   - What actions will we take – individually and collectively?

There is nothing like the view from the outside as a health check on the performance of any team. The customer survey is a good thing for any team to do from time to time.

Using a facilitator

If you decide on the team-building path, you must have some assurance from the team, or from some members, that they will collaborate in this process.

With this done, there will still need to be some skilful facilitation to create the necessary conditions for this team to thrive.

A facilitator can help the dysfunctional team deal with their issues by making it safe for them and building up their confidence. She or he can 'flag the mines' so that the team can have the choice whether to tackle them or not, and can also help the team to develop coaching skills with each other. However, it must be said again that not all situations are retrievable, even by a skilled facilitator. Where personal antagonism, competition or low morale are deeply entrenched, it might save time and trouble to re-form or change the team and start again.

Sometimes, however, just the presence of a outsider in the facilitator role can allow new conversations to take place that might lay a basis for more openness, trust and collaboration. *Are the team ready for this?* If there is sufficient willingness, a next step could be to audit the current state of internal relationships, although it might serve better to start by auditing the principal customers or clients of the team – a way of doing this has already been suggested above. The advantage of focusing on the customer is that it takes the team out of itself and away from navel-gazing.

It is best to do this sort of inner and outer research before approaching the question of task performance. An approach to facilitating the team on their task or purpose will be found in Chapter 7, but another tool that may be especially helpful here is *T, P & N analysis*. This very simple tool can be used with any team, but it may particularly helpful to a struggling team because it looks at their collective power to do things.

Activity: T, P & N analysis

1 For any group or team, first list the tasks or projects that make up their remit and responsibilities.
2 For each one of these tasks or projects, is it
   ■ totally [T] in the control of the team?
   ■ partially [P] in the control of the team?
   ■ not at all [N] in the control of the team?
3 Now, analyse the results. If there are lots of Ns and Ps then either the team has taken on inappropriate tasks or the wrong people are present. Either drop the tasks or change the people.

A T, P & N analysis can reveal interesting things about the organization and not just about the team in question. As an example, take the staff of the corporate Human Resources (HR) Department.

Human Resources team

The staff of a corporate HR Department carried out a T, P & N analysis and listed 47 projects for which they were responsible. A close inspection revealed that only five of these were Ts with the rest being Ps and Ns. It soon became obvious to those present that the HR Department was the 'nice pieces of work orphanage' – they received the unwanted projects from the rest of the organization. Many of these were either peripheral to the business purpose or very difficult to bring about. No wonder the HR Department had a reputation for being ineffective.

The corporate HR Department example shows how, because of the way the wider organization works, some teams have dysfunction thrust upon them. It may be argued that they should not have accepted all these tasks, but building the internal team alone will not resolve these issues. A wider remit is needed.

A culture of teamworking

Problems such as those facing the corporate HR Department have convinced many people that the single team-building focus is not particularly helpful and that what is needed is a general culture of team-working. The essence of this view is that people do not become committed so much to this team or to that, but develop the skills to work well in any team. This has great advantages for organizational flexibility and adaptability as people move quickly in and out of teams, project groups and networks.

Developing a culture of team-working is a more demanding and longer term project than the sort of team-building efforts discussed in this chapter. It is touched upon in several of the other chapters in this book, including Chapters 11, 12, 14 and 21.

Conclusion

Because of the power and iconic status of good teams, it is important to be clear-eyed about what can be done and what cannot. With new or OK teams, there are few problems. Giving proper attention to the forming and team development processes using straightforward activities such as those exemplified in this chapter will yield valuable dividends. Teams that are ineffective or struggling can also be helped by outside intervention, although it is worth considering other alternatives. Teams may be struggling not through fault on their own but because of their constrained or 'bottleneck' situation in the workflow.

The idea of teams has its critics. It can become so strong an ideology that it stifles dissent and creativity. Teams are expected to deliver, do their own managing and disciplining, sometimes as 'leaderless' work groups. In other words, they have become the new management.

Other concerns centre on the impact of teams as foci of loyalty and commitment to wider systems. Strong teams may build power on the inside but create barriers and competition on the outside; high-performing teams can act to the detriment of the organization as whole. From this perspective, teams with tight boundaries, holding on to their players and rejecting newcomers, can be the enemies of adaptability and innovation. Proponents of knowledge-based organizing have referred to teams as the 'new hierarchy' because they carry the power structure. From a knowledge or learning perspective, it is important to nurture the networks and communities of practice that transfer intelligence more widely and easily.

This sort of critique supports a focus on wider organizational cultures that carry the values of teamworking. Ideas of cultures of collaboration, organizations as networks and the learning organization represent the virtues of being team players and of working as cohesive teams in the wider systemic context.

Further resources

To tackle the full variety of team-building situations likely to be encountered in any organization needs a detailed manual beyond the scope of this chapter. Fortunately, there are many resources available to help with the challenge of creating powerful teams, and a quick perusal of the management shelves will yield a large number. It has to be said that some of them are rather naïve and simplistic, treating this task as if it were just a matter of rational project management.

Amongst the best are Jon Katzenbach and Douglas Smith's *The Wisdom of Teams: Creating the High Performance Organization* (Harvard Business School Press, Boston, 1993) and David Casey's *Managing Learning in Organizations* (referenced below) contains more wisdom than most.

Very well known in the quality field are the two handbooks by Peter Scholtes, *The Team Handbook* (Joiner, Madison, WI, 1988) and *The Leader's Handbook* (McGraw-Hill, New York, 1998). The first of these is a classic text with clear and useful advice on setting up and working with teams. These books are very rational and straightforward in their approach and reflect the Deming view that when things go wrong it is the system that is to blame. Weaver and Farrell's *Managers as Facilitators: a Practical Guide to Getting Work Done in a Changing Workplace* (Berrett Koehler, San Francisco, 1999) is also good on teams, and Mike Pedler's *Action Learning for Managers* (Lemos and Crane, London, 1996) contains the models, handouts and tools to enable any group to practice the action learning approach.

References

Casey, D. (1993) *Managing Learning in Organisations*, Open University Press, Buckingham.

Harvey, J. (1974) 'The Abilene Paradox: the management of agreement', *Organisational Dynamics*, Summer.

Tuckman, B. (1965) 'Development sequence in small groups', *Psychological Bulletin*, **63**(6).

14

Challenge 5: Crafting Cultures of Innovation

I kissed a lot of frogs until I got a prince
Attributed to Art Fry, the developer of Post-it Notes

Introduction

Culture is a fuzzy term with a wide range of uses. It can refer to the arts, to refined tastes or to the form of life associated with a particular local or ethnic group. As a metaphor, culture is borrowed from biology and agriculture, where it refers to the careful nurture and growth of living systems – cells, plants and whole ecologies. In organizations, culture generally means the prevailing pattern of values, beliefs, knowledge and behaviour, and also how these have developed and been passed on.

The limitations of what can be achieved by structural change in organizations are now widely understood. If the goal is behaviour change, then a deeper and more enduring effort is required beyond redrawing the lines and the boxes of the organization chart. Culture plays an important mediating role in what we believe, what we value and how we act. Developing a culture that supports people in experimenting, learning and innovation is likely to promote these outcomes.

In the era of the learning company, organizations need to be able to adapt, learn and change in addition to maintaining their stability and continuity over time. This learning company ambition has little chance of succeeding unless it includes a strategy for working with the culture. Without this culture strategy, structural or technological initiatives may be subverted.

When a new Chief Executive announces that the culture around the place must change to support more flexible, adaptable, multi-disciplinary, client-focused working, they know what they want, but not usually how to do it. They commend such values and behaviours as:

- learning from our mistakes
- sharing the knowledge of what works across the company

- valuing diversity
- challenging existing practices
- questioning as a key practice for new thinking.

However, culture does not change by command and patterns of behaviour and ways of thinking about things are remarkably persistent. Businesses often try to deal with this by getting rid of the top people and bringing in new ones. These new leaders bring with them their own trusted people and articulate a different view about how life should be. Yet true cultural change only happens when lots of people start doing things differently all over the organization. When this gets under way, the new way of doing things becomes contagious, like a rolling wave. This does not happen just because of a few new people at the top – however inspirational they are, whatever the CEO autobiographies say.

A sense of the culture in any situation is most available to the new starter. Once a person joins an organization and becomes a participant, doing it daily, this impact recedes and is less clearly felt or seen. Getting a sense of how things are, and how they might be different, is an essential starting point. This chapter will help you to make this start of understanding the local culture and how it might be influenced.

It includes:

- a description of an innovative culture
- two contrasting examples of cultural change efforts from financial services and health
- tools for scanning cultures and for developing new cultural 'groundrules'
- further resources.

Cultures of innovation

What is an innovative culture? The answer to this question depends greatly on the context: what is innovative now, in this situation, may be commonplace and old hat in another.

So-called organizational competencies such as flexibility, creativity and learning depend upon the largely invisible connections and relationships between people. Being hard to detect, these informal systems of relationships are often not given much attention in change initiatives. However, recent thinking suggests that the roots of innovation are likely to stem from the richness of the networks and communities of practice, inside, outside and around the organization. Being informal and self-organizing, these networks are fluid and mobile, continually adapting to new situations. They are often the most vibrant aspects of any organization.

Scanning the culture

Embarking on the creation of a more innovative culture requires first an understanding of this invisible but living and developing system. It also means working with the informal webs of people and relationships in ways that build on what exists to enhance the creativity of the whole. A first step on the road to developing a culture of innovation is to become aware of what exists already. What is it like here? How do people get things done? How well do people share knowledge and learn from each other?

Activity: scanning a culture

The usual way to do this is to scan the culture using a checklist such as that in Box 14.1.

If you are new to the situation you can use this culture scan as an *aide-mémoire* as you familiarize yourself. If you are already part of this culture you might bring in someone to help you get a fresh view. This is commonly part of the work of an external

Box 14.1   A checklist for reading the culture

Culture is encoded in the values, history, artefacts and behaviour of the people in the situation. Reading culture is an art especially developed by consultants, but anyone can learn to read a culture by doing a careful scan of how things are done around here.

This checklist contains some of the common features of culture scans:

1. PHYSICAL: How is the physical setting – the buildings, equipment, layout, etc. – what does this say about us?
2. PUBLICITY: What do we say about ourselves in reports, leaflets, press releases, etc. – what is our self-perception?
3. STRANGERS: What first impressions do visitors, strangers and new starters get?
4. HISTORY: What were the beginnings? The key events and stories from the past?
5. LANGUAGE: What is the normal language of the place – keywords, catch-phrases, etc.?
6. ACTIVITY: How do people spend their time? What are the normal topics of conversation?
7. STORIES: What stories and anecdotes do people use to relate their experiences to each other? What is the point of these stories?
8. SUBCULTURES: Are there any obvious subcultures? How do they differ? What purposes do they serve?
9. PEOPLE: What sort of people work here? Who gets on? Who is influential?
10. VALUES: What do people believe in? What is most valued by people here?

consultant, but there are many ways to get this outside view. For example, you might invite in a couple of graduate students from the local Business School. Such people are always on the lookout for good projects, and two inquiring minds round the business for a few days will produce interesting information.

Once you have a sense of what you are dealing with, the task of developing a more innovative culture may be relatively straightforward. In an example in a financial services company, there were a number of conditions that favoured the development of something new. As a result of recent and multiple mergers and restructurings, people in the company were keen to settle down in new departments staffed by survivors from several different backgrounds.

Innovating in financial services

In answer to the question 'What would make this company more innovative?', a group of managers brainstormed the following list:

- taking more risks
- support from managers for taking risks
- support from colleagues for trying new things
- talking about the job and your practice
- challenges from colleagues about your practice
- much more experimenting, trying new things out
- being less critical, more appreciative of other people's efforts
- encouraging people to freewheel, run with their ideas
- combining ideas, build on suggestions
- benchmarking what others are doing
- trying out things that work in other companies
- learning from our mistakes
- sharing the knowledge of what works across this company
- setting up processes for gathering new ideas
- inviting outsiders in
- sending insiders out
- putting idea generation on the meetings agenda
- setting up little experiments
- encouraging people to move round and change teams
- encouraging job shadowing
- making sure that teams are made up of different sorts of people
- high diversity of people in the company
- building networks and networking opportunities.

These financial services managers produced far more items than are listed here. It is interesting to note that they understood the question immediately and knew exactly how they would recognize and experience an innovative culture. They were full of ideas and keen to express them – which is often the case when the time for moving forward is right.

Groundrules for innovation

Yet there is nothing particularly surprising in the above list. The elements of innovative cultures – new experiences, risk, experiment, sharing ideas, working with differences and so on – are well known. So why are these sort of cultures apparently so rare? New organizations often exhibit these sort of behaviours, but bigger, older ones can find it very hard to maintain this initial enthusiasm and energy. Developing an innovative culture is likely to be easier on a 'greenfield site' – where the business is new and where everyone is new to the business.

Although they were part of a very large an old company, in some ways the financial services managers were starting a new. After discussing and evaluating their list of elements, they developed and agreed some groundrules for behaviour in the new department (Box 14.2).

These groundrules were subject to some argument and testing, and consequently a special group was set up to monitor them. It would be the job of this group to assess progress, to check how well the groundrules were working and whether they needed to be added to or modified.

This is the difficult bit of the challenge to create an innovative culture. Even in the most favourable conditions, the crunch comes in the practice of these

Box 14.2   Groundrules for an innovative culture

DO:
- put three or four options for action in every business case or proposal
- propose courses of action which involve 'experiments at the margin'
- say what risks you are taking and why this is worthwhile
- support people in trying new things
- ask people for help on tasks
- ask for diverse views
- ensure that task groups contain at least one 'outsider'
- hold 'after action reviews' to capture the learning

DON'T:
- discourage people from trying new things without good cause
- re-invent things when you can borrow them from what works elsewhere
- innovate on other people's turf without checking
- criticize without offering new options
- run other people down

rules. Putting such groundrules for innovation into practice calls for leadership by everyone concerned, starting with personal actions with colleagues.

The process described above is one that can work well. Obviously it has to be interpreted for your situation. For example, the groundrules in Box 14.2 belong to a particular context and they might not fit your situation. It is important to go through the full process of determining the rules that you want to work to, and with the participation of all the people who must practice them. To give this approach a good chance of working, the following steps are indicated:

- Brainstorm a picture of a more innovative culture.
- Agree what elements and dimensions are most important for you.
- Develop some behavioural groundrules based on your view of what it will take to shift to the new desired culture.
- Follow up and monitor how well you are doing on the groundrules, amending them as you go.

Cultural change

It would be misleading to suggest that 'cultural change' is as simple as the financial services story might suggest. In these circumstances, where there has been a lot of change and something new is welcomed as an opportunity to move forward together, this sort of process will probably work very well. But what happens when you do not enjoy these favourable initial conditions? Deal and Kennedy (1982, pp. 159–161) suggest that there are only a few circumstances that justify the considerable effort involved in seeking to reshape or reframe the culture. These include when:

- The environment is changing quickly and the market is very competitive or the current values are likely to threaten our future.
- The organization is in generally very bad shape, with low output, quality and morale.
- The company is growing very rapidly and needs to make a step-jump in how it operates.

The words 'reshape' and 'reframe' are also important here. Change implies a new departure, but it is more sensible to think in terms of influencing or adding to cultures rather than radical shifts of direction.

This is particularly relevant in the story of the Hospital Therapy Services Department discussed below. In this case, the first two of the conditions noted by Deal and Kennedy were applicable to a considerable extent. Expectations from both the Government and from patients had changed and the department had failed to keep up. Some of the services offered by the department looked outdated and its internal organization was wasteful.

Rehabilitating Therapy Services

Since the late 1990s, the UK NHS has been subject to a 'modernization' effort to increase service quality, especially in terms of the patients' experience. This story concerns the new manager of a large Hospital Therapy Services Department mainly offering physiotherapy and occupational therapy to in- and outpatients.

When she came to the department, the new manager's first impression was of two clans occupying their own territory. The physiotherapists and occupational therapists (OTs) operated in very distinct ways, each with their own service heads, assessment protocols and systems for referral and treatment and separate workspaces. Although the individual physiotherapists and OTs frequently dealt with the same patients, they kept separate notes and there was no joint management of patients. There were many other differences, for example the OTs had few administrative staff and many 'helpers' (unqualified staff working under supervision) whereas physiotherapy was well supplied with administrators and operated with few helpers.

The new manager was concerned about the effects that this division in Therapy Services might be having upon the quality of work. In her general view, single multi-disciplinary treatments are likely to produce better clinical outcomes than multiple individual interventions. The obvious lack of co-ordination of treatments, inefficiencies in room usage and the very rigid stance of many of the clinicians promised little in the way of service innovations.

In order to help her staff develop more innovative and 'modernized' ways of working, the manager sought help from a consultant to hold a series of focus groups with staff to gather their views. What were the problems and opportunities of the present set-up and what new services could be offered? These meetings confirmed the new manager's first impressions and also revealed that there were widespread concerns amongst staff about the department's shortcomings, including:

- no quiet space – problems of distraction and lack of confidentiality
- poor understanding of what the different professions do
- a general lack of clarity about who can do what in terms of assessments and treatments
- a feeling that the staff had little involvement in decision-making above the immediate service level
- little integration in planning and resource allocation across the department
- difficulties with the hospital portering service
- poor liaison with external 'stakeholders', for example Primary Care Trusts and Social Services Departments.

On the other hand, there were various ideas for improvement, including:

- develop joint protocols for pre-assessment, referral and treatment
- redesign the 'patient pathways' and work patterns
- share available work spaces and to create quiet rooms

- experiment with joint management of patients and joint case notes
- examine new services for acute rehabilitation of, e.g., stroke patients
- develop new services jointly with Primary Care Trusts and Social Services Departments.

The new manager was heartened by the new ideas and suggestions and also to see that her concerns were shared by some of the staff. Perhaps things were not as bad as she thought and she had misjudged the situation? Discussions with the consultant revealed a different picture. The consultant was surprised by the apparent rigidity of staff around job definitions and their insistence on strict professional boundaries. Any new thinking was limited to just a few staff, mainly physiotherapists.

The manager thought through her ideas and wrote a short paper outlining some proposals for action. She wanted a sense of a shared service – a 'seamless rehabilitation service' – with a much more integrated staff. She wanted more joint management of patients and the redesign of protocols and work patterns, work space and case notes to help bring this about. She expected these changes to lead to great improvements in service delivery through the sharing of ideas, information and resources.

The consultant then asked her what she thought the impact of this paper would be on the staff of the department. After some discussion, the new manager saw that she might drive the cultural problems even deeper if she tried such a 'pushy' way forward. A slower, more inclusive approach was needed. The consultant then suggested that a residential workshop might be a good place to start so that departmental staff could get to know each other socially in addition to having time to think in a more relaxed way.

As it turned out, two 24-hour residential workshops were needed so that all staff could attend. One part of each workshop took the form of an activity to sketch the 'Biography of Therapy Services – Past, Present and Future'. This encouraged people to draw pictures, play around with ideas and think in metaphors about the department over time. The results from the two workshops told an interesting and remarkably similar story (see Table 14.1).

Following the workshops, the manager called a full meeting of the department and spoke about some of her ideas for the department in the future. She said that she realized that there were many reservations about some of these ideas but that she hoped people would join in to work out good ways forward. Following this meeting, several small volunteer task groups agreed to look at aspects of the department's work and to make proposals for change. These groups would report back to another full meeting in 6 weeks time. Some small changes were agreed at the workshops, including the willingness for trainees to 'job shadow' outside their immediate professional group.

The new manager reflected that, although this was a long way from what she wanted, nevertheless a start had been made. Some amorphous concerns and anxieties had been surfaced and defined and some problems had been faced. It was clear that changing this culture would be a long haul with resistance felt all the way. The tough issues could only be addressed in an atmosphere of trust, and it would take time to build this. However, the inclusive process gave everyone the opportunity to be involved and soon there would be some learning about how to tackle the tough issues and develop new initiatives. She reflected that, whilst it was important not to leave innovation just to the few, it was equally vital not to get bogged down by 'democracy'.

Table 14.1   A biography of Therapy Services – past, present and future

Theme	Past	Present	Future
Our workspace	Little huts and encampments all over the hospital	Football match: two sides	Open plan
What we say about ourselves: publicity and information	Each hut has its own sign	Leaflet is 'Medical dictionary' – people don't know what we do.	'Show and Tell' – with pictures, posters and videos
How we meet and greet patients	We had our own porters to fetch people	People dumped in wheelchairs	Friendly helpers at reception
What is work like	Safe, secure, boring	A race against time (and each other)	We are in it together
What stories do we tell	About the downtrodden and undervalued	How the other lot make mistakes!	How we won the cup
What do we believe in	A steady job	My job	Valuable service to local people
What do we look like	Shanty town dwellers	Men and women in white coats	A flock of flying geese
Who is respected	Nobody!	Qualified professionals	All of us – whoever we are
Who we are	Neither doctors nor nurses	Professional OTs and physiotherapists	Professionals delivering high-quality therapy services

In the case of Therapy Services, the staff themselves needed some 'cultural therapy' before they could begin to see what might be different and positive. Once stuck in an old position, it takes time, and determination by those who are leading on the path to a more innovative culture, to get enough freedom of movement to make possible the experiment and learning which is an essential part of service improvement.

Conclusion

The existence of subcultures that do not work well together, as in the Therapy Services situation, is a common sign of a weak overall culture. Subcultures can be about healthy differences and energizing competition, or they can become exclusive and isolated, laws unto themselves, not part of the shared conversation in the company as a whole. When there are obvious signs of trouble – where people are unhappy, inwardly focused, given to erratic and inconsistent behaviour, working in different directions – then there is a strong case for intervening to influence cultural change.

The story of the hospital Therapy Services Department is a cautionary tale that illustrates the difficult nature of cultural change. In this way, it balances out the story of the financial services initiative, which, given favourable circumstances, worked well and straightforwardly. Neither case can be taken as typical for the variety of cultures is just too great for any single formula. However, as a pair, if one gives a hopeful glimpse, the other underlines the advice that the cultural change journey must be undertaken in hope whilst preparing for the worst. This journey might start with some history and understanding of how things have come to be as they are, as a precursor to developing a sense of movement towards the future. In these situations, as with Therapy Services, it might take some time to get the old joints and the stiff tendons moving.

If the conditions are right, then the simple approach can work well, releasing energies and getting people working well together in a new direction. The tools provided in this chapter give you the means to get started on the challenge of creating cultures of innovation. They will help you understand the nature of your situation and, whatever the circumstances, they will help you get under way.

Further resources

The pervasive question of cultural change links to many of the leadership challenges featured in this book. The list of chapters containing tools and ideas that may be helpful if you are considering how to bring about a more innovative culture is a long one. First check Chapter 21, which discusses the role of networks and communities of practice in animating organizations, especially in terms of their abilities to learn and to share knowledge. Many people would argue that these webs of relationship and practice are core to innovation and creativity in any enterprise. Other chapters worth scanning for useful and related sources are Chapters 11, 15, 16, 22 and 23.

Roger Harrison has developed a famous typology of organizational cultures: power, role, task and people together with a questionnaire for understanding your organization's character. Roger has many wise things to say about organizations and their cultures and his papers can be found in R. Harrison, *The Collected Papers of Roger Harrison* (McGraw-Hill, Maidenhead, 1995).

For a more general text on cultural change, Terrence Deal and Lee Bolman's *Re-framing Organisations: Artistry, Choice and Leadership*, 2nd edn (Jossey Bass,

San Francisco, 1997) develops the authors' idea of four basic frames for viewing organizations as multiple realities: factories, families, jungles and temples. It provides a wealth of cases and other illustrative materials for leaders and managers to expand their options and enhance their effectiveness.

Reference

Deal, T. W. and A. Kennedy (1982) *Corporate Cultures: The Rites and Rituals of Organisational Life*, Addison Wesley, Reading, MA.

15

Challenge 6: Fostering Diversity and Inclusion

Learning proceeds from difference
Gregory Bateson

Only variety can absorb variety
W. Ross Ashby

Introduction

Questions of diversity, difference and inclusion often arise as industrial relations problems, centring on questions of unfair discrimination and the importance of ensuring justice and fairness through equal opportunities. The importance of these issues increases as workforces become more diverse. Organizations without good equal opportunities policies and practices may experience problems such as labour shortages in key posts.

However, this chapter is not focused upon the good management of difference, diversity and equal opportunity – important though this is – but on the innovation and learning potential of personal and cultural differences. As the anthropologist Gregory Bateson pointed out many years ago, learning proceeds from difference, from a difference between what one expects and what actually happens. The more open we are to difference, the greater is the learning potential and the greater the ability to embrace change and development. Difference and diversity therefore hold the key to many of the aspirations of leadership.

Ashby's Law of Requisite Variety holds that the internal diversity of any system or organization must match the variety and complexity of its environment if it is to deal with the challenges coming from that environment. The English cybernetician Ross Ashby explored the notion of organizations as self-organizing or self-regulating systems – systems capable of progressively differentiating themselves towards higher levels of complexity. Ashby's ideas about self-organizing systems have been seminal in thinking about the leadership of organizational change and development. For example, the idea of the learning organization centres on organizing to maximize learning by shifting towards self-regulation and away from command and control (see Chapter 11).

Organizations systems often unintentionally suppress diversity, seeking uniformity of performance and behaviour. Unlocking the potential of difference and diversity depends on being clear about what is held tight and what can be loosened to admit new views and new voices that can challenge previous orthodoxies with novel perspectives. Some of the sources of novelty in an organization are the collective differences of gender, age, ethnicity, sexuality, disability and so on and the myriads of individual differences within persons.

Including local voices

There are two important aspects of diversity. The first is representation – are all the people who should have a say included? The second is to do with learning – are the people who deliver the service or produce the product with vital local knowledge included in the discussion. The importance of local voices and local knowledge is one of the threads running through many of the leadership challenges in this book. Action and implementation are always local, and local commitment is central to sustaining change in any setting. Yet many change efforts are imposed without the inclusion of relevant local voices and without the understanding and ideas that might come from this source.

The validity of these voices is often denied. How can such people understand the strategic imperatives? How can they come up with ideas and solutions for problems when we employ the best in the field? Yet whilst locals need to learn enough about the big picture to interpret it in their own context, the strategists' most common error in change management is the belief that their map is a true representation of the territory. Locals understand more than central teams suppose and can not only make practical suggestions for improvement, but also bring opinions and perspectives not otherwise available at the centre.

However, including local voices is not just a matter of listening to people. Senior people may also fear a loss of control. Driven by shareholder expectations or targets from above, the inclusive route, unpredictable and inevitably political, is the hard choice to take:

The politics of inclusion are not faint-hearted efforts at making everybody happy enough. Inclusion means more than taking people's views into account in defining the problem. Inclusion may mean challenging people, hard and steadily, to face new perspectives on familiar problems, to let go of old ideas and ways of life long held sacred. Thus, inclusion does not mean that each party will get its way. Even the most well-crafted efforts at inclusion can rarely prevent the experience of loss by some.... Furthermore, from a strategic standpoint, some parties often must be excluded from the problem-solving process.

(Heifetz, 1994, p. 240)

Leadership groups which have held their nerve, and travelled this route, are usually surprised by the volume of ideas and the creativity of responses that comes when different groups and people are properly invited to take part.

This chapter includes:

- Wakefield Cosmetics – a case illustration of a company which needs to embrace more diversity to survive
- a tool for stakeholder mapping
- a description of the whole systems approach to inclusion
- a process tool for developing and working with a design team
- further resources.

Diversify for growth

Diversification is one of the oldest strategies for growth, often bringing small companies to their knees and large companies into conflict with institutional shareholders. The histories of long-lived companies shows that this long life frequently depends upon diversifications or transformations at critical times. However, diversification, as branching into new product or service areas, is always a risky shift. Making use of the existing diversity in and around a business is much less risky – all it takes is courage, vision and a good process.

Wakefield Cosmetics

Wakefield Cosmetics (not its real name) started as Edwards Soap Manufacturers in the mid-19th century and is proud of its local history and roots. The founder, Josiah Edwards, was a well-known lay preacher and philanthropist, who imprinted his Christian beliefs on the company and promoted its products as God's work on Earth. From the outset there was a great belief in making soap from natural products and the incorporation of herbs for colouring and scenting. The company's products were superior to more mundane soaps and commanded premium prices.

In the early-20th century, the firm continued to be managed by Josiah's children and grandchildren and the family remain major shareholders to this day. As soap production became the province of large manufacturers, the company began to diversify into cosmetics. In the 1960s, the company changed its name to reflect the increasing importance of cosmetics to its current and future prosperity. Still based on natural products, its cosmetics and toiletries were increasingly advertised as not using preservatives, artificial dyes and, eventually, animal products. Environmental protection and preservation became a key theme. In the 1980s and 1990s the company underwent rapid expansion as major contracts were gained with department stores and international distributors. The company also started its own mail order business.

Currently, Wakefield Cosmetics employs some 300 people, mostly females, who work on production and packaging lines. Because of the demand for high-value and handmade products, the company also deals with a diverse network of customers, distributors and suppliers, many of whom run 'lifestyle' businesses and are strongly ethically driven. Additionally, the company employs some 40 homeworkers, mainly from ethnic minority groups, to handle special packaging and decoration tasks. The senior management team are entirely white and male, although most of the supervisors are female, an increasing number of Asian origin.

Although demand for its products is holding up, Wakefield Cosmetics has been experiencing quality problems over the last couple of years, and there have been a number of complaints about discrimination. Views have been aired, both inside and outside, that the company needs to do some new things. Worse still, there seems to be a growing perception amongst its diverse suppliers and distributors that the company is now devoted to turnover and profit maximization and is increasingly remote from its ethical roots and principles. Although the management team has responded to the growing diversity of the workforce by appointing supervisors from amongst their ranks, they have a sense of a divide between themselves and the staff. In the boardroom, the idea of an employee survey is being mooted.

Wakefield Cosmetics is seeing early signs of trouble in terms of managing its equal opportunity issues. More importantly perhaps for its long-term success, it is failing to make the best of the rich mosaic of diversity and difference both within the company and outside in its wide network of business partners. The idea of the employee survey might be a good one, and will, if well conducted, certainly generate useful information.

Mapping the diversity of stakeholders

If you were in Wakefield Cosmetics position, a positive first step would be to map the diversity of stakeholders. Table 15.1 offers a simple framework for the process of engaging with the diversity of stakeholders in a given organization.

Activity: stakeholder mapping

A stakeholder analysis is a useful activity in the face of a challenging situation for any collective, organization or community. This might be a simple issue such as inadequate car parking in a city centre office, or it might be more complicated as in a University seeking to increase its research and publication outputs. In the case of Wakefield Cosmetics, there are clearly a number of issues that need to be addressed; equal opportunities might be a good place to start, or the problems can be approached another way by looking at product quality. As there seems to be a cluster of interconnections here, a focus on any one is likely to lead to the others.

Table 15.1 A stakeholder analysis

Stakeholders	What is their view of the problem or issue?	What is their desired picture of the future?
Internal groupings		
1.		
2.		
3.		
4.		
Etc.		
External stakeholders		
1.		
2.		
3.		
4.		
Etc.		

The mapping starts by identifying all the diverse groupings with a legitimate interest in the particular issue. In the Wakefield Cosmetics case there are a number of these, including the various groups of employees inside and all the external customers, distributors, suppliers and home workers. Once all the relevant groupings are listed, the next tasks are to identify the particular view of the problem or issue which each of these takes and what they would like to see in terms of a future situation. What is their desired vision or picture of how things should be? Getting this information might be simple in some cases, for example by contacting known people or calling them in for an informal brainstorming session, but much more difficult in others. In Wakefield Cosmetics there are likely to be large gaps in the management team's knowledge of these different views, and it is not clear how they might obtain good information in all cases.

With these steps completed, there will be a diverse and rich picture of views and perceptions. To convert these insights into action, the next step is to find ways and means of unlocking the energy potential of these diverse perspectives. This could involve a whole systems development process to bring them together to clarify differences, forge common purpose and determine useful actions for the future.

Convening the whole system

Whole systems development involves working with all the stakeholders in a situation to bring about change in a system. Exploring the diversity and difference within a business system can lead to connections and synergies for the benefit of the whole. Whole systems development is a response to a growing complexity, both of business issues and of partnership and network relationships. This is inclusive 'big tent politics' where all the people who might be part of the problem are also part of the solution. Actions generated from such a process are taken on the basis of 'nothing about us without us'.

Weisbord and Janoff (1995, p. 2) have proposed a historical trend in organizational problem solving, away from a reliance upon experts and towards self-regulation by people taking more control over their own working lives:

1900	Experts solve problems
1950	'Everybody' solves problems
1965	Experts improve whole systems
2000	'Everybody' improves whole systems

Getting 'Everybody' into improving whole systems means 'getting the whole organization into the room' by representing all aspects and groups, especially those who are not usually heard. The aim is to maximize diversity in order to generate the internal requisite variety to match that being encountered in the environment.

Starting this process means considers such questions as:

- What are the opportunities to bring people together to share their views?
- How could people agree on the important questions that need to be answered?
- What would be the process for negotiate a joint inquiry into these questions?
- How can we give permission for people to express different views?
- What would be a way of articulating a shared purpose?
- Who should be accountable to whom? And for what?

The best way to get started on this ambitious process is to create a design team.

Working with a design team

A design team is a micro-organization or parallel structure to plan, anticipate and experience a change effort on behalf of the whole. On holographic principles, a design team aims to be a microcosm of the whole, representing all groups and stakeholders. In the case of Wakefield Cosmetics, this would require the involvement and engagement of all the stakeholders listed in their version of Table 15.1. Design teams usually have consultancy support to help them both to achieve their potential as a team and to handle relationships with others in the system, including especially the leadership team.

Setting up a design team is a good first step in tackling a complex system, and a vital step in avoiding or ameliorating the effects of top-down programmes of change. Box 15.1 offers some simple guidance on how to create and facilitate such a team. More detail can be found in Attwood *et al.* (2003) and Jacobs (1994).

Design teams have great credibility in organizational development efforts because of who they are – they represent us rather than them. They bear local knowledge in deciding who to talk to, what might work, what makes sense and so on. No survey or climate questionnaire can supply this sort of know-how and feel. By becoming an alternative and authoritative source of opinion, they also open up the possibility of dialogue with the senior team.

To work well, the design team must have a mandate from a leadership team. They need this sort of trust to allow them the freedom to do their own data gathering and diagnosis of how things are in the organization. Coming together for the first time the design team will be asking all sorts of questions (Attwood *et al.*, 2003, p. 121):

- Why have we taken this on?
- What is this task anyway?
- Where are the resources to do it?
- What does the leadership want us to do?
- What are they trying to achieve anyway?
- How will other people see our role?
- Who is part of this situation and who needs to be involved in resolving it?
- How willing are others going to be to get involved?

These questions are the basis for action and profound learning and will determine the route ahead. They are very different from the questions that a consultancy might put to their clients for a major change. These same questions might be there for the consultants, but they would not be put in the same way, nor would they lead to the same discoveries and dialogues.

Box 15.1   A design team specification

> **Size** – Up to 20 or more; whatever is needed to reflect the diversity and harness the energy
>
> **Membership** – Design teams may have core members and less regular attenders. A continuous core group is essential and it may work well to have other levels of membership according to circumstances and tasks

Composition – Reflect the diversity of the system to ensure that all the relevant organizations, professional groupings, occupational categories, interest groups, age, gender and ethnic mixes and so on, are represented

Getting to know each other – A crucial task at the first meeting of a design team is to give lot of time to people meeting each other and understanding their differences and similarities in relation to the task. This meeting each other needs time to lay a good foundation. It is also likely to surface some differences which may be difficult to handle

Exploring differences – These differences need to be explored constructively within the design team. This may not happen at the early meetings and may be better surfaced during discussions on the task. However, exploring these differences *is* part of the task, and learning from this work in this group is vital for understanding how to react to when they appear in the wider organization

Collecting data – Going out, collecting data and information and bringing it back to analysis and understanding is a good way for a design team to find its feet. Members already bring data and understanding with them, but deciding what to collect and from whom, together with the collaborative experience of bringing it back home and making sense of it, is a useful team-building activity

Designing events – A common feature of whole systems designs is the 'Big Event', bringing together perhaps 200 or 300 people (or more), to give their views, seek common ground and agree next steps. These events can be very dramatic and energizing and the design team can play many roles here. With experience, teams can run the entire event themselves, handling the up-front facilitation in addition to all the logistics work. A lot of design work goes into such events, from deciding who will be invited to detailed scripting of the activities and timetable of the event

Relationships with the leadership team – A design team may find itself coaching or advising the leadership team of any change effort. Although this work will often be done by the consultants, a strong design team may well become engaged in a dialogue with the senior leadership, perhaps in the context of a middle-ground framework to link action on the ground with overall strategic direction (Attwood *et al.*, 2003, pp. 50–52)

Action learning – Action learning is one of the best tools for seeking to carry through the agreed actions from any 'Big Event'. The design team will already have experienced this process in their own working together and they are well placed for encouraging and monitoring it within the wider system

Organizational learning – The design team can contribute to organizational learning by being a conduit for learning throughout. Public exchanges in 'Big Events' may have already generated considerable learning within and across stakeholder groups. This may be continued in bringing action learning groups together for periodic conferences or through the on-going dialogues of a middle-ground framework

Conclusion

Fostering diversity and inclusion is not only about the important business of developing justice and fairness, it also makes good commercial sense. This is especially obvious in matters such as recruitment and retention: what sort of person, given a choice, wants to work in an all-white, all-male organization these days? In the longer term, new and diverse recruits will take the company in new directions. For many older traditional concerns, such as Wakefield Cosmetics, there is a trick here in turning the issues that have been the subjects of discrimination and complaints into positive differences that make working life more exciting, more innovative.

The question of culture is central to making the most of diversity and difference. It is common to encounter organizational cultures, which have developed over time and in particular circumstances, that turn out to exclude or disadvantage particular groups of people. 'Cultures of inclusion' aim to welcome everyone and not to leave out any particular group or type of person. Such cultures can sometimes be found in surprising places, such as the UK Civil Service, where the tradition of regular movement between jobs emphasizes the role and not the person, providing a shelter for people with a surprising variety of views and lifestyles. Whether this diversity is actively sought out and 'leveraged' is another question.

Whole systems development approaches bring together diverse groups to participate in the debate about the need for, and the direction of, change. If successful, such approaches enrol people as part of the sustained effort in taking agreed changes forward. However, this is demanding work. The processes for creating common purpose amidst diversity and difference, and for negotiating the 'system of authorizations' (Heifetz, 1994, p. 70), whereby people and groups take responsibility for tasks on behalf of the whole, take time and persistence to bring about.

Further resources

There are relatively few good publications on managing diversity. Binna Kandola and Joanna Fullerton's *Managing the Mosaic: Diversity in Action* (Chartered Institute of Personnel and Development, London, 1994) is an exception and gives advice on the best way to handle this process and how to intervene on specific issues.

In the books referenced below, Weisbord (1992) and Weisbord and Janoff (1995) detail various processes that 'bring the organization into the room together' – to tell their stories and articulate their wishes for the future. These processes are not complicated, but the diversity and numbers involved make careful planning essential. Jacobs (1994) provides a detailed planning system for doing this, and Attwood *et al.* (2003) provide many examples and illustrations together with tools for whole systems development.

References

Attwood, M., M. Pedler, S. Pritchard and D. Wilkinson (2003) *Leading Change: a Guide to Whole Systems Working*, Policy Press, Bristol.

Heifetz, R. (1994) *Leadership Without Easy Answers*, Belknap Press, Cambridge, MA.

Jacobs, R. (1994) *Real Time Strategic Change: How to Involve an Entire Organisation in Fast and Far-reaching Change*, Berrett-Koehler, San Francisco.

Weisbord, M. (1992) *Discovering Common Ground: How Future Search Conferences Bring People Together to Achieve Breakthrough Innovation, Empowerment, Shared Vision and Collaborative Action*, Berrett-Koehler, San Francisco.

Weisbord, M. and S. Janoff (1995) *Future Search: an Action Guide to Finding Common Ground in Organizations and Communities*, Berrett-Koehler, San Francisco.

Challenge 7: Promoting Partnerships

No company can go it alone
Doz and Hamel (1998)

Introduction

The capacity to collaborate with a variety of business partners is a new core competence for organizations. Collaborative advantage is the key to survival and success in a networked world. Partnerships can be very informal, and they often begin in this way. Good partners add value by bringing in new skills, resources or customers. Small firms can extend their range of products by linking up; large companies can achieve global reach through strategic alliances, and in the UK there is a duty to partnership to provide more joined-up and better quality public services.

Partnerships are often formed to tackle the really tough challenges as we can see in the example below.

Iridium

In the early 1990s, Motorola initiated a global alliance to build a mobile communications network. Based on 62 orbiting satellites, this would have significant advantages over ground-based technologies, but to do this Motorola needed a wide range of partners to supply the funds, ownership rights and capabilities which it did not itself possess. A coalition of no less than 17 equity holding partners was assembled, including for example, Nippon Iridium, which was in itself an alliance of 18 partners. These partners provided all sorts of expertise from ground communications to space-based technologies, and also held ownership and traffic rights which were crucial to success in a situation where Iridium was competing in a race with other similarly assembled partnerships. This $3.4 billion investment was intended to boost Motorola's (and its partners') position in global cellular communication (Doz and Hamel, 1998, pp. 3–4).

Most partnerships are more modest in scope than Iridium, and more locally based. This is characteristic in health and social care where partnering activity often comes about because services are faced with overwhelming demand. Many local partnerships are forged as different agencies come together to share knowledge, pool resources and redesign services.

A health inequalities alliance

The National Health Service (NHS) is charged with reducing health inequalities in the UK. However, this is not a question just about health, but about all the underlying factors which affect a person's well-being, including whether they have a job, enough money and decent housing in a decent environment free from crime. Addressing the problem of health inequalities means engaging all the agencies involved in these fields.

In one rural area of the UK, the County Council and Health Authority convened a coalition to tackle the problem. At the outset this included local NHS Trusts, the Community Council and the Council for Voluntary Services. As the project developed, many other partners joined, including the Youth Service, Education, Transport, Police and also some of the existing partnership organizations involved in local regeneration and neighbourhood renewal. In this project, there are already some notable achievements in terms of redesigned and joined-up services, and a more collaborative way of working between the partners is beginning to emerge. In a review day, they reflected on the lessons learned so far:

- Build on existing good practice where people are already working together.
- Involve users, patients and carers from the earliest stage.
- Find and help the innovators who are working to deliver services differently.
- Develop a clear collective purpose and vision.
- Take the time to engage the commitment of the senior people in addition to the professionals who deliver the services.
- Invest in co-ordinator and 'animateur' roles to help develop the networks.

In this chapter, we provide models and tools for helping you get started on promoting and developing partnerships. The rest of this chapter contains:

- a stage model of partnership together with some key questions about the match between the prospective partners
- PAT: a partnership advancement tool for assessing partnerships
- further resources.

A model for developing partnership

Good partnerships like this do not just happen. Success depends on two main things: how partnerships begin and how they continue. This is true both of small local collaborations and of large strategic alliances. From even the smallest beginnings, time spent on establishing the right initial conditions and creating a high-quality joint development process is vital. The initial conditions include:

■ *The strategic match* – do the partners complement each other in terms of competencies, assets, markets, etc.?
■ *The organizational match* – are the parties compatible in terms of organizational structures, cultures and ways of doing things?
■ *The expectations match* – are the partners similar in motives and intentions? For example, is this a defensive or a developmental initiative?

However good the apparent match and however well the initial conditions are set up, the success of any partnership also depends on how it matures over time. Good relationships can develop opportunities never glimpsed at the outset; poor ones can sap energy and take years to untangle. The 'developmental climate' of a partnership can be judged by the answers to questions such as:

■ How open in this partnership? Does the agreement allow for sharing of knowledge about technology, information systems and markets?
■ What opportunities are built in to review and evaluate the way the partnership is working?
■ What processes exist for the parties to learn from each other around tasks, work processes, skills and so on?

A key issue in partnerships is how the partners think about and react to the differences between them. In successful partnerships, there is an evolution over time of the ways of thinking about and responding to differences within the relationship. It is the nature and quality of the learning opportunities and conversations which exist around the partnership which will enable the parties to share knowledge, skills and understandings and – more importantly – to adjust their expectations of the partnership over time.

Successful partnership

In a major European engineering and manufacturing joint venture making small aircraft, the parties had worked successfully together on the 'high walls make good neighbours' principle by tightly specifying the tasks and processes for which each partner was responsible and by designating special joint teams to manage the important interfaces. However, when the partner responsible for the manufacture of the engines hit an apparently insurmountable problem that threatened the status of orders from the most important customer, the engineers concerned had to trust their partners and put all their knowledge on the table. This felt like a big risk but when the other partners responded and pooled their knowledge and expertise, a solution to the problem was devised. One long-term outcome of this learning was a new agreement about knowledge and skills sharing across the partner companies.

There are three stages in this evolutionary development of a partnership (Box 16.1). Successful partnerships depend on this development of the relationship over time, but if they do not get off to a good start, there is no possibility of building the relationship. An initial step in forming a partnership is to look at the match between the parties and generally to assess the initial conditions. This is similar to what accountants call the 'due diligence' process.

Box 16.1   A stage model of partnership

STAGE 1 = SEPARATE and ISOLATED
'They're different from us' (and we don't really want to know about or have anything to do with them)
   In some partnerships, the terms are tightly set, and the parties protect their valuable knowledge, processes, technology and so on outside these strict contractual obligations from the other partners

STAGE 2 = CURIOUS and EXPLORATORY
'They're different from us' (and that's very interesting)
   Here the partners have started to notice each other and ask questions about how the other does things. To question and to wonder creates the initial conditions for learning

STAGE 3 = JOINT ENQUIRY and CO-CREATION
'We are different' (and through understanding and using these differences we're working together generate something new and exciting)
   The ultimate aim for good partnerships. One plus one equals three and more. A key point here is how learning and innovation grow out of difference and diversity. Yet in Stage 1, difference is rejected and suppressed. For partnerships to succeed they need a process for shifting from Stage 1 to Stage 2; Stage 3 is then likely to follow

Activity: PAT – partnership advancement tool

A good business partnership is best entered after the parties have given it considerable thought. PAT is a partnership advancement tool to help you prepare, plan, get started and learn from any partnership. It covers the main aspects of partnership working under three headings:

- *Assessing the potential*: what value and benefits are likely to accrue to all parties? What are their track records of past collaborations? How skilled are the partners at this way of working?

▨ *Designing the partnership*: what are the main parameters to be considered, including the jointness of purpose, goals and values, the clarity of the scope and limits of partnership working and the extent of agreement on working rules and conduct? What arrangements do the parties have for sharing benefits?

▨ *Developing the partnership*: what processes do the partners have in place to help them monitor progress and learn from their relationship? What are the provisions for mutual development and adjustment over time?

Work through the following questions alone or in your team. For each question choose one of the five options that seems to best describe the current state of affairs as you see them:

▨ strongly agree
▨ agree
▨ don't know
▨ disagree
▨ strongly disagree.

	Strongly agree	Agree	Don't know	Disagree	Strongly disagree
Assessing the potential					
1 We will gain substantially from the partnership					
2 We can specify how the partnership will create value for us, e.g. new resources, skills, markets					
3 Our partner(s) will gain substantially from the partnership					
4 We can specify how the partnership will create value for our partners, e.g. new resources, skills, markets					
5 Our partner(s) and ourselves understand each other's business strategies and see them as compatible					
6 Both we and our partner(s) have a track record of factors good partnership working					
Designing the partnership					
7 Our partnership has a clear joint purpose and vision					

	Strongly agree	Agree	Don't know	Disagree	Strongly disagree
8 Our partnership is based on shared values and principles					
9 Our partnership has clear joint aims and goals					
10 The partners agree on the scope and limits of the partnership working					
11 We have adequately discussed each other' areas of work non-partnership and how this affects the partnership					
12 We have discussed with all partners how this partnership fits in with our other alliances, networks and partnerships					
13 We have agree the joint task demands and have designed the interface between partners					
14 We have agreed rules for the conduct of the partnership to promote fairness, trust and joint working					
15 The outcomes of our partnership working can be clearly linked to each partner's contributions					
16 We have a process for discussing how benefits are shared relative to partners' contributions at any given time					
17 Each partner has senior people committed to the success of the partnership					
18 There is strong ownership of the partnership within each of the partner organizations					
Developing the partnership					
19 There are agreed success criteria that will be used by all partners					
20 We have jointly identified some early successes					

	Strongly agree	Agree	Don't know	Disagree	Strongly disagree
21 The partners have a clear and agreed process for monitoring progress on both the goals and the process of the partnership					
22 We have an agreed process for understanding and bridging any gaps that may appear at the inter-face between partners, e.g. in terms of expectations, skills, organiza-tional cultures and contexts					
23 We have established a joint learning agenda for developing partnership tasks					
24 We have established a joint learning agenda for developing the partnering process					
25 We have established a joint learning agenda for developing skills and knowledge between partners					
26 We have built a learning cycle into our partnership working so that from time to time we jointly reflect and agree new ideas to try out in our relationship					
27 Our joint learning cycle enables us to reconsider all our goals and working arrangements and modify them in the light of our discussions					
28 We have a declared intention to look for new areas of business and new opportunities which we might pursue together					

PAT: understanding the results

Numerical scoring does not do justice to the complexity of the issues behind each of the questions in the three categories of:

- assessing the potential
- designing the partnership
- developing the partnership.

Our view is that it is best to treat your responses as indicators of where you might need to put more effort or think more carefully before moving ahead. The best way of using your responses is to think about the patterns that are revealed in the relationship and what actions are indicated. It helps if you do this in a team or small group and discuss the collective outcomes.

PAT is constructed so that the *Strongly agree* response gives you the best score or cleanest bill of health on that particular question. If you have a *Strongly disagree* or *Disagree* response, this indicates that this area may be a problem for you and your organization and that it may need your attention. If you have a *Don' t know* response, this may mean that more thought is needed here or that this is an area of confusion or ambiguity that would benefit from further discussion.

However, if you wish to give your results a numerical scoring, you can allocate scores to a five-point scale as follows:

- ▓ Strongly agree   5
- ▓ Agree   4
- ▓ Don't know   3
- ▓ Disagree   2
- ▓ Strongly disagree   1

The maximum score in each of the three categories is then as follows:

- ▓ Assessing the potential   =   30 (6 × 5)
- ▓ Designing the partnership   =   60 (12 × 5)
- ▓ Developing the partnership   =   50 (10 × 5)

A score of, say, less than half of these totals might indicate a serious problem in that category.

How to use PAT

There are three obvious ways in which you can use PAT:

1 First, you can use PAT as personal preparation. Working through it on your own, perhaps with a 'speaking partner' in whom you can confide, will provide you with an agenda of issues and questions to guide you in any discussions and negotiations.

2 Second, it is a good idea to work through PAT with your own team – and especially also with key senior people in your organization from whom you may need to get clearance, support, commitment and a good mandate to continue this work.

   Have each member of the team – and the main people in your organization concerned with this partnership – to complete the PAT separately and then meet to compare notes. This discussion, and the questioning which will be part of it, will be the best possible preparation and means of ensuring that you go into this new venture with your eyes open.

3 The next step is to work this through with your prospective partners. This may involve some risk taking on your and on your organization's part, but time spent on

these questions now could add great value and perhaps save a great deal of wasted effort in the future. Also, although there will be commercial and political reasons why you cannot share everything with your partners at the outset, beginning by working in this way will help to build the trust and establish the longer term learning climate which are so vital to success.

Invite your prospective partners to complete the PAT and to arrange a meeting to have a similar discussion to that described above. Make it clear what you are prepared to share and what you cannot share at this stage.

Partnering and success

This chapter starts with the assertion that partnering is one of the keys to business success in a 'networked world'. We also believe that collaborative advantage is an outcome which is planned for and worked at; the fruits of partnering are generally gathered over the long term. At the core of this effort is the building of trust: partners need confidence that each will do what they say they will do. Being trusting or trustful means going into things with your eyes open, and making sure that your prospective partners do likewise. This means defining what you say you will do carefully, and also being very careful about changing any agreements made in this way.

To close this chapter, here is a partnering success story that comes tinged with irony. The partnership between the UK and Japanese car manufacturers Rover and Honda took years to bring to fruition. It existed for several years in Stage 1 mode with the Rover engineers in particular showing little interest in their Honda counterparts. Then something happened that triggered a mutual interest that led to learning about different ways to make cars. The partnership ended abruptly when the improving Rover company was sold for cash by its owner. A former senior Rover manager tells the story:

Honda and Rover

'From 1978 to 1995 the strategic alliance between Honda and Rover developed and launched six new models, each with many derivatives. After 17 years, there was a great deal of evidence of product improvement and learning especially on the Rover side. But the partnership did not really take off until 1986 when the Total Quality Initiative was introduced together with the notion of a "learning culture".

This prompted line managers to ask themselves questions never asked before. Lots of new questions on capturing best practices, benchmarking, team-working and communications suddenly put Honda in the frame for the Rover engineers because they had such a positive reputation on these subjects. A number of questions led us naturally to consider Honda as a source of expertise from which we could learn, and we belatedly realized that they were our working colleagues! A watershed event reflecting the new spirit of co-operation and learning was a corporate learning day in 1992, when 200 people came together through presentations, exhibitions and small group action learning sets. This resulted in many implementation plans across the organization and had a knock-on effect that embraced 10 times the number who actually attended.

Rover was owned at the time by British Aerospace (now BAe). It remains interesting that up to the BMW takeover, Rover was the only UK-based automotive business to form a long-term partnership with a Japanese business with "learning" as a main component part'   (Source: Barrie Oxtoby).

Whatever the outrageous fortune of the market, success remains success, and to this day the Rover people remain proud of what their partnership achieved.

Further resources

Rosabeth Kanter was one of the first people to spot the partnering trend and her 'Collaborative advantage: the art of alliances', *Harvard Business Review*, July/August 1994, pp. 96–108 is well worth a read. Yves Doz and Gary Hamel's *Alliance Advantage: the Art of Creating Value Through Partnering* (referenced below) is a very usable book. Although it takes its material and context entirely from the world of commercial big business, it is admirably thorough and discerning readers will be able to cherry-pick many good ideas, not least from the 20-page Appendix containing numerous detailed questions on how to assess a strategic alliance. Doz is one of the few who have looked at partnerships from a developmental perspective and his paper 'The evolution of cooperation in strategic alliances: initial conditions or learning processes'?, *Strategic Management Journal*, 17, Summer 1996, is a minor classic.

Locally you may find many reports, publications and tools on partnership, especially in the public and voluntary services. Ask colleagues what is available. Specifically on health and social care is Brian Hardy, Bob Hudson and Eileen Waddington's *What makes a Good Partnership? A Partnership Assessment Tool* (Nuffield Institute for Health, Leeds, 2000), produced in partnership with NHS Executive Trent.

Reference

Doz, Y. and G. Hamel (1998) *Alliance Advantage: the Art of Creating Value Through Partnering*, Harvard Business School Press, Boston, MA.

17

Challenge 8: Improving Work Processes

*What do 'targets' accomplish? Nothing. Wrong: their accomplishment
is negative*
W. Edwards Deming

Introduction

Some 20 years ago, the UK motor-car industry began to wake up to the fact that Japanese manufacturers were somehow able to produce cars of a much higher quality. Quality, that is, not so much in terms of luxury, but when measured by reliability and durability. Not only that, they were able to do so much more economically. In a study published in 1990, the productivity of European car manufacturers was less than half that of the Japanese, and the number of defects in a new car was 60 per cent greater.

The same study showed that although these differences were partly due to the relative levels of automation, the main causes lay in different approaches to quality and the use of continuous improvement tools. Since then, there has been a growing recognition of the importance of quality as experienced by the customer. In the commercial sector, it is one of the key factors in determining profit or loss, flourishing or bankruptcy. Also, people are becoming less and less willing to put up with poor service and performance in health, education, transport and the other public services.

Examples of poor quality abound. A recent USA survey showed that 100 000 people per year die as a direct result of medical mistakes, partly due to the faulty prescribing of medicines. A recent UK study looked at prescriptions in a 550-bed teaching hospital in London, and found that almost 1300 drug orders were written each day. Pharmacists found mistakes in 1.5 per cent of these – mistakes, which included prescribing 10 times the recommended dose of a drug for heart failure. On the face of it, 1.5 per cent does not sound too bad – it means that 98.5 per cent are OK (a figure that would delight train operators and passengers). However, suppose pharmacists fail to spot errors in a similar 1.5 per cent of cases, and also themselves give the wrong medicine in a similar number?

Then the overall error rate increases to nearly 4.5 per cent, that is, one prescription in 23 is wrong. In fact, one study concluded that pharmacists misread prescriptions in no less than 17 per cent of cases, which would now lead to over 19 per cent – nearly one in five – of medications being incorrect.

This example shows the cumulative effect of errors that may in themselves look small. In addition to being inconvenient, annoying or downright deadly to the customer, poor quality leads to very high costs associated with rectifying defaults, rework, scrap, handling complaints, insurance, litigation and so on. Although exact figures will vary from industry to industry, broad estimates of these costs, put together from a number of sources specializing in quality, have been calculated as in Table 17.1.

From this it will be seen that even if you are already getting things right 99.5 per cent of the time in each part of your process, you are likely to be losing between 15 and 25 per cent of your income on rectifying the adverse affects of the errors that still get through. That is, your organization is in effect budgeting 15–25 per cent of your income or turnover on making scrap, wasting time, paying compensation and engaging in non-productive activities. Also, far more common are situations where performance is more likely to have 5 per cent errors, leading up to 35 per cent of income being wasted on putting things right. Is this a budget you want to carry?

There are, then, compelling business reasons to try to improve the quality and reliability of work processes – by which we mean activities that contribute to the output and performance of your organization, be these manufacturing, service or administrative. This means reducing the costs of getting things wrong, or increasing customer satisfaction by getting things right, and making continuous improvements in all cases. This is the best path to financial and managerial autonomy and stability in the public services and to competitive advantage in the commercial sector.

Table 17.1 Cost of poor quality

'Organizational quality standard'	Average percentage error rate in major steps in overall process	Cost of poor quality (rework, etc.) as percentage of financial turnover
Poor	7 i.e. 93% meet specification	25–40
Typical	5 i.e. 95% meet specification	20–35
Good	0.5 i.e. 99.5% meet specification	15–25
Excellent	0.02 i.e. 99.8% meet specification	5–15
'World Class'	0.00034 i.e. 99.996% meet specification	1

Sources: combined from Behara *et al.* (1995), Harry *et al.* (2000) and Klefsjö *et al.* (2001).

This chapter contains:

- ideas and key themes about process improvement
- two improvement stories
- a detailed overview of an approach to systematic improvement
- further resources, including locations for more detailed descriptions of tools and techniques than we are able to provide here.

Improvement – not targets...

The first theme to stress is that there is far more to improving processes than merely setting targets. As W. Edwards Deming, arguably the most significant 'quality guru' ever, put it: 'What do "targets" accomplish? Nothing. Wrong: their accomplishment is negative'. Why such an uncompromising response to something that organizations and governments are so keen on?

There are a number of reasons for Deming's condemnation of targets. They concentrate on what is easily measurable, rather than what really matters, and often use pretty arbitrary figures. They are frequently tied to relatively short, unrealistic time-scales. Crucially, given that they are nearly always associated with rewards or punishments, people put their energy into meeting, or appearing to meet, these arbitrary, short-term targets and not focusing on important systematic improvements.

Targets lead people to cheat, sometimes rather crudely, as in altering children's examination scripts, or returning false figures for ambulance response times, sometimes more creatively as in inviting patients to see a medical consultant on dates when they know the patients are on holiday (which counts as a 'seen-by-consultant' in reducing waiting lists). Such ingenuity is not restricted to the public services.

Targets also lead people to what Deming termed 'sub-optimization' – where the performance of the whole is made worse by individuals (or groups) concentrating on their own targets to the detriment of others. Shiftworking teams can meet their targets by hammering their machines or depleting supplies, so that when the next shift comes on duty they have to spend half their time repairing this damage. The morning shift meets its target, the afternoon shift is way behind and overall production suffers. This gets worse where targets are linked to competition; for example, if there is a prize for the shift that exceeds its target most, then teams may even sabotage the efforts of their successors.

...Or slogans!

It is easy enough to post what Deming refers to as 'useless and meaningless slogans', such as

- take pride in your work

■ be a quality worker
■ do it right first time
■ quality is our motto.

These amount to no more than rhetoric. If you want to make sustainable improvements in process performance, you have to be serious about it. You have to invest in more than exhortations and platitudes.

Conscious, systematic improvement: the DMAIC approach

If you are going to exercise a leadership role in creating improvements, there are a number of things to consider – what sort of things will you be involved with? What does this greater investment of commitment and effort look like? Where should you start?

A number of mnemonic sequences have been devised to help to plan and implement improvement processes. The PDSA cycle (Plan–Do–Study–Act) is perhaps the best known. More recent is the DMAIC process, which stands for:

■ Define the opportunity for improvement; select a process to be worked on, identify its customers and what they require of it.
■ Measure the performance of the chosen process – how well is it doing, compared with what its customers would like?
■ Analyse the data and causes of shortfalls in actual performance compared with desired performance.
■ Improve the process – remove the causes of the problems.
■ Control the process – that is, make sure that the new performance is maintained and that faults and problems do not creep back in.

Going into DMAIC in detail requires a whole book on its own (see the Further resources section at the end of this chapter). Here we give an overview of what is involved, with points for guidance.

Activity: DMAIC

Define the opportunity for improvement

Step one

A good starting point for reviewing any process is to look at data from a variety of sources:

External customers – What are they saying about us? What are the main sources and types of complaint? What do they think of us in comparison with our competitors? In the public services, you may or may not have competitors, but you will certainly have vocal and demanding clients and governments – what are they telling us to improve?

Internal data – This could include waiting times, productivity per employee, wastage rates, time taken to carry out tasks, time spent on rework/putting things right, late deliveries, direct costs, indirect costs, accidents.

Internal customers – What are your employees complaining about, irritated by, dissatisfied with, wanting to change? What are they telling you through absenteeism, sickness, staff turnover?

Environment – What are the reports on, for example, waste discharge, noise, light pollution?

Step two

Once you have a preliminary idea of a process that may need improving, you can map it out using a simple flowchart or a deployment or integrated flowchart which shows the handover points in the process: where the people, the unit, team or individuals responsible for a particular stage hand over to the next people in the chain. The flowchart identifies both the internal and external customers and suppliers involved.

Step three

Next, consider the feasibility of improving this particular process. How complicated is it? If considering a range of processes, you need to consider if it would be sensible to start with an easier one, and get some success under your belt? How long will it take? A relatively quick success might be politically useful. However, this is not to be confused with the quick fix, involving changes on impulse rather than systematic effort. Deming calls this 'tampering' and notes that it often make things worse.

Step four

You need to take a number of views into account when deciding which project or projects to focus on in the first instance. So, who are the stakeholders in this process improvement? In general terms, stakeholders are people who:

- know about the process and its effects
- care about it
- are affected by it
- can stop improvements being made
- can help to make improvements – through influence, support and the like
- can help to make improvements through specialized expertise in improvement tools and techniques.

Typically they include:

- customers of the process – internal or external
- suppliers to the process – internal or external
- people who work in the process
- managers who interact with it and/or who have an influence over it
- people with expert knowledge related to the process
- people with expert knowledge related to quality improvement
- employee representatives.

You have to decide with which of these to work. How will you get their views of priorities – through interviews, group meetings or questionnaires? A flowchart can again be very helpful to identify the stakeholders at each stage of the overall process. Some people may be in more than one of those groupings and these would be good people to train in the process to become experts at using improvement tools.

How Whitegoods talked with their customers

Whitegoods Ltd (not their real name) is a manufacturer of kitchen appliances. Their Board decided they wanted to find out how their customers – retailers, not end-users – saw them compared with their leading competitors. A survey was carried out via telephone interviews and focusing on how the customer experienced the service they received from Whitegoods. This approach involved what are known as 'moments of truth' – 'each and every moment when the customer experiences the organization and is therefore able to form some judgement of it' (Jenkinson, 1995).

Ten main moments of truth about Whitegoods' service were identified in approximate sequence:

1 When the customer obtains information on products and prices.
2 When the customer decides which of Whitegoods' products to stock.
3 When the customer negotiates prices and discounts.
4 When the customer places an order.
5 When Whitegoods trains the customer's staff (e.g. on physical things, such as new products, and on administrative processes, such as the use of electronic ordering systems).
6 When goods are delivered to the customer.
7 When the customer receives an invoice.
8 When items under warranty are sent for repair.
9 When the customer seeks information on delivery dates and back orders.
10 When the customer wishes to return unsold stock.

For each moment of truth, customers were asked how they rated Whitegoods against the best performing competitor. They were also asked to rate the importance of each moment – not very important, important, very important.

Whitegoods' performance was then classified as poor, moderate or good, in a matrix as in Table 17.2.

This matrix was discussed with other stakeholders, including staff from sales and support services, and it was decided in the first instance to concentrate on three aspects:

1 When the customer obtains information on products and prices.
3 When the customer negotiates prices and discounts.
8 When items under warranty are sent for repair.

Project groups were set up for each of these, each group then proceeding with the next steps in the DMAIC process.

This is only one way to collect data for the prioritization of processes for improvement. There are many other tools, such as brainstorming, affinity diagrams and nominal group techniques, which can be used at any stage for generating ideas and clustering them. This may be seen as 'breathing in and breathing out' – first expanding, then contracting or reducing the large number ideas to some manageable basic groupings. Details of these techniques and many more can be found in Pande *et al.* (2002), Boydell and Leary (1996) and Brassard and Ritter (1994).

Table 17.2 Whitegoods customer survey

WHITEGOODS LTD: PERFORMANCE GOOD	*5: Product training*	**9: Getting information on deliveries and back orders**	2: Deciding which products to stock
WHITEGOODS LTD: PERFORMANCE MODERATE	6: Delivery of goods	**3: Negotiating prices and discounts** 4: Ordering products	**8: Handling warranty repairs**
WHITEGOODS LTD: PERFORMANCE POOR	**1: Obtaining information on products and prices** *10: Dealing with unsold stock*	7: Being invoiced	
	BEST COMPETITOR: PERFORMANCE POOR	**BEST COMPETITOR: PERFORMANCE MODERATE**	**BEST COMPETITOR: PERFORMANCE GOOD**

Items in bold, very important; items in normal type, important; *items in italics, not very important.*

Measure the performance of the chosen process

Having defined the opportunity and chosen a process to improve, it is tempting to start to get stuck into improving it. This would be tampering, which is something to avoid. In fact, the next step is to measure the performance of the chosen process. It is important to do this for a number of reasons:

■ Collecting measurements now can serve as a base point with which future improvements can be compared; in turn, this will provide evidence of progress and in some cases may enable the return on investment of the improvement to be calculated.

■ Deciding what to measure is in itself an activity that may focus attention on what really matters to the customer (internal and/or external).

■ Measured data will probably be needed later in the DMAIC steps when it comes to analysis. For example, by plotting numerical data on what are known as 'run charts' – showing the value of the process performance over a period of time – you may well spot patterns or trends that can point the way to identifying causes of problems. We will look at this again in the next section.

You have to decide what to measure. In principle, it is sensible to choose variables that are important to the customer of that particular part of the process. You may want to stratify the data – that is, use various 'slices' when collecting measurements. Such slices might be by team, department, category of customer or product range. Alternatively, they might be based on time – for example, are there seasonal variations, or differences according to time of day, or shift?

The Danish nightshift

We recently worked with a Danish manufacturing company and noticed that there were always fewer defective products on the night shift. As the shifts rotated, this did not seem to be due to the particular individuals involved: no matter who was on at night, their quality was better than when they were working during the day. So we asked the employees the simple question, 'why is quality higher on night shifts?'. 'That's easy', they replied, 'at night there are no managers to get in our way – so we can get on and do our job properly!'.

This striking response led to a thorough exploration and changes in the roles of the Quality Assurance Department and the extent to which the workers were themselves allowed to take responsibility for quality – during the day and at night.

It is important to be clear about exactly how you are going to define and collect your data. For example, you might be measuring 'length of time waiting in a queue'. This might be defined as time taken between joining a queue and arriving at the head of it; an alternative would be time taken between joining a queue and finishing being served. The books in the References section provide useful guidance and advice on sampling and associated techniques such as the Critical to Quality Tree (CTQ), check sheets and various types of flowchart which are useful in highlighting possible points in the process where data can be collected.

Analyse the data and causes of shortfalls in performance

Having decided on the priority area for improvement and designed and implemented a process for recording or retrieving data, you are now ready to analyse the data and look for causes of poor performance. A range of tools and techniques are listed in Table 17.3, but below is a brief summary of the key items.

Value chain analysis – A variant of the flowchart that shows the points in the flow where value is actually added for the external customer. This can highlight aspects of a process that might usefully be reduced or cut out altogether, giving much quicker response times for the customer.

Run chart – A simple graph showing performance over a period of time. Called after the 'run' of measures, these charts may give indications of a number of problems. To get a feel for this, look at Figure 17.1. This shows the performance of a particular process – in this case the percentage of deliveries rejected by customers each day. Of course, a

Table 17.3 Some tools and techniques for analysing data and causes of shortfall in performance

Tool/technique	Reference	Notes
Run charts; control charts	Boydell and Leary (1996), pp. 61–96; Brassard and Ritter (1994), pp. 36–51, 141–144; Pande *et al.* (2002), pp. 208–211, 238–245, 346–349, 354–361	Run charts are graphs showing output from a process over time. Patterns indicating the sources of problems often emerge. Control charts are special forms with more possibilities of interpretation
Pareto analysis	Boydell and Leary (1996), pp. 91–93; Brassard and Ritter (1994), pp. 95–104; Pande *et al.* (2002), pp. 205–208, 236–239	Shows where you are likely to get the biggest impact from an improvement
Root cause analysis; five whys (5Y)	*www.rootcauselive.com*	Drills down through apparent causes of a problem to get at underlying 'root cause'
Fishbone, cause-and-effect or Ishikawa diagram	Boydell and Leary (1996), pp. 96–100; Brassard and Ritter (1994), pp. 23–30; Pande *et al.* (2002) pp. 214–216, 250–251	Shows a number of possible causes of a problem
Relationship diagram or interrelationship digraph	Brassard and Ritter, (1994), pp. 76–84; Pande *et al.* (2002), pp. 216–217, 252–253	These tools show how various causes may reinforce each other. More inter-related than the fishbone
Systems diagram or causal-loop diagram	Sherwood (2002)	
Scatterplots, tests of hypothesis, design of experiments	Brassard and Ritter (1994), pp. 145–149 (scatterplot only); Pande *et al.* (2002), pp. 253–256, 270–279	A number of relatively mathematical/statistical tests for exploring relationships between variables

whole host of measures might be appropriate here: output, time taken to deliver, number of on-time deliveries and so on. The graph in Figure 17.1 shows the performance run over consecutive days, with something happening around day 11 or 12, leading to an upward trend (defined as a run of six or more consecutive points in the same direction). It will probably be useful to look more deeply into this: what happened on day 11 or 12? Why is this trend occurring?

The chart shows the mean or average percentage of rejected items and gives the baseline measure. The general aim of process improvement efforts is to move the average performance in a better direction – in this case to reduce the percentage of rejects. The other general aim of process improvement is to increase the reliability of the output, that is, to reduce the variation in performance from the average. In these terms, the performance shown in Figure 17.2 would be considered better than that in Figure 17.1 – the average reject rate is the same, but performance is clearly more consistent;

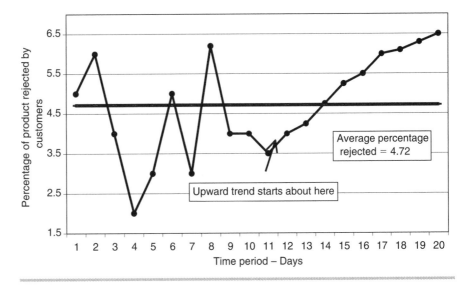

Figure 17.1   Run chart showing an upward trend.

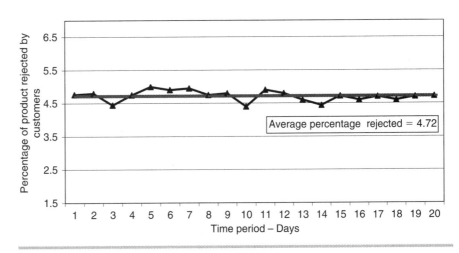

Figure 17.2   Run chart with no trend, same average as in Figure 17.1, but smaller variation.

there is no trend and the standard deviation spread, or around the average, is much lower. If you include standard deviations on a run chart, then it becomes known as a *Control Chart*, and further interpretations may be possible.

On each of these charts there are 20 points, in this case days, which is considered the minimum necessary for any run chart to be meaningful. This obviously affects the data you choose to use; for example, unless you have good records, you will have a long wait if you decide to work with weekly or monthly figures, even if you choose a much smaller time period, you may still have to wait some weeks before your data can be said to be valid. This may be frustrating, especially if you are under pressure to do something now! Well, in fact, you are doing something – you have chosen a priority area, you have set up a process for collecting data and you are indeed collecting them. However, pressure to be seen to be doing something may well be a factor in determining what to measure, at what time interval.

There are many other tools that can be used at the analysis stage. *A Pareto Chart* shows where you are likely to get the biggest impact from an improvement. *Root Cause Analysis* [also known as *Five Whys* (5Y)] allows you to dig deeper into a particular problem: each time you arrive at a possible cause you ask 'why?', until after about five times you either feel that you are going mad or you reckon you have tapped into the root cause.

More commonly used are the *Fishbone*, *Cause-and-Effect Analysis* or *Ishikawa Diagram*. The main problem is put at the 'fish-head', and possible causes are identified and placed on the diagram under one or other of the 'side-bones'. A limitation of the fishbone is that it does not show how various causes may be interconnected. For this purpose the *Relationship Diagram* can be used, and even more dynamic inter-relationships between causes can be shown with *Systems or Causal Loop Diagrams*. If you want to use more statistically inclined tools, then you may like to consider *scatterplots, hypothesis tests* and what is rather curiously known as '*design of experiments*'.

Improve the process

By this stage, you will have chosen one or more opportunities for improvement, set up processes for collecting data, acquired some data and then analysed them. Perhaps the first step in improving the process is to generate some possible solutions using brainstorming or a similar tool. Resulting ideas can be clustered using affinity diagrams, and then each cluster explored in depth – perhaps after getting peoples' commitments to each cluster through, say, a nominal group technique. Another way of combining brainstorming and clustering is described in Pande *et al.* (2002) as the 'Tree Diagram for Solution Development'.

Having created a number of possible solutions, these need to be judged according to their likely impact and feasibility. An impact/effort matrix is simply a 2 × 2 diagram, with impact (low to high) up the left-hand scale and effort required along the bottom, also low to high. The resulting quadrants are low effort but little impact – probably not worth doing; high effort and little impact – don't go there!; high effort and high impact – worth considering; and low effort/high impact – great if you can get it!

If you need to be more systematic you can use specific criteria against which to evaluate each possible solution. Pande *et al.* (2000) (pp. 296–297) suggest that each alternative is considered in terms of the:

■ cost to implement
■ ability to meet customer requirements

- impact on other processes
- time to implement
- complexity
- expertise required.

These criteria can be weighted according to importance, by scoring any solution against each criterion, and then multiply the scores by the importance to see which of the solutions comes out best. Of course, you can brainstorm your own criteria if you wish. Another well-known tool for checking the feasibility of a solution is Force Field Analysis, whereby you look at which 'forces' or factors are helping the implementation of the improvement, and which are likely to hinder it. All the tools mentioned here can be found in Pande *et al.* (2002) or Brassard and Ritter (1994).

If at all possible, before going live with an improvement you should carry out pilot tests, possibly with more than one of the possible solutions. This should be planned as a systematic experiment, thinking through in advance where to do it, when, what data to collect, how to collect and so on. Only after rigorous testing should a changed method be implemented on a large scale. Implementation should involve training people, updating procedure manuals, instituting new record-keeping processes and possibly informing customers.

Control the process

Once a change has been implemented, you must remember to monitor it for progress, to look out for possible slippage back to how things were before and to look for new opportunities for even further improvement.

Further resources

Pande *et al.* (2002) is an excellent source for further information on the DMAIC steps and these various tools and techniques. Other useful sources tools and techniques for continuous improvement include Brassard and Ritter (1994), Boydell and Leary (1996) and Capper (1998).

References

Behara, R. S., G. F. Fontenot and A. Gresham (1995) 'Customer satisfaction measurement and analysis using six sigma', *International Journal of Quality and Reliability Management*, **12**(3), 9–18.

Boydell, T. H. and M. Leary (1996) *Identifying Training Needs*, Chartered Institute of Personnel and Development, London.

Brassard, M. and D. Ritter (1994) *The Memory Jogger II: a Pocket Guide of Tools for Continuous Improvement and Effective Planning*, Goal QPC, Salem.

Capper, R. A. (1998) *Project by Project Approach to Quality*, Gower, Aldershot.

Harry, M. J., D. R. Linsenmann and R. Schroeder (2000) *Six SIGMA: the Breakthrough Management Strategy Revolutionizing the World's Top Corporations*, Doubleday, New York.

Jenkinson, A. (1995) *Valuing Your Customers*, McGraw-Hill, Maidenhead.

Klefsjö, B., H. Wiklund and R. L. Edgeman (2001) 'Six Sigma seen as a methodology for total quality management' *Measuring Business Excellence* **5**(1), 31–35.

Logothetis, N. (1992) *Managing for Total Quality*, Prentice-Hall, Englewood Cliffs, NJ.

Pande, P. S., R. P. Neuman and R. R. Cavanagh (2002) *The Six Sigma Way Team Fieldbook*, McGraw-Hill, New York.

Sherwood, D. (2002) *Seeing the Forest for the Trees: a Manager's Guide to Applying Systems Thinking*, Nicholas Brealey, London.

18

Challenge 9: Streamlining

*Muda – the Japanese term for any activity that consumes resources
but creates no value*
Womack and Jones (1996)

Introduction

Downsizing, right-sizing, restructuring, delayering, re-engineering and lean thinking have succeeded each other in the management vocabulary over the last 25 years. However, streamlining differs from most of its predecessors in the effort to realign business activities to meet customer or client definitions of value, by being more of a continuous process. Like lean thinking, streamlining involves cutting back here in order to develop over there, moving people and resources to where they are most needed *now*.

Streamlining is the business equivalent of gym work. It is about toning up, slimming down, building muscles around the key areas. It is about :

■ decluttering
■ decomplexing
■ rebalancing
■ tidying up
■ outsourcing.

Unilever decided to slim down a portfolio of 700 brands to 200 over 5 years. The message was simple: stick to the core businesses – outsource the rest. Many business processes are easy to outsource, and even less obvious ones, such as training and development, can be purchased from a preferred supplier rather than retaining expertise and infrastructure in-house.

History reminds us that seasonal or cyclical layoffs and redundancies have always marked industrial life. In the 1970s and 1980s, many organizations began to feel bloated, overstuffed with functions, layers and staffing levels. As business globalized, many had excess capacity. In British Steel and British Coal, brutal pruning was done by hatchet men were brought in to make cuts of a fundamental nature. Businesses were in crisis – 'We'll get you through', the hard men said. In the 1980s, Rank Hovis McDougall had around 100 bakeries, and were lopping off four every year in the face of declining sliced white bread sales.

This drastic downsizing was replaced by the more sophisticated Business Process Re-engineering (BPR) which was based on the ideas of the Total Quality Management movement. The revolutionary nature of BPR came from looking at businesses as collections of processes linking customers and suppliers, rather than as hierarchies of functional silos. It was particularly effective in businesses with lot of paper-based processes such as insurance and banking. Lean Thinking advances on BPR by embracing the whole value stream across a network of businesses from the '... order or delivery, into the hands of the customer or user' (Womack and Jones, 1996, p. 311).

The streamlining mindset is characterised by constant challenging and questioning:

- Can we do this simpler?
- Where can we make efficiencies?
- How can we get rid of activity?
- Where can we take stuff out of the back office and put it in the front line?
- How can we get more feet on the street at less cost?
- How can we get more for less?
- What do we need to invest in?

And especially:

- Which are the areas for development *and* where are the cuts and efficiencies to be made?

There are two key aspects of streamlining: identifying core competencies and then a focus upon business processes for product or service delivery to cut waste and improve flow. On core competence, the streamlining philosophy is: don't try to do everything to the gold standard: do some things really well, outsource others. The second aspect of streamlining is the focus upon, and the continuous improvement of, businesses processes. This is part of a longer move to relocate organizing away from the vertical functions or 'silos' to the lateral streams or flows of activities involved in creating and delivering products and services. In the BBC, the organization has been redirected from the previous preoccupation with hierarchical management controls and production systems and has defined the creative process of programmes as the core competence.

This combination of focus on core competencies and business processes makes streamlining very much more than just cost-cutting. This old favourite never goes out of fashion and 'Project Squeeze' is always good for a few points in the City. But the learning organization soon notices that the consequences often outweigh the gains. Annual cost reduction targets of 3 or 5 per cent mean loss of people, experience, memory and capability. Whole units and functions disappear, until someone realizes they are vital and puts them back in. Hospitals and schools outsource their cleaning services and find that they have lost the commitment that came from the feeling of being a core part of the service. This is not organic development but drastic surgery.

The rest of this chapter contains:

- an owner–manager's story that illustrates the leadership challenge of streamlining
- a model case study of streamlining in a learning company
- how to avoid 'Great Company Disease' by redefining the core competence of your unit or organization
- a basic tool for process mapping and process re-engineering
- further resources.

The leadership challenge of streamlining

TechStar

George is the ambitious co-owner of an electronics company, TechStar (a pseudonym), employing 47 people, many of whom he has known from school and university. TechStar specializes in manufacturing communications technologies; its customers are much larger companies looking for increasingly sophisticated solutions to streamline their service delivery processes.

TechStar has a number of strings to its bow and has been growing rapidly, in terms of turnover and staff. It depends upon the high quality and commitment of its engineers and has invested heavily in R&D to gain superiority in a market that has yet to grow significantly. Like many small, entrepreneurial companies in this sector, TechStar's fortunes are strongly affected by the economic cycle. After several quarters of recession, in a market slow to recover its confidence, customers are holding out on placing big orders with severe effects on the company's cash flow. This situation can change quickly, but TechStar is expanding and its bankers are asking for economies now in exchange for further injections of funds.

TechStar's management team agrees that something should be done. A temporary, across-the-board, 15 per cent wage cut is one of the options; another is to reduce the staff by 10 per cent. No-one much likes either option, although George reflects that there are one or two people who, although good engineers, do not show the level of commitment that he would like. 'Maybe they are not suited to this type of environment and would fit better into a bigger firm? When things pick up we could replace them with better people.' In Jack Welch's shocking phrase, this could be a good time to 'pick the low-hanging fruit'? Rumour is already rife and something needs to be done soon, but no-one present wants the job of sitting down one-to-one and saying 'Sorry, we've decided to let you go'.

Fairness and justice

George's motivation is less about cost-cutting and more about how to weather the crisis by slimming down TechStar whilst preparing for future growth; balancing investment in the future against minimizing the risk. Streamlining involves some pain, but the pain is worsened by the spurious rationalizations and justifications that often accompany such exercises. Simple rules of thumb are sometimes used to resolve these difficult situations, but they are rarely satisfactory. 'Last in, first out' is usually too simple, for it does not differentiate by merit. Without exhausting the possibilities, Solomon's list of a baker's dozen of reasons for justifying merit pay displays the rich range of rationalizations for such decisions:

- *Rights* – what are the existing agreements and legitimate understandings?
- *Tradition* – what has happened in the past?
- *Seniority* – who has been here longest?
- *Equality* – ignore all differences
- *Merit (performance)* – who has produced most?
- *Merit (effort)* – who has worked hardest?
- *Duties and responsibilities* – who carries the greatest burdens?
- *Risk and uncertainty* – who carries the greatest risks?
- *Ability* – who has potential and promise?
- *Need* – who can bear losses least?
- *Loyalty* – who is most committed and loyal?
- *Moral virtue* – who is most trustworthy and honest?
- *Market value* – who will be OK outside?
- *Public good* – what would be best for most people, staff, stakeholders, community?

(adapted from Solomon,1993, pp. 238–239).

Any decision can be rationalized, but feelings – and the consequences of these feelings – are another matter. The question is: does it *feel* fair? A decision can be rational but feel unfair; another can be based on ramshackle logic but somehow feel OK. If the decision feels spurious, arbitrary or selective then the survivors can feel especially bad: feeling guilty about their colleagues and also worried that it might be them next time. This damages both individuals and the collective psychological contract of trust and commitment in the firm. If, however, on balance, people feel that 'The boss had no choice' or 'That's how it is these days', then the outcome is likely to be better, including for those who leave.

Streamlining in a learning company

Can the values of participation, free choice and learning for all survive in tough situations such as streamlining? A Swiss consultant, Elizabeth Michel-Alder, believes they can. She describes her work in a Swiss Obstetrics and Gynaecological Clinic, part of a larger hospital complex, where the high levels of staffing and training delivered an excellent service but at a high cost (Michel-Alder, 1998).

The crunch came when the main Hospital appointed a new CEO. He demands that the Clinic accept the challenge of the market situation: efficiencies must be made by lowering costs, but justified improvements and new investments, such as renovation and remodelling of facilities, are not ruled out. Elizabeth is engaged to help with 'a re-engineering process'. Her proposal is to create a developmental process based on two underlying principles:

- joint planning and implementation of the re-structuring with staff
- a search for solutions to increase options and open up new possibilities.

The first step is to form an initiative group of some 30 people representing all the important groups concerned – doctors, nurses, midwives, physiotherapists, secretaries, bookkeeper, housekeepers, laboratory technicians and so on. This group is established in an interesting way: half are picked as 'must be there' by the CEO, the Clinic Medical Director and Elizabeth and the other half are elected as representatives and delegates by the various groups.

Over the next 3 months, this group has three workshops, together with much individual and small group coaching. In the first emotionally charged workshop, the group sets its own groundrules for working. The first is that there are to be no compulsory redundancies. On the basis of the groundrules, the group accepts the responsibility for leading the reshaping of the Clinic and begins to work through an agenda including:

- What kind of results are we looking for? What should be the strong points of our clinic in the future?
- What opportunities can we imagine for the future?
- What is good and excellent about what we do now and what should be retained and maintained?
- What has to be left behind or changed?
- What are our fears about restructuring? What are the possible losses and gains?
- How will we cope with the difficult challenges and feelings?

These questions involve everyone in working on solutions, mainly in smaller groups mixed by profession or by task, and in making collective decisions. The workshop is characterized by the open expression of strong feelings – despair, hope, fear, loss, sadness, optimism.

At the end of the 2 days, a contract is made with each individual – what will they do and what will they expect? A timetable and priority areas for change are agreed with groups or named individuals are commissioned and given responsibility to undertake research and other tasks. Additionally, there is a discussion about the evaluation and control of the project and about information flow – who will be informed and how.

After 8 months, the results are impressive:

- Three nurses have found new jobs elsewhere, about half of the people are working to different, sometimes shorter, hours, no-one was let go.
- A female gynaecologist has been employed (before all were male).
- New services of such as birth preparation and health maintenance have been developed and are generating new income.
- The hierarchy is flatter, there is more teamwork and the atmosphere has become more enthusiastic and creative.
- Costs are lowered by 17 per cent (the CEO asked for 20 per cent).

This short account gives a very exterior description of what happened. Formal evaluations tell only part of the story, missing the roller coaster of actions and emotions that engaged everyone in this group, and in the Clinic as a whole, over the months. Personal traumas, triumphs and sacrifices marked the path: a senior doctor volunteered to take shorter hours ('I can afford it'); a nurse took a hard decision about her career ('I worked hard for this position but there are too many of us'); and a technician discovered that he can change his hours ('I asked my wife and she suggested I do more child care so that she could work too!').

Great company disease

The story of the Swiss Clinic demonstrates that streamlining can be a collaborative effort and a profound learning experience that helps create an organization fit for the future. In terms of business strategy, a key question that can be asked at any time is, 'Is this organization geared up for the past or for the future?'. This is a safeguard against 'great company disease' (Hamel and Prahalabad, 1994, pp. 127–128), whereby many organizations achieve excellence in some aspects of their work, but fail to maintain it, even failing because of the complacency that tends to accompany 'excellence'. This disease displays the following symptoms:

- being successful (which confirms current strategy)
- feeling good about current performance
- having plenty of resources (which substitute for creativity)
- one-off re-engineering of processes that creates 'deeply etched recipes'
- momentum mistaken for leadership.

Do these seem familiar to you? The challenging questions that might protect against great company disease include:

- Are we relying too much on our existing products or services or skills?
- Do we see the future as much of the same rather than different from now?
- Do we feel satisfied with our current performance?
- Are we putting our attention and resources into refining current processes or in developing new business?

If the answer to these questions is mainly 'Yes', then the Core Competencies Tool below provides a process for rethinking the business strategy in any unit or organization. Using this tool works best in a workshop format or with a small group of people and can be done as part of a team meeting.

Activity: core competencies

1. PRESENT: current core competencies

The first step is to define the current core competencies of your section, department or organization. In pairs or in the group, brainstorm your answers to the question:

> What are the four or five products, services or skills where we are 'top of the class'?

These are aspects of our work or things we deliver and produce which others admire us for. These are where we have a 'competitive advantage'. They might be traced by looking at where we had a recent success. Why was this? Also, what do others – such as our colleagues who are customers or suppliers to us – see that is really good about us that perhaps we don't see ourselves?

Agree the top four or five current core competences.

2. FUTURE: corporate foresighting

Now, forget the present and focus on the future. This is a visioning activity; again, brainstorm in pairs or in the whole group to answer the question:

> What changes do we expect to see in the next 5 years?

(See Chapter 4 for a more sophisticated PESTLE approach – Political/Economic/ Social/Technical/Legal/Environmental scanning.)

List these expected aspects of the future. For example, a staff of a human resources section included the following in their list:

- More electronic connectedness.
- Lifestyle changes – more active, health conscious but also stressful, people juggling, trying to have it all.
- Downshifting – people looking for ways to declutter and rebalance.
- Harder to attract and keep key staff – work must be more fun.

■ Increasing inequality – locally and globally.

■ More variety in what people want in the way of rewards.

■ Work is less controllable but we have more central controls and targets!

■ Network organization – flatter, giving more autonomy and responsibility.

3. BACK TO THE PRESENT: development and cuts

The third question in the Core Competencies Tool is:

> Given the current core competencies and the likely developments over the next 5 years, what should we be maintaining, developing and giving up?

Again, working in pairs or small groups, make three lists: what should we:

Maintain?   *Develop?*   *Give up?*

Or, to put it another way, can we outsource things that are not critical to the survival, maintenance and development of our core competencies?:

Never!   *Maybe?*   *Yes*

Lean thinking processes

Redesigning work processes without rethinking your core competencies can be dangerous. Without a strategic gearing up for the future, exercises in re-engineering or lean thinking may result in a deep etching of the wrong industrial recipes. Once sure of your direction, redesigning your customer value chains and redrawing your patient pathways is the way to change your 'corporate architecture' to face the right way.

All approaches to streamlining the supply chain or value stream start with mapping the processes. A basic example of a process map in primary healthcare is shown in Figure 18.1. Some useful points become apparent even on the basis of such a simple mapping process.

The first point of interest is to notice how things look when the process map is drawn up on the basis of the patient's (or the customer's) experience and not from the perspective of the professional or service provider. The map describes the winding pathway that the patient has to follow, the language used is that of the ordinary person and, most importantly, the outcome or value is described and determined by that person: a toe good enough to walk on. For the professionals involved, this looking at the whole process from the patients' perspective may be a new experience, and one that can potentially change their practice.

The second obvious point is how many places the patient has to visit and how often he or she has to return to the doctor. Could the process not be simpler? Could any of these steps or 'inefficiencies' be eliminated? If all

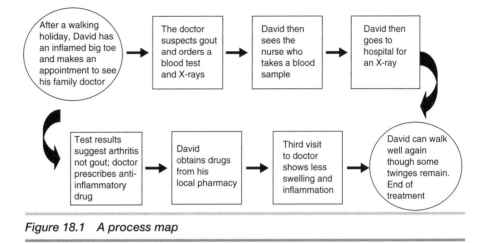

Figure 18.1　A process map

those involved in the provision of any service come together in this discussion, they can generate possibilities that no one of them could have developed alone.

This activity of process redesign can only start from a dissatisfaction or a questioning of their current operation by the professionals and service provider themselves. Without this curiosity, the patient or customer will not be asked for their view, and not listened to. In recent years, a major driver for this change of perspective has come from the Government, which has insisted that public services should be considered from the view of the 'end-user' as part of the 'modernization' of services.

Once this decision has been taken, then the application of lean thinking or service redesign follows a straightforward course. Maxine Conner and her co-authors suggests an eight-step model (Conner, Knott and Bulman, 2003, p. 9):

1　Identify the process to be improved.
2　Define the project boundaries.
3　Identify the project team.
4　Understand (and map) the current process.
5　Identify the results you want to achieve.
6　Create a vision of the new service.
7　Redesign.
8　Implement, evaluate and continuously improve.

There is much more to be said about the application of these ideas, and an increasing amount of materials and experience available, some of which is listed in Further resources below.

Conclusion

Streamlining is heir to a long tradition going back at least to F. W. Taylor and his efforts to apply science and measurement in the service of efficient work. Part of what is different now is the need to apply both the strategic and operational aspects of this thinking. Whether you should adopt first the more strategic work of identifying and developing core competence or the more operational tasks of lean thinking and process improvement depends on your situation.

The methods and tools that have been developed to work well in large manufacturing concerns may not make the same sense with fast-moving consumer goods or in the delivery of public services. Lean thinking was developed in the manufacturing world where value is 'the right thing at the right time and in the right place – as identified by the customer' (Womack and Jones, 1996, p. 311). However, where forms of rationing are involved, as in the police, education, health or voluntary services, there are some constraints on this refreshing view. Womack and Jones (1996) further advice about dealing with the 'anchor draggers' – 'Deal with excess people at the outset' (p. 257) and 'Your operating managers will need continual education in lean methods and periodic evaluations of their efforts to make sure there is no backsliding' (p. 259) tells us a lot about the particular contexts in which they operate.

An element of learning and creativity is required to make streamlining work well in any situation. Start on the operational aspects by identifying and mapping the value streams or pathways that flow backwards and forwards between customer and supplier. The work continues in improving the flow of these streams by removing hold-ups and waste and by investing in new resources at the bottlenecks. This is good work that can be done creatively and collectively with all those people involved in these flows. The long- and short-term benefits of streamlining at the right time and in the right way – for both users and service providers – cannot be overstated.

However, the tough phrases of people like Jack Welch and Womack and Jones also express a reality about the changes that may be essential to survival and growth. Continuous improvement sounds fine, but success at this means that jobs will inevitably be eliminated from time to time. In such circumstances, the costs to the 10 per cent are weighed against the benefits to the other 90 per cent and their clients. Such are the decisions weighing heavily upon those, such as George at TechStar, who are impelled to act and to act quickly in difficult circumstances. The resolution of such leadership dilemmas will not come from any rational measures of the 'value stream', but from a deep indwelling on business issues and personal values.

Further resources

Gary Hamel and C.K. Prahalabad's *Competing for the Future* (referenced below) expands their earlier *Harvard Business Review* paper, 'The core competences of the corporation' (May/June 1990), and provides the basic text on the strategy of core competencies.

Chapter 17 of this book will be a useful first place to look for further help and information on lean thinking and process improvement. James Womack and Dan Jones's *Lean Thinking: Banish Waste and Create Wealth in Your Corporation* (referenced below) builds on their earlier bestseller, J. Womak, D. Jones and D. Roos, *The Machine that Changed the World* (Rawson Macmillan, New York, 1990) in forthrightly propounding the virtues of lean manufacturing methodologies. It also provides the quote that heads this chapter.

Maxine Conner, Sandra Knott and Brenda Bulman, in *Excellence in the Public Sector: Re-designing the Patient/User Experience* (referenced below), provide a short but well-written and illustrated guide to applying the principles of process thinking to healthcare. This will be useful to anyone looking for a concise guide to get started.

Jim Collins' *Good to Great* (Random House, London, 2001) provides a different and convincing slant. His focus is on the wider disciplines that give companies enduring strength and on the dedication, perseverance and personal humility needed by leadership to bring this about.

References

Conner, M., S. Knott and B. Bulman (2003), *Excellence in the Public Sector: Re-designing the Patient/User Experience*, Kingsham Press, Chichester.

Hamel, G. and C. K. Prahalabad (1994), *Competing for the Future*, Harvard Business School Press, Boston.

Michel-Alder, E. 'Downsizing in a learning company', paper presented at The Learning Company Conference, Warwick University, 1998.

Solomon, R. C. (1993) *Ethics and Excellence: Cooperation and Integrity in Business*, Oxford University Press, Oxford.

Womack, J. and D. Jones (1996), *Lean Thinking: Banish Waste and Create Wealth in Your Corporation*, Touchstone Books, London.

19

Challenge 10: Encouraging Social Responsibility

Think global; act local
Environmentalists' slogan

Introduction

The place of work organizations in society – local, national and global – is suddenly subject to a new scrutiny and critique. Great businesses are creators of value and bringers of prosperity, but their growing size, wealth and reach have given them a power and influence to rival some elected governments. The rise of interest in corporate social responsibility (CSR) is one mark of this coming of age. For the global corporation, the traditional 'Trust us' is giving way to a new, stakeholder-led 'Show me'.

However, CSR is a slippery concept. For large companies it is a matter of enlightened self-interest and an increasingly important part of branding and corporate positioning. For those who have grasped this point best, CSR tends to figure large in public statements made by senior figures. Oil companies, for example, make great play of their environmental awareness or benevolent community activities without touching on the controversial aspects of their drilling and extraction operations. CSR is only loosely connected with the notion of ethical management, which tends to seen as more of a personal responsibility.

Although private sector organizations provide many of the most developed examples of CSR policies and practices, questions of social, environmental and ethically responsible behaviour apply to everyone. Public service and voluntary sector organizations cannot take CSR for granted and are beginning to take it seriously. Some Higher Education colleges have undertaken CSR assessments based on the list of 65 criteria from the UK Institute for Business Ethics (IBE).

Responsible corporate citizenship poses essentially the same questions to organizations as those that apply to us as individuals. Are you an ethical consumer? How much damage do you do to the environment? How socially aware are you? In posing these questions for itself, the Cooperative Bank is leading the way.

> ## The Cooperative Bank
>
> In 2002, the Cooperative Bank turned away more than £4 million of new business from companies that failed to meet its ethical standards. The bank will not deal with companies involved in arms dealing, animal testing, exploitative labour practices and nuclear power. Quarrying may be next on the list. A technology company involved in supplying aircraft for use by oppressive regimes was turned down, as was a toy manufacturer using suppliers in developing countries with questionable labour conditions.
>
> The Cooperative Bank's ethical policies are devised on the basis of customers' views and the bank believes that about one-third of all new customers open accounts because of these policies. It puts a value on this ethical stance of £30 million – far in excess of the potential that is turned away, and about a quarter of overall profits. This is strong support for the argument that virtue pays.

This chapter contains:

- some good and bad stories of corporate social practices
- what is a good company?
- a story of corporate social responsibility at Cadbury Schweppes
- a CSR Gap Analysis tool for auditing your organization
- further resources.

CSR as good business practice

Discussions about business ethics are often heated, with powerful emotions on both sides. Some argue that nothing should interfere with the duty of a company to maximize returns to its shareholders, and that any distortions of the market will raise costs and prices. On the other side are arrayed a growing army of environmental protesters, social activists, members of voluntary and civic society organizations and, increasingly, concerned citizens, seeking to reduce waste, promote fair trade or force the polluter to pay.

Still a fringe issue for many, these arguments have not been taken seriously by mainstream manufacturers and service providers. Yet business ethics and corporate social responsibility are moving rapidly centre stage. A growing number of companies are encountering protests, adverse publicity and the potential loss of customers because of their activities. There is a lengthening agenda of worldwide environmental, social and human rights issues to which the responsible corporate citizen must pay attention.

It is the business case for CSR that is convincing companies that they must develop policies, codes and ethical reporting procedures. Virtue pays, according to the IBE. Large UK companies with codes of business ethics actually perform better in financial terms than companies without such codes. The codes themselves are hardly guarantees of virtue – Enron had a good one, apparently – but they do tend to be associated with other desired qualities. For example, the IBE found that there is a strong correlation between having an ethical code, addressing 'non-financial risks' effectively and being an 'admired company' (Caulkin, 2003).

Having socially responsible policies does not by itself make a good company, but adopting these values is likely to develop one in the long run. As the example of the Cooperative Bank shows, such policies – if they are lived out in the organization and by its staff and customers and are not just window dressing – can lead the business in new directions. By making firms think about how they do business and with whom, the CSR debate can be a driver of innovation and new best practice. 'Normal business practice' can become 'anti-social behaviour' surprisingly quickly. Today's fringe is tomorrow's mainstream and tomorrow's customers will take it for granted.

Corporate cowboys?

Private sector, public service and voluntary organizations make great contributions to the living standards and comforts enjoyed by many people all over the world. Nevertheless there are growing questions about the way in which business does business. Until very recently, it has been possible to get away with the uncompromising 'the business of business is business' that some enterprises have taken as their unofficial code. In the last few years, the obligations of business to society have broadened and become more challenging. The field of corporate social responsibility is a minefield for unwary companies.

Good companies recognize that whether they like it or not, they play an important role in the development of society, locally, nationally and globally. Aware and responsible organizations have now accepted their corporate social responsibility, captured it as CSR and incorporated it into their business processes and reporting systems. However, in reality this creature is hard to contain.

CSR is linked with just about all the issues which challenge the future of the planet and the human race as a whole. These are the many intractable global problems of environmental degradation, climate change, 'Third World debt', global poverty and inequalities, human rights and many, many more.

As remarkable human achievements that have and can accomplish great things, it is perhaps overdue for our major organizations to consider what they might contribute to these pressing problems. Yet this is a new field for many, suddenly and dramatically present.

It is now common for ethical protestors to buy shares in companies and ask question in shareholders' meetings. It is also common for these encounters, to be keenly reported and the news widely disseminated via activists' newsletters and electronic webs. 'Shareholders press companies to clean up', 'corporate cowboys' and 'fossil fool' are a few recent headlines. This is a field that lends itself to powerful stories – good and bad. Stories carry 'sticky knowledge' and rapidly multiply and transmit virtuous or vicious spirals of publicity around the globe. This makes good CSR stories very good news, but the consequences of bad publicity can be hard to shake off.

Mining and energy companies are often in the news. The mining company Rio Tinto is frequently questioned about its activities in Indonesia; the oil giant Shell is regularly accused of the polluting effects of its refineries in South Africa, Nigeria and even Texas; and campaigners claim that a million motorists in the UK are boycotting Esso products as a result of that company's stand on fossil fuels and climate change plus their lack of concern and investment in renewable sources of energy. Food and drug companies are close behind. Bayer-Aventis, the pharmaceutical and biotechnology company, is testing genetically modified crops in conditions regarded as unsafe by protesters, whilst Nestlé is a long-standing target on account of its policy of selling baby milk in poor countries and most recently for attempting to extract a bad debt from an already poverty-stricken nation. Some companies are seen as particularly bad offenders, but environmental and social concerns are stalking most big organizations. Tesco, the UK's largest supermarket chain, is accused of paying the lowest prices to farmers and driving small farms and shops out of business, creating misery for rural communities; even Cadbury Schweppes, a pioneer of social responsibility, has been accused of encouraging a growing problem of child obesity through its marketing.

There are also lots of good stories – some from the same organizations as above. After years of pressure, including 'ethical shoplifting' by campaigners carrying timber believed to be illegal past the tills, B&Q became one of the first companies to commit to sourcing only from Forest Stewardship Council (FSC) certified timber. Wimpey, the housebuilder, attacked for unimaginative identikit housing, is now building 700 affordable homes near Newcastle-upon-Tyne with saltmarsh gardens, recycling points and nesting sites for birds. Mothercare and Sainsbury's have signed 'safer chemicals pledges' to identify and eliminate risky chemicals from everyday products. All these stories come from just one issue of *Earthmatters* – the Friends of the Earth magazine (Issue 55, Summer 2003). Is your company doing enough?

In good company?

There are three underpinning principles that guide policies and practices on corporate social responsibility:

Transparency

The principle here is that people should have the right to know if they are being affected in any way. This means being open about corporate aims, activities and actions. Many people are affected by a company's operations, because of their occupations, or because of where they live, because of what they eat and in other aspects of in daily life or through global impact on matters such as climate change.

Accountability

The principle here is that anyone affected by the actions and activities of a company should have the right to be consulted in advance, to participate in any decisions that impact on their lives and livelihoods and should have the right to a genuine say in those decisions. Companies should consider themselves accountable to all stakeholders and not just to shareholders or single owners.

Liability

The principle here is that if anyone suffers harm or damage, either personally or in terms of their possessions and surroundings, they should be entitled to compensation.

These are tough principles to build into business practice; they amount to a fundamental shift for organizations. Some firms, in already contentious areas such as tobacco or nuclear power generation, might be driven out of business altogether by a full application of these principles. In Chapter 6 is a story of a copper plant at Tacoma, WA, whose arsenic emissions were a public safety hazard but which was also the major employer and a key part of the economy. This case is a model of good leadership by the head of the Environmental Protection Agency, because he opened up the facts of the case and held the ring for a public debate about the trade-off between regulating pollutants and saving jobs and the local economy.

In difficult cases like these, trade-offs have to be made and value conflicts are involved. Decisions cannot be made on the basis of scientific analysis alone, however much governments and businesses sometimes pretend that they can. Yet the costs and time involved in such public debates and enquiries can be prohibitive. Corporate social responsibility is concerned with these difficult areas and contentious decisions, but it does not resolve them. It sets out the principles and practices by which a company self-regulates its corporate behaviour. In the case of Cadbury Schweppes, this is based on both a strong cultural heritage and a recognition of a recent shift in attitudes to CSR.

Cadbury Schweppes

Cadbury Schweppes has been making chocolate for over 200 years. The company has a strong sense of history and heritage and some brands, such as Dairy Milk, are 100 years old. Founded by Quakers, it once built houses and schools for its workers and has a tradition of social responsibility towards its employees and communities. Over many years, this has developed into a strong corporate culture. In 1984, the then Chairman, Sir Adrian Cadbury, published *The Character of the Company*, enshrining the special nature of this business, its distinctive values and its responsibilities to all its stakeholders.

In the last 20 years, competition has increased dramatically and Cadbury Schweppes, along with all its competitors, must now pay more attention to the needs of shareholders than it ever did in Sir Adrian's time. Public targets recently announced include a commitment to annual increases of 6 per cent in net sales value and similarly sized cost reductions right across the company. As reflected in the new statement on values and behaviour, this demands an accountability, adaptability and business aggressiveness that was not part of the company in the 1980s.

Nevertheless, the character of the company remains based on the traditional principles and values. The current Chairman, John Sunderland, sees himself as the inheritor and present guardian of this heritage, and sees the company as made up of people, products (or 'brands') and values. Suitably enhanced and developed, these will be passed on to the next generation. Cadbury Schweppes has a Main Board CSR Committee and published its first *Corporate and Social Responsibility Report* in May 2002. With its bright colours, storybook characters and animated graphics printed on thick card manufactured from 'elemental chlorine-free pulp', it looks like a bedtime book for a 4-year-old. However, the double-page spread on the Cadbury Schweppes value chain carries a clear message of the responsibility that the company acknowledges to all its suppliers of milk, cocoa, fruit and plants from all over the world, and also to all the millions of people and children who buy and consume its products. This is an acknowledgement of the rise of 'marketplace' issues about CSR with consumers and in supply chains.

The company has a 4 × 4 management system for CSR: four areas of corporate social responsibility described at four levels of company practice (Table 19.1).

Cadbury Schweppes is a member of both the FTSE4Good index and the Dow Jones Sustainability Group Index (DJSI), which are the benchmarks for good CSR practice. The *Corporate and Social Responsibility Report* shows that the company scores just over 50 per cent overall on the DJSI – comfortably ahead of the industry average of just over 20 per cent, but below the best at almost 70 per cent. On the social dimension, reflecting its long history of social concern, it is 'best in class'. It is the environmental dimension of the DJSI that shows most scope for improvement.

Cadbury Schweppes is asking itself two critical questions about its CSR policies and practices:

- How can we make them sustainable?
- How can we make them a business advantage – an integral part of our business that people want to buy and be associated with?

Both of these questions can lead to one conclusion: that to be effective, corporate social responsibility must be deeply embedded in business processes and over time. Being a good corporate citizen is not a current fad but core to the identity of the company, part of who we are. Cadbury Schweppes employs 7000 people in the UK, nearly 1500 of whom are members of the company volunteers' programme. These volunteers work in schools, hospitals and other community activities, and in many cases this is not regarded as charity work, but as part of the training and development of those involved.

Table 19.1   A 4 × 4 CSR framework

Four CSR areas	Four CSR system levels
Ethical trading	Commitment
Employees	Policy and strategy
Community	Implementation and verification
Environment	Communication

Cadbury Schweppes has a proud heritage and wishes to ensure that its business practices remain socially responsible in an environment of intense global competition. The recent controversy over marketing to schoolchildren makes it clear that this work is of great commercial sensitivity and importance. Like other companies, Cadbury Schweppes is under increasing challenge, not only from without but also from talented young managers who often have a clearer position on these matters than their seniors.

For those with less experience and resources in this field, how can a start be made on CSR? What is in the 'Black Box'?

Activity: a CSR gap analysis

It is up to the company concerned to decide on the contents of the CSR 'Black Box'. Any policy and system for CSR must address the underlying issues of transparency, accountability and liability, but in the context of that particular organization – what it does, how it does it, who is involved and so on.

As the Cadbury Schweppes model is simple, robust and to some extent generic, this is a good place to start. Table 19.2 gives a CSR gap analysis that provides a framework for analysing what already exists in the organization and implies a checklist of what might be needed.

Step 1: To do an adequate job on this you need a working party or an interest group to support this leadership effort. Recruit a group and consider the following questions:

Q1: Why do we need a Corporate Social Responsibility system?

What are the contextual drivers? – E.g. legal: International, European or UK legislation, Government pressures or targets, risk assessments, requests from staff, complaints from users.

What is the business case? – E.g. What are our peers doing? FTSE4Good and DJSI, etc. How will this help our business? How will it be sustainable?

Q2: What should the Corporate Social Responsibility system look like?

There are four levels on which to think about this:

1 *Leadership and commitment* – What are the values and principles that will support CSR in business strategies and working practices?
2 *Strategy and policies* – What does CSR mean in terms of the standards which you will aspire to, and commit to, in various areas of activity. What are the Best Practice Guidelines, e.g. ISO Standard on CSR?
3 *Management and implementation* – How will you make CSR happen? What is the management system of programmes, guidelines, training, codes, tools and performance indicators that will ensure compliance with commitments and policies?
4 *Reporting and communication* – How will transparency be achieved? What audits, surveys and evaluations will be conducted and by whom? How will reports on ethical performance be made and delivered in ways that are meaningful to all stakeholders?

Q3: What are the specific areas in which we wish to make commitments?

In Table 19.2, there are again four main areas, but you can change these, or add any others that are relevant to the workings of your organization. Under each of these areas, you now need to go through carefully, deciding what are the specific commitments and targets to which your organization should commit itself.

This is a straightforward but possibly contentious process of making commitments to run your business in ways that you think are more socially responsible. For example, think of your household as a business unit that consumes resources and produces various valuable outcomes for its members.

Ethical trading – Do you buy everything from the supermarket or do you use your local shops?

Table 19.2 A CSR gap analysis

CSR system / CSR area	Leadership commitment (Board-level values and principles)	Policies and strategies (policies, codes, strategies in all areas)	Implementation and verification (systems, business processes, work programmes, steering groups)	Communication and reporting (audits surveys, evaluations and reports, meetings and forums)
Ethical trading – e.g. on procurement, supplier policy, supplier assessment				
Employees – e.g. on rewards, health, safety, quality of working life, training				
Environment – e.g. on environmental impact and management, waste and recycling, green issues				
Communities – e.g. on social impact and creating value in communities, donations, volunteering				

Employees – If you have a cleaner or gardener, how well do you pay them in comparison with your neighbours?

Environment – What is your recycling policy? Are you a 'carbon-neutral household' – using up as much carbon as you produce from your car mileage and central heating by planting trees or sponsoring forests?

Communities – What do you contribute to your local community? What donations do you make? Do you regularly do any voluntary work?

Good citizens are likely to support good corporate citizenship – and vice versa. We are often as good as the company we keep, but should we expect our organizations to be better than ourselves?

Q4: Where are the gaps and what actions will we take to fill them?
This is the action plan. What aspects of the CSR Management System do we need to develop, strengthen or put in place? How will we meet the commitments we want to make under the various areas on which the business has an impact?

Conclusion

The best organizations are voluntarily producing CSR codes and social and environmental reports, but they still do not exist in more than three-quarters of large companies. Many public agencies and government departments are further back. However, the UK Government has set out to encourage CSR and has reported on the efforts of various government departments. Legislation on CSR is on the increase, and there are laws in Australia, Japan and many European countries requiring certain minimum standards. In the UK, an Early Day Motion on Corporate Social Responsibility signed by some 250 MPs calls for:

- *Targets* – All companies with a turnover of more than £5 million must report on their social and environmental impact.
- *Directors* – There would be a duty on all Directors to minimize their companies' negative impacts.
- *Consultation* – Before any major project, there would be a duty to consult – 'to show, tell and listen' – all those people and communities affected.
- *Transparency* – Everyone concerned should have access to company reports and information.
- *Right to challenge* – Affected communities would have a right to challenge company activities.

Such legislation can only be a matter of time; if your organization is not yet considering its social and environmental impact and consulting with, and reporting to, all those affected, the leadership challenge is to get them started. Good corporate citizens do not appear overnight. Those you see around you are the result of many years of growing awareness, commitment and effort – and even most of them have a long way to go. Deeply rooted in company history and values, corporate social responsibility is a tradition you can start now, but which develops over time.

It is essential that CSR is built into the business model of the company. Unless the practices of CSR are embedded in how the various business activities are conducted, then this is not the real thing. CSR is not a flavour-of-the-month fad, but an essential part of good business practice, the pressure for which that has been building for some years. If CSR is an integral part of business practice and processes, then it cannot be discarded or neglected; it is a core part of your business offer – it is what people buy.

Social Responsibility Audits are a useful way of diagnosing need or measuring progress, but they should not be taken as incontrovertible evidence of good corporate citizenship. Audits measure what can be measured – visible activities – and not the deeper heartbeat of business processes. Audits can be influenced by throwing money around at the right time by painting the company green or as socially concerned: 'greenwash' or eyewash. However, these initiatives will not last or be sustainable, nor will they influence the behaviour of all the people in the company whose actions are the real measure of good corporate citizenship. There should be no gap between CSR and ethical management.

Further resources

There are many sources in this area – legal, financial, environmental and social from corporate, public services and civil society organizations. In terms of widespread awareness and adoption, this is a field in its infancy and this is reflected in a lack of books but a plethora of websites. Many of these are changing and rapidly developing but represent the best source of information. Two useful background books are Simon Zadek's *The Civil Corporation: The New Economy of Corporate Citizenship* (New Economics Foundation, London) and Naomi Klein's famous *No Logo* (Flamingo, London). Zadek has long been associated with social accounting and reporting and his book takes the view that CSR signals a corporate and global sea change. Klein's book is a protester's bible which exposes some of the worst corporate practices concerning global firms and brands.

For examples of CSR policies and management systems, it is worth looking at the various companies that now have CSR strategies, management frameworks and reports addressing the issues of business ethics, human rights, workplace diversity, supply-chain and procurement management, stakeholder participation and consultation, and environmental matters (e.g. *www.cadburyschweppes.com*). The UK Government has taken a lead in seeking to encourage the public sector to develop CSR policies and practices and has audited the work of various departments. Its website contains much information on many aspects of CSR including efforts to promote it in SMEs and small businesses (*www. societyandbusiness.gov.uk/*).

The FTSE4Good index (launched in July 2001) and the Dow Jones Sustainability Group Index (DJSI) are the benchmarks for good CSR practice and use audit tool concerned with socially responsible investment and judge firms on their environmental, community involvement and human rights record. Businesses that do not meet specified criteria are dropped from the index (*www.ftse.com/media_centre/FTSE_data.jsp*).

On the matter of management standards, the ISO (International Organization for Standardization) is one of several organizations producing guidelines. There is a CSR standard (September 2002) and an ISO 14001 standard for corporate environmental management. ISO has a website and an online forum (*www.iso.ch/iso/en/comms-markets/industryforums/corporate socialresp/messageboard/index.list*). Finally, an organization called Employees in the Community Network, concerned with involving people in community action and social enterprises, has developed a toolkit to build skills and capacity in communities and organizations (*www.toolkit.org.uk*).

References

Caulkin, S. (2003) 'Ethics and profits do mix', *The Observer*, 20 April 2003.
Friends of the Earth (2003) *Earthmatters*, Issue 55, Summer 2003.

20

Challenge 11: Mobilizing Knowledge

The single greatest challenge ... is to raise the productivity of knowledge and service workers. This challenge, which will dominate the management agenda for the next several decades, will ultimately determine the competitive perform-ance of companies. Even more important, it will determine the very fabric of society and the quality of life in every industrialized nation
Peter Drucker (1991)

Introduction

For many organizations, the basic economic resource is no longer land, labour or capital, but knowledge. Under global pressure to become more adaptable and innovative, firms are increasingly aware of the value of specialized knowledge, and advances in computing provide some of the tools for working on learning and knowledge sharing within the organization.

Yet whilst the information age and the knowledge era put a premium on learning and knowledge creation, blockages to the sharing and transfer of knowledge abound in organizations. Success depends upon the ability to generate and share knowledge, but how well do we do this? Customers need the best advice and information, but how well does it flow to the point where it is needed? Policy makers need good feedback and intelligence to inform their decisions, but knowledge and learning do not flow easily up organization structures.

Knowledge management has come to be almost synonymous with large and impressive-sounding information management systems. These have frequently led the unwary into expensive purchases that do not deliver on their implied or indeed contractual promises. On the face of it, information management systems appear to be marvellous tools for knowledge, and the visions of their proponents are even more marvellous. Consider, for example, the dazzling array of 'laws' from this over-exciting world:

- *Moore's Law* – The power of computers doubles every 18 months.
- *The Law of Storage* – For a given cost, storage capacity doubles every 12 months.

■ *The Law of Fiber* – The bandwidth capacity of fiber (the backbone of the Internet) doubles every 9 months.
■ *Metcalfe's Law* – The power of the network goes up by the square of the people interacting.

How could you fail to buy the most expensive kit available?

However, knowledge is not an inanimate thing but a living process, whereby people use what they know in action, in practice. Useful knowledge is increasingly vital stuff, and is not to be found just in the hands of experts but is distributed all over the organization. This suggests that the core task of any 'knowledge management' effort is to enhance and maximize the flow of knowledge rather than seek to capture and store it.

This chapter contains:

■ three fundamental shifts in thinking about knowledge
■ a case history of mobilizing knowledge in Mott MacDonald, an international civil engineering consultancy firm
■ a model for designing a knowledge strategy for your organization
■ after Action Review: a tool for building reflection into working practices
■ further resources.

Mobilizing knowledge

Nancy Dixon suggests that there has been a revolution in how we think about knowledge. Her three fundamental shifts are (Dixon, 2000, pp. 148–160):

■ *From expert to distributed* – From the idea that knowledge is found only in small numbers of experts or 'best' practitioners towards the idea that useful knowledge is distributed throughout the organization.
■ *From being seen as an individual possession to knowledge as embedded in group or community* – This suggests that we cannot divorce knowledge from participating in the community in which that knowledge is exercised.
■ *From knowledge as a stable commodity to knowledge as dynamic and ever changing* – These shifts remind us why 'knowledge management' can be a misleading term. The notion of a knowledge store or warehouse is old thinking. As long ago as 1932, the British mathematician and philosopher A. N. Whitehead noted drily that 'Knowledge does not keep any better than wet fish'. It has taken a while to understand this view, but the current best thinking about knowledge now uses a flowing water metaphor rather than a storage one. Knowledge is seen as continually in motion across the organization; always in play.

The case of Mott MacDonald helps us to understand how knowledge works in a complex organization.

Knowledge management at Mott MacDonald

Knowledge is the main asset and product at Mott MacDonald, an international engineering and management consultancy with 150 sites and offices in 100 countries. Founded by Basil Mott, the resident engineer on the world's first electric underground railway in London in 1890, and Murdoch MacDonald, a key figure in the 1912 Aswan dam construction on the Nile, the company has grown to some 7000 consultants including engineers, planners, environmentalists, economists, IT specialists, management consultants and even educationalists, as the company has diversified from its civil engineering origins into environmental management, development policies and education.

Mott MacDonald decided that they needed to develop their knowledge management effort 'to improve technical and professional excellence'. As leaders in their field, they expect this of themselves, but also increasingly find their clients asking for it and a growing number of tenders requiring it. The intellectual capital in Mott MacDonald dwarfs the financial assets employed, yet, if sustainable advantage lies in what the firm knows, how well it uses what it knows and how fast it can learn new things, then the key task is to transform the company from an emphasis upon knowledgeable individuals to a knowledge-focused organization.

To assist in this task, Mott MacDonald appointed a member of this author team's consultancy firm as their knowledge management partner. Inter-Logics found that Mott MacDonald had good systems for data retrieval, document management, project websites and active discussion groups. The main website, 'MiMi' (Mott MacDonald Information), is organized under the following headings, each of which is a rich source of data:

- Staff
- Group
- Units
- Offices
- Projects
- Customers
- Policies
- Guidelines
- News
- Services
- Professional
- Communities
- Discussions
- Websites

'Staff', for example, enables you to call up detailed profiles of each employee, with CVs and special interests, and also details of job vacancies, learning opportunities, clubs and societies and more. The people directory is perhaps the best-used knowledge tool in the company: you can search for any staff with an interest in a given topic or project, and Email someone for information with great ease.

Technical or cultural?

However, despite the good systems, there was some concern in the company that given its growing size and diversity, face-to-face contact was increasingly difficult. Learning and knowledge sharing were less than they could be due to cultural and other barriers. Sharing Mott MacDonald's accumulated knowledge, especially in terms of knowledge across business functions, and improving the flow to and from external organizations including customers, suppliers, universities and governments is now a major focus of concern.

After an initial investigation, the consultants advised the company that, although their systems created great opportunities for learning and sharing, only a collaborative and 'people-oriented' approach will deliver improved development, sharing and use of knowledge. This means a cultural change and not just the construction of a knowledge system. The consultants had noted some differences in views between senior and more junior staff on issues such as access to knowledge and freedom to innovate. Some internal accounting systems could interfere with learning opportunities particularly at junior level. Although appropriate leadership is critical, as people more readily support and value what they create rather than what they are given, the focus should be on a 'bottom-up' approach.

Modelling knowledge mobilization

These views were a challenge to the company's existing ideas about knowledge management. Knowledge was seen mainly as an asset and a commodity, to be stored and traded. 'We are leaking knowledge' was one persistent refrain. The consultants view was that knowledge is a process, not a commodity – you can have a database but not a knowledge store because data or information becomes knowledge as it is used to do something; it is embedded in practice. It follows from this view that knowledge has to be 'managed' as part of business processes and work practices and not as an abstract entity. In turn, this means that the organizational culture must support and encourage these processes (Figure 20.1).

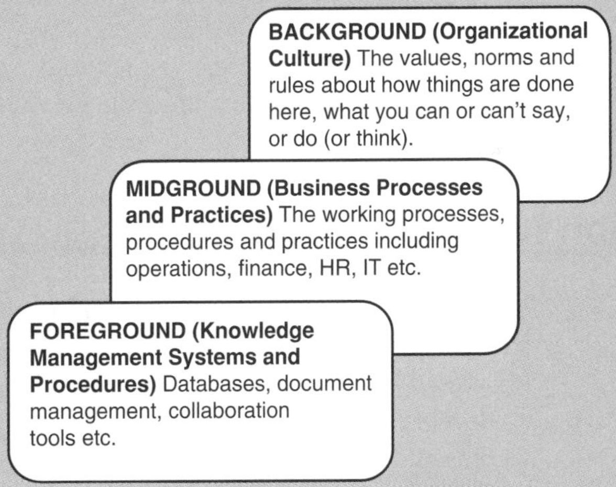

BACKGROUND (Organizational Culture) The values, norms and rules about how things are done here, what you can or can't say, or do (or think).

MIDGROUND (Business Processes and Practices) The working processes, procedures and practices including operations, finance, HR, IT etc.

FOREGROUND (Knowledge Management Systems and Procedures) Databases, document management, collaboration tools etc.

Figure 20.1 Organizational knowledge mobilization (adapted with permission from the original by Inter-Logics.net Ltd, 2001)

On the basis of this diagnosis, three priority projects were agreed – learning from project experience, making best use of our expertise and improving induction and networking. A variety of interventions have been used to progress these projects, including large group events and action learning sets. These have aimed to support people and to encourage project groups in a busy working environment where people are driven by deadlines to build reflective practices into their working cycles. To achieve the goal that Mott MacDonald has set itself – to become a knowledge-focused organization in order to improve technical and professional excellence – requires a sustained effort. The new professional competencies of learning how to learn must become embedded into the core business processes and practices.

Leading on knowledge

The Mott MacDonald story illustrates, amongst many things, how difficult it can be to create space for reflection. Given the rapid advances of information technology, it is all too tempting to rush into devising and installing knowledge management systems, that make the easy assumption that people will use them as they are intended. Just as we use only a fraction of the capability that Microsoft has built into our PCs, so most so-called knowledge management systems are only partly activated and then only by people with the energy and enthusiasm to make the effort.

The role of leadership in knowledge management is crucial. It should encompass three priorities:

- first, to resist the rush to spend on information technology
- second, to encourage a new view of knowledge as inseparable from personal practice and business processes
- third, to facilitate the personal and organizational spaces for reflection without which the learning from practice will never see the corporate light of day.

Reflection for knowledge

Blinded by hi-tech visions, it is easy to forget the basics, generating ideas and knowledge, and then sharing these, are human activities that can only be supported by the technology, not driven by it. There is no mystery about how to develop the skills to generate knowledge, but it does require an investment of time and space. Take that most basic process of reflection to start with; here a facilitator reflects on a recent 'lessons learned' meeting:

> We worked in three groups – one per project – and I explained a structure designed to allow each person in turn to tell a story about a key experience

they have had on that project, to be heard without interruptions, and then to ask questions. I noticed that people found it extremely difficult simply to listen without chipping in, making comments, asking questions and so on. Of course there are times when this can be supportive and show engagement with the speaker, but on this occasion I wanted people to have the chance not to get sidetracked or put off by interruptions.

After each person had told their story and been heard in this way, each person was asked to say what they had learned as a result. I recall that most people seemed to have learned something important. One person also stressed the value she felt from having had the ability to tell her story, what had happened and how she felt about it. This led me to think in terms of four possible benefits or 'lessons learned'. One is to meet the requirements of the QA process; another is to learn something that is generalizable and that others in the company may find useful. A third is more personal – something the individual learns that is helpful primarily to her or to him, but because it is very context-specific, may be of rather little interest to others. The fourth is the value felt in simply having the opportunity to talk about things in a way that normal project meetings just do not allow.

The next day I heard that some of those who had been there had felt that there wasn't enough of the 'what went well, badly, do differently' data that could be incorporated into the QA system. There's a nice irony that, at the end of a meeting designed to help people say things they don't normally feel able to say, people still went away unable to say the things they wanted to say.

In this company, the QA system accepted data of a certain sort and effectively defined what was meant by reflection in this context. This in turn defines what learning means in this context, and beyond these one-line 'lessons learned' people see no point in further reflection.

We assume that we know how to reflect, but is this true? Do we have time to really ponder things? And if we have time, do we actually know how to do it? We also tend to assume that it is individuals who do the reflecting and that this is a private process, happening somewhere in the head. This is partly true but, in busy firms, space can be created for reflection by making it a shared process. The following is a simple tool to encourage and build in reflection into project and task cycles.

After Action Review

People in organizations are often very focused on the task, but are less good at pausing to take stock and learn from what has happened once the job is completed. Taking just 20 minutes or so to review can result in good ideas to improve practice next time. If the vital opportunity to learn from experience is missed, this results in a 'learning loss' – not just for the person and their work group, but also for the whole organization.

Use the After Action Review immediately after the completion of any task. It is done in the group of colleagues who have been involved in the task or project concerned. During the completion of this task each person will have made some observations from their experience; for example, they will have noticed:

■ What actions they themselves took (what they did and *didn't* do, what they said, and so on).
■ How these actions impacted on the outcome.
■ What actions other team members took and how these actions impacted on the outcome.
■ The effect of the environment or local circumstances – expected and unexpected.

If these individual observations and personal learning are made available, then everyone has a chance to learn from experience and do better next time.

Activity: After Action Review

Step 1: Fix a time for the After Action Review – say for 20 or 30 minutes.
Step 2: At the start of the meeting, propose some ground rules, e.g.

■ Everyone's experience is valid – irrespective of rank, etc.
■ Don't hold back – say what you saw and heard.
■ 'No thin skins' – don't take anything personally, focus on the impact on team performance.
■ Propose changes – how could we do it differently and better?

Ask people if they want to suggest others and add these as appropriate, but then move on quickly.
Step 3: Now work through the three basic questions of the After Action Review. Ask each person to make brief notes on:

■ What was supposed to happen?
■ What actually happened?
■ What accounts for the difference?

Step 4: Taking the three questions in turn, ask each person to comment and note down on a flip chart a summary of the points on which most people agree.

Step 5: When all three questions have been dealt with in this way, ask:

■ What could we do differently next time?

Note any ideas or responses that people think might improve practice.
Step 6: Close the meeting and provide everyone with a copy to take into their next task or project.

A strategy for mobilizing knowledge

A strategy for knowledge obviously includes much more than reflective practices, but unless it is built upon this solid foundation its results will be disappointing. Information technology is a marvellous enabler of knowledge sharing, but it is the servant and not the driver in these essentially human exchanges. Building a knowledge strategy from the bottom-up means working with the energy of the people with the know-how to help them develop their knowledge and to share it with whoever might find it useful. Imposing a system and structure on them will just be a waste of our money and their time.

Should you take the lead on a strategy for knowledge in your organization? Some companies, especially those in fast-moving businesses in electronics, communications, consulting and so on not only have strategies but have also appointed CKOs – Chief Knowledge Officers – to signal the importance of this new function for knowledge-based industries.

Any strategy will contain the following:

■ context
■ core purposes and objectives
■ key policy areas
■ action: how will we do it?

All of these can be seen at work in Mott MacDonald, and we also learn from that case that for any knowledge strategy to work it must integrate with other relevant strategies and disciplines within the business. Most organizations, even if they are not international consultancies, need a strategy for knowledge management. This need not be too complicated. The aims and objectives cited by Mott MacDonald to make their company fit for the future are increasingly being expected by clients and demanded by regulatory bodies. What we learn from this case is that any strategy for knowledge must link on the one hand to core business processes on the one, and be supported by the culture or climate of the organization on the other. A knowledge strategy can be as simple as in Figure 20.2.

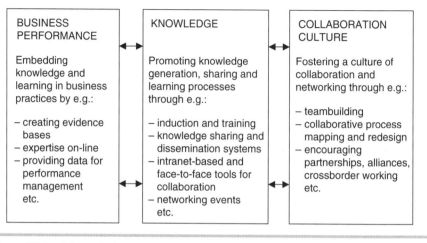

Figure 20.2   A knowledge strategy

It is much better to start with a minimal framework to allow for learning and emergence. What we can all learn from the IT industry is to over-deliver rather than to over-promise. A recent review of Human Resource Management strategies contains some useful general advice:

It is better to ensure that (HR) policies are properly implemented than to try and develop new policies.

The role of line managers in bringing these policies to life and exercising leadership is crucial.

Done well, these (HR) practices produced highly committed, motivated employees. But there are risks involved… It is actually better not to do these things at all than to do them badly.

(People Management, 15 May 2003)

Conclusion

Some final thoughts:

Knowledge Mobilization Strategy is not a document …

… but a living process practised by line managers, work groups, project teams and multiple communities of interest, knowledge and practice.

Build on what already exists …

… rather than investing heavily in new kit and systems before you know how they will work to complement what is already done well.

One size does not fit all …

... 'Best Practice' may be a poor guide to what will work for you in your context.

Start with something simple ...

... that you can actually implement.

Look for powerful connections ...

... practice joined-up thinking in terms of other areas of policy and practice, especially human resources, research and development, business process and service redesign, health, safety and risk management and so on.

See it as an exciting journey ...

... Knowledge strategy not a finished object – see it as something you will build on, adapt and add to as you go along.

Further resources

The After Action Review in this chapter was adapted from those described in Nancy Dixon's book referenced below. This excellent book is concerned with how to promote knowledge transfer and dissemination in organizations. It is clearly written and full of practical examples of how this may be done.

References

CIPD (2003) 'Unlocking the black box', *People Management*, 15 May 2003.

Dixon, N. (2000) *Common Knowledge: How Companies Thrive by Sharing What They Know*, Harvard Business School Press, Boston.

Drucker, P. (1991) 'The new productivity challenge', *Harvard Business Review*, Nov.–Dec., p. 69.

21

Challenge 12: Leading in Networks

Networks are the organizational form of the 21st Century
Pettigrew and Fenton (2000)

Introduction

These days, almost everyone seems to do it in networks. For individuals, networks provide a source of information, support and friendship. For organizations, they promise a rapid response to customers and users, with a fluidity and flexibility free from the confines of the traditional form. For the nations of the European Union, this network of small and large states offers common security and splendid trading opportunities.

For Capra (2002), networks are the basic principle of organization for all forms of life – cellular, animal and human. Castells (2000) argues that we live in a networked world society, in which global financial markets, networked via computers, have facilitated the rise of global capitalism focused on shareholder value. This interconnected world economy now challenges governments through the power that it confers on markets, large corporations and even on sophisticated criminal and terrorist networks. Networks, it seems, are archaetypal.

For companies, the seminal notion is that of the value chain, which does not stop at the boundaries of the formal organization. As Emery and Trist (1965) noted years ago, when the environment is turbulent and it is not just the actors who are moving but the ground under their feet, the proper unit of analysis is not the individual company but the network of firms in a market. The contemporary language of subcontracting, supply chains, alliances, partnerships, interlocking ownership and so on attests to this need for interorganizational collaboration and connectedness. The rise of the network is fuelled by the rapid advances of information technology – the Internet and World Wide Web provide both the conceptual model and the practical enablers of networking.

Networks provide a context in which to work inside and outside formal organizational and professional boundaries. This can bring the skills and knowledge of those at the grassroots to the fore in a more unified way, thus enhancing many aspects of service delivery. However, they present both opportunities and threats. The implications for leadership include the need to master the new skills for developing, harnessing, nurturing and facilitating networks for business purposes, but also to develop socially responsible responses to those excluded from the flows of resources in a networked world.

This chapter contains:

- the network organization
- a living systems view of organizations
- organizational networks for policy, learning and service delivery
- case examples of the CRINE network in the offshore oil and gas industry and clinical networks for cancer services in the NHS
- a Due Diligence Tool for network organizations
- nine simple rules for network organizing
- further resources.

The network organization

Networks are an attractive prospect for organizations seeking greater flexibility, adaptability and improved service delivery. However, their self-organizing nature constitutes a formidable challenge to the leadership skills of managers used to commanding and controlling. To help with this, a network organization needs a set of strong guiding values and principles. W. L. Gore, the makers of Goretex, set out to create an internal network based on some key principles.

W. L. Gore: the Lattice Organization

W. L. Gore is famous for its Goretex fabric, known to sailors, mountaineers and sports-people for its breathability and waterproof qualities. The company itself, which began life in 1958, is organized on equally radical lines. Known as 'the Lattice Organization', all units are small, no more than 150 people, each containing multiple and overlapping lattices of people who work together and know each other well. Lattices have similarities with communities of practice and the linkages and connections between these and the units are of vital importance.

Making this organizational structure work depends a great deal upon the relationships and connections between people. Each person is an Associate – there are no 'employees' – who chooses their own work tasks, subject to peer feedback and discipline. Each associate chooses a sponsor, a person who takes a personal interest in that person, and their progress and development. Sponsors thus acquire leadership by being chosen by others, what Bill Gore himself called 'natural leadership'.

> Like any other network, Gore's relies for its effectiveness upon responsible self-organization rather than the tidy ordering of roles and responsibilities and the clarity of reporting relationships. To make the lattice work, Bill Gore put forward four simple rules as guiding principles for the behaviour of all associates:
>
> - Try to be fair in all transactions inside and outside the organization.
> - Encourage the growth and development of all associates.
> - Make commitments and stick to them.
> - Consult with others before taking actions that might threaten the business.
>
> (Hastings, 1993, pp. 15–16)

These principles apply inside and outside the business, extending to reach out to suppliers and business partners. Like its cousins, the boundaryless, the virtual and the learning organizations, the network organization is a process-based form, and is more about *organizing* than organization. A central idea is the value chain or stream – the flow of processes and activities that creates value for clients, customers or users. Another is the metaphor of 'living systems'.

Living systems

Pioneer organizations such as W. L. Gore aim to adapt their organizational structures and behaviour to adopt a different perspective on organizing. The old, but lingering, idea of organizations as machines that can be managed, controlled and fixed has severe limitations in the face of the complexity, uncertainty and turbulence of markets and societies. Interest in networking is linked to a movement towards thinking about organizations as living systems modelled on life itself, complex but adaptive A living system is:

> *a system of independent agents that can act in parallel, develop models as to how things work in their environment and, most importantly, refine those models through learning and adaptation.*
>
> (Pascale, Millemann and Goija, 2000, p. 5)

This principle – that self-organization deals much better with complexity than central control – is found in many natural systems such as flocks of birds and shoals of fish. Here, change and turbulence are normal part of life, and so is the 'resistance to change' from any outside interference. Whereas a machine may be controlled, a living system can only be disturbed or influenced, as it actively chooses what it notices, and it responds to impulses, not to instructions.

To adopt a living systems perspective, organizations are learning to value the informal relationships of communication, friendship, networks and alliances that exist within and around the formal organization. These shadowy, continually shifting and adaptable aspects of the company are believed to hold the key to greater flexibility, learning capability and creative potential.

Yet organizations are not just living systems. They have many machine-like aspects and, when we are in them, we do behave in remarkably orderly ways, conforming to rules, processes, procedures and control systems. This dual, 'Cyborg' nature of human organizing, both living system and machine, means that organizations need both to be designed and allowed to emerge. The leadership task is to specify the minimum 'machine' that allows for emergence and self-organization.

How do networks work?

Personal networks, as discussed in Chapter 9, are easy to understand, but organizational ones are more complex. The World Health Organization has a straightforward definition:

> A *network is a grouping of individuals, organizations and agencies organized on a non-hierarchical basis around common issues or concerns, which are pursued proactively and systematically, based on commitment and trust.*
>
> (WHO, 1998)

There is an extensive and growing literature that suggests that network organizations connect people not through the normal command and control structures but through:

- establishing *common goals*
- operating through *personal relationships* of mutual interest, sharing, reciprocity, trust
- *organizing through (i) nodes* – individuals, teams or organizations, *(ii) ties or links* – relationships, connections, working partnerships and associations; and *(iii) spaces* – made possible by nodes and links which contain the potentials for learning, innovation and emergence
- through making use of computer networking and *virtual association*
- and with *status and authority* based on knowledge, usefulness, sharing and innovativeness and not on formal position or qualifications.

The main problem with such definitions is that although networks are in theory flat and fluid forms, resisting external control and direction, in practice network organizations are always managed to a lesser or greater degree. The work requires a lot of local autonomy and flexibility, but there is always some central control or co-ordination. This constitutes the central challenge for the leadership of networked organizations:

> *How can we maximize the advantages of self-organization by putting in place only the minimum requirements for overall alignment and control?*

Another problem with general definitions is that they do little to prepare you for the wide variety of forms to be found under the currently fashionable label of 'network'. Transport, utilities and facilities firms all use the word to mean different things; some other organizations are networks are in name only, traditional hierarchical structures masquerading as something modish. What network organization means in practice depends first upon its core purpose: what is the network for?

Networks for policy, learning and service delivery

How a network may be configured, facilitated and developed depends on its particular purpose. The wide variety of network forms can be grouped under three headings (Figure 21.1).

- Learning networks attract members around common training and development needs. In many ways, the network ideal lends itself most easily to transmission of ideas, the sharing of good practice and the solving of technical problems. Learning networks need relatively few resources or rules, have a bottom line of member satisfaction and are generally *facilitated*.
- Policy networks have been a mainstay of governments and international communities for many years. They produce ideas, models and potential agreements, and are *convened* and chaired rather than managed.
- The service delivery network is *managed* with a clear hierarchy of decisions, tighter rules and more demanding bottom lines in terms of productivity, cost reductions or other synergies.

Many networked organizations are combinations of one or more of these ideal types. Learning and service delivery can go well together. In fact, a good way to

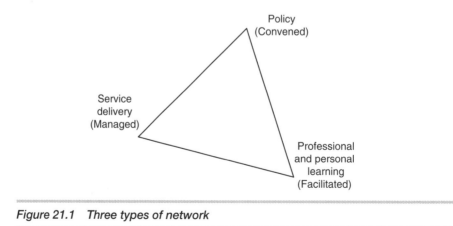

Figure 21.1   Three types of network

start any network is to begin by connecting with others in a learning relationship. Learning networks are lower risk than joint service delivery commitments, and are well suited to opening up new areas of work. Learning networks have the added benefit of giving members the opportunity to explore relationships with each other as potential service delivery partners. The CRINE network shows how joint working can grow out of successfully learning together.

CRINE

The contractors, suppliers, consultants and trade associations of the UK oil and gas industry set up the CRINE (Cost Reduction Initiative for the New Era) as a learning network in response to the 1992 oil crisis. The aim was to share ideas and best practice in order to achieve cost reductions of 30 per cent for offshore developments by sector-wide efforts rather than individual actions. By 1997, costs had fallen by 40 per cent and attracted so much international attention that the initiative spread to Mexico, Venezuela, India and Australia.

   After reaching their initial goals, the members felt that the relationship was worth maintaining and set up the CRINE Network in 1997 to increase their share of the non-UK market. Steered by a representative body and managed by a small co-ordinating group, CRINE seeks to establish a learning and continuous improvement culture, encouraging collaboration rather than confrontation between suppliers and customers. It works through 'supported networking', with financial, technical and other support from government, major operators, trade, research and academic bodies to the network of actors in the supply chain. Activities include newsletters, websites, workshops and conferences, technical projects and other initiatives such as the *First Point Assessment Programme*, which uses seconded engineers from major subscribers to assess and improve supply chain capability in companies.

(Bessant, Kaplinsky and Lamming, 1999)

Service delivery networks require careful preparation, planning, negotiation and development. These are new organizational forms that carry heavy and wide-ranging responsibilities on impressively light infrastructures. When they work, they can deliver impressive outcomes unachievable by other means, as Toyota, Benetton and others have demonstrated.

   These service delivery networks are also the most distant from the fluid, flat and self-organizing ideal from which they take their name. For example, the 34 Cancer Networks in the UK's NHS are charged with the heavy responsibilities of ensuring the equitable provision of cancer services and the efficient use of resources across regions of up to two million people. Leading these vital networks means persuading and influencing the hospitals and health organizations in these regions to work on the 'value stream' across their organizational boundaries. In the case of health services, the value stream takes the form of 'patient (or care) pathways' to promote consistently high-quality services and the removal inequities of access or treatment.

There are many practical obstacles to bringing such seamless services into reality, only one of which is that – rather like the borders of many African nations – the geographical boundaries of the networks have been drawn up without the participation of those who are supposed to make them work. However, to make them work, a formidable effort at collaborative leadership and organizing is required. One account of the systems, structures and rules needed to bring about this collaboration gives the following list of essentials.

> **Essential features of an effective NHS clinical network**
>
> - clear objectives in terms of improvements in service outcomes
> - clear management structure and accountability arrangements
> - a lead clinician
> - a network project manager
> - shared evidence bases and document protocols
> - active involvement of all disciplines in the relevant care pathways
> - effective systems for dissemination of information for patients and staff
> - regular meetings of network staff
> - active patient involvement
> - joint clinical audit across the network
> - shared commitment for regular review of network objectives, achievements and development
> - shared approach to the development of best practice and the training of staff
> - regular performance management by an outside body
> - sound financial management with equitable contributions from constituent organizations
> - committed ownership by contributing organizations.
>
> (Davies, 2001)

The work of the clinical networks is vitally important and they carry great expectations from patients, managers, leaders and politicians. The concept attracts widespread support in the light of the failure of market mechanisms and hierarchical performance management to bring about the desired outcomes. It is just a small matter of implementation. Developing these networks is made all the more heroic by the fact that they are not statutorily accountable and have few staff and resources.

A due diligence checklist

It might have been better to begin on the cancer networks from a different starting place. As noted above, to carry heavy responsibilities on light infrastructures requires careful preparation, planning, negotiation and development. The Due Diligence Tool will help with the first two of these at least.

Due diligence is a term borrowed from merger and acquisition situations, where it means taking appropriate responsibility and spotting likely pitfalls, especially in legal and financial terms. Here due diligence serves as a way of thinking through and creating sound foundations for network organizing. This is a checklist of questions to be addressed in appraising, establishing or developing any networked organization.

Before embarking on any network development, work through the following checklist with a steering or initiative group.

Activity: due diligence checklist for network organizing

1   Domain and purpose
- What is the focus or specific area for the network?
- What is the basis for interaction and networking?
- Where is the energy? What is the passion?

2   Community
- Who are the people concerned?
- What is the 'whole system'? Where are the boundaries?
- Who is in? Who is out?

3   Animation and mobilization
- What exists already?
- How do we get the ball rolling? (NB: In contrast to 'rolling out').
- What is the sequence of activities? What is the first step?
- How will this be an inclusive or exclusive process?

4   Exploring and building common ground
- What is the diversity of different interests?
- Where is the common ground?
- What is the process for defining common ground *and* special interests?

5   Organization and governance
- How will the network be maintained and supported?
- How will decisions be made?
- How will the network be managed?
- What sort of leadership is encouraged?
- What is the structure?
- What are the simple rules?

6   Behaviour
- What are the norms for good behaviour?
- What are members' responsibilities for sharing, spreading and linking with others?

■ How is good behaviour rewarded?

■ What is bad behaviour?

7   Learning

■ How will practice and knowledge be shared and developed?

■ What will be the learning activities?

■ What knowledge, practices, techniques, tools and resources are available?

8   Performance and accountability

■ How will performance be measured? By whom?

■ To whom are we accountable? For what?

■ What is the evidence for learning, innovation, change?

9   Life cycle development

■ What are the stages of development in the network?

■ Where are we now?

■ What is our next step?

10   Network learning

■ How has the network as a whole learned?

■ What are we learning about organizing in networks?

■ What is the value of the network? To whom?

The due diligence checklist will help you avoid some of the more obvious pitfalls of network organizing and prepare you for the negotiation, influencing and development work that a good network demands. Once the network is established on sound foundations, the following principles will help to guide this development work.

Nine principles for network organizing

Developing and facilitating networked organizations is a new challenge for leadership. Networks may need legitimacy and recognition as much as resources, and a good way to start is to look and see what exists already. Although they will need some local interpretation to suit your circumstances, here are some general development principles (adapted from Pedler, 2001):

Connect what exists: As networks are normal forms for many trade, professional, voluntary and community associations, the first question is: what exists and how can we work with this? Linking up existing networks might be much easier than bringing together unconnected people.

Preparation: Do 'due diligence' on the network (see above). Start-ups are crucial. What are the common goals, simple rules and governance arrangements?

A central figure: The best networks often have a person or small group as a central hub, a source of information, connection and the 'face behind the web'. It helps if these people are good brokers and diplomats.

A directory of members and contact details: With a sentence or two about each person's know-how and interests to encourage self-organization and 'weak link' connections.

A newsletter: A simple, but regular, news-sheet that can be distributed electronically and on paper.

Meetings: Have some regular opportunities for people to meet each other spontaneously and energetically to share ideas and experiences.

Teach networking skills: Encourage people to learn about connecting, brokering and trading. One set of simple rules for network meetings is:

- listen
- ask questions
- give as well as take.

Encourage self-organization: Self-interest is a powerful motivator. Having too few rules or too many rules inhibits activity. What are the few simple rules on which the network will operate?

Facilitate leadership, governance and accountability: Where multiple organizations sponsor the network, some unity at the top is necessary. A partnership board or convening group can represent the whole.

Conclusion

Networks are very attractive to organizations seeking improved service delivery, learning and innovation. However, their self-organizing nature constitutes a formidable challenge to leadership skills. Networks also have a dark side. As mutual benefit associations they can operate as cliques or gangs with negative consequences for others. Balancing the desirable but selfish qualities of self-organization with the broader concerns for inclusivity, alignment and accountability constitutes a critical challenge in leading with networks.

Networks are associated with all kinds of innovations in collaborations of nation states, transportation, food production and distribution, localization, healthcare and community development. More broadly still, the network idea stems from and supports the ecological and 'lean thinking' principles which are an essential component for reshaping the destructive effects of globalization. This reshaping will require changes in values, political will and operational rules to adopt the systemic networked perspective, which, according to Capra (2002), is the basis for sustainable life.

Supported by this wider shift, people concerned to lead their organizations towards better service delivery will be learning to work with networks.

Without the knowledge and intelligence of front-line and grassroots activists, service improvements will not be delivered. Nor can they be delivered by 'empowerment' – unless this means sharing power with local networks.

Further resources

The resources on networks are fragmented and localized, and not always practical in nature. Some of the best materials may be local, as in reports on local supply chains or networks, some of which are cited by Bessant, Kaplinsky and Lamming (1999) (see References). Ask around your local trade associations and other likely places, or enter your interest followed by the word 'network' on the search engines.

Perhaps the best general source is Fritjof Capra's readable account of how systemic and network principles underlie all forms of life (see References). He has a good and penetrating chapter on 'Life and leadership in organizations'. For a more academic review from an organization perspective, Andrew Pettigrew and Evelyn Fenton have edited a series of case studies in *The Innovating Organization* (Sage, London, 2000) with useful topping and tailing chapters. The cases cover banking, insurance, pharmaceuticals, engineering, construction and water services and there are many useful further references.

From a more practical business perspective, Michael Goold and Andrew Campbell's *Designing Effective Organizations: How to Create Structured Networks* (Jossey Bass, San Francisco, 2002) is a design primer which aims to marry the decentralized network with hierarchical organizational structures. Although it is not a simple book, it has a firm focus on implementation. Wenger, McDermott and Snyder's *Cultivating Communities of Practice: a Guide to Managing Knowledge* (Harvard Business School Press, Boston, 2002) is a readable and practical guide to this fast-moving area.

References

Bessant, J., R. Kaplinsky and R. Lamming (1999) *Using Supply Chains to Transfer Learning About 'Best Practice'*, Report to the Department of Trade and Industry, London, January 1999.

Capra, F. (2002) *The Hidden Connections – A Science for Sustainable Living*, Harper Collins, London.

Castells, M. (2000) *End of the Millennium*, Blackwell, Oxford.

Davies, L. (2001) *Clinical Networking in Trent: Principles and Practice*, NHS Trent

Emery, F. and E. Trist (1965) 'The causal texture of organisational environments', *Human Relations*, **18**, 21–32.

Hastings, C. (1993) *The New Organisation: Growing the Culture of Organisational Networking*, McGraw-Hill, Maidenhead.

Pedler, M. (2001) *Networked Organisations – an Overview*, Issues in Health Development, Health Development Agency, London.

WHO (1998) *Health Promotion Glossary*, WHO/HPR/HEP/98.1, World Health Organization, Geneva.

22

Challenge 13: Managing Mergers

*It is not the strongest of the species who survive or even the most intelligent,
but the most responsive to change*
Charles Darwin

Introduction

Mergers, acquisitions and integrations are special forms of change management. In common with other types of change, mergers usually aim to make savings and improvement, but they have a special flavour that calls for distinctive leadership. What makes mergers and integrations different is summed up in the word 'synergy'. For a merger to be worth it, 2 + 2 must equal 5 (or more).

Mergers – and demergers – are an increasing feature of organizational life as businesses and public services struggle to stay relevant and competitive. There is a growing number of books and articles on this issue, but much of this writing is concerned with the financial, legal, due diligence and strategic 'fit' aspects of mergers and acquisitions. In this chapter, the focus is on the process of merging. How we integrate is as important as what we merge.

However, despite the popularity of big mergers as a quick way of growing a business and enhancing the Chief Executive's profile, no less 70 per cent of mergers and acquisitions in the commercial world are reported as failing to add value (KPMG, 2001). Explanations for this have long been available. One detailed study reveals that the biggest cause of failure is 'people problems' – clashes over management, human relations and corporate cultures. Lack of understanding of the acquired company and lack of clear purpose come next, with the objects of due diligence activities – inadequate financial analysis and lack of synergy – way down the list (McCann and Gilkey, 1988, p. 64). Although 'CEO hubris' is probably a major underlying reason for the failure of mergers, it is the people issues that make synergy easier to say than to do:

People-based assets are difficult to manage – it is not a simple task to harness people's intellects, emotions and imaginations. Nor is it easy to persuade employees to behave in certain ways or to endorse cherished corporate values.

(Devine, 2002, p. 9)

Pulling off the value-adding merger requires a remarkable effort at the involvement and integration of the people who are the heart of the new business. Merger and acquisition processes tend to focus on business fit and commercial advantage, neglecting the human and social 'capital' built up in these organizations. This shortsightedness is what undermines shareholder promises or dreams of public service reform. The chances of creating synergy are enhanced by the way in which mergers are led and especially on the quality of in the integration process.

However, it is important not to equate a good integration process with project management. Good project management is part of the story but it also constitutes a trap. Take all the risk and uncertainty out of the integration process, and you also remove the opportunities for local solutions, for the local autonomy, ownership and diversity that can generate the new possibilities to 'beat the plan' for the merger.

In this chapter, this integration process is exemplified in the Diageo story – the merging of the drinks businesses of Guinness and Grand Metropolitan. This story and the ideas in this chapter owe much to Phil Radcliffe, who, as Director of Strategic Change at Diageo, was closely involved in the planning and implementation of that merger. The general principles of the integration process as developed at Diageo apply to a wide range of merger situations in commercial and public service reorganizations. They also apply to small-scale mergers, as when two departments or two or more teams are brought together – perhaps as a consequence of major change within an organization or following an acquisition.

As with other major changes, it is difficult to do justice to the complexities of merger situations in one short chapter. Whole books are devoted to mergers and acquisitions without exhausting the challenges of these situations. The aim of this chapter is to help you make a start and to take a positive lead in any merger situation, however small. This chapter contains:

- three key themes in merger situations
- the integration process at Diageo
- an integration road map
- further resources.

Working with energy: three merger themes

There are many aspects of the merger process that require sensitive and creative attention. At their best, mergers have been described as controlled explosions of energy, but in all cases they constitute major upheavals. A number of forms of energy surround the merger situation, both negative and positive. These include:

- emotional energy from risk, vulnerability and uncertainty
- 'two tribes battles' and the potential for conflict
- a widespread sense of being on the edge which affects everyone
- loss and bereavement – the loss of the past, of place and of meaning and personal identity
- the possibilities for personal development in spite of it all
- the energy of new purpose through reconnecting with others to live out new values of product or service improvement and of creating something new.

Anyone seeking to manage a merger needs to be aware of and be able to work with these energies. Although their manifestation can be alarming, they are also the source of the hoped-for benefits. In these situations, questions of purpose and identity, participation and ability to maximize opportunities for learning are critical.

Purpose and identity

There is a huge potential loss of purpose when a merger takes place. The prospect of merger generates a great deal of unhappiness and anger. Expect people to say, 'I didn't join this organization to see it taken over. If I had wanted to work for them, I would have applied there' and 'So what have we been working for all this time?'. Expect people also to ask, 'Who are we – now?'. Loss of purpose and loss of identity lead to powerlessness and negativity.

Anyone leading the merger process must tackle this head on. The leadership group must first have a clear purpose for the merger, and then be able to explain it to others. Once the merger becomes public (the preplanning will usually be private to a few individuals), the urgent task is to turn round the negativity and find a way to create meaning with those people who will have to make the merged organization work.

What is needed is some meaningful view of the future that depicts a new (and better) organization than currently exists. Just describing this in terms of new products or services will not do it, it also must include a sense of how the new organization will work and what it will be like to work there. The job of communicating this falls inevitably on the leadership team, and at this point it becomes necessary for these people to take a stand and be very visible.

At this point, as in every crisis, there will be an opportunity to establish trust (and an equal opportunity to send the level of trust spiralling downwards). Woody Allan suggested that '90 per cent of life is turning up', and this is definitely one of those times when you have to be there, very visible, not just turning up but standing up – at the front. Honesty and openness after the secrecy of the planning will be highly valued. People understand why they are sometimes kept in the dark, but now they want to know what the future will be like and particularly what this means for them personally.

Participation

Amongst the first questions that will be put at any merger briefing, once the initial shock has been overcome, will be 'What's my part in all this?'. A good merger process will combine top-down integration plan with opportunities for people to shape the outcomes in their localities. This is too critical a task to be left to an entirely emergent process, but it will succeed best when those who ultimately have to make it work are involved in working out how that can best be done.

Bringing together two or more organizations, which have their own directions and energies, is a complex task. In a big merger, there is an expectation on those leading the process that they will shape up this task to the point that it is made understandable and can be communicated to other people. There is a big temptation here to call in merger consultants. Mergers are scary situations. Most of those involved, even the most senior, will probably have had little experience of such risk and uncertainty. They will be scared, although they may not say so. These are the ideal conditions for the merger experts to come and do their project management. However, as we will see from the Diageo story below, this is not necessarily a good move.

An important part of any merger process, whether specialist consultants are involved or not, is the *integration plan*. How will the two organizations be integrated; what will be the process? The integration plan is also a participation plan: who will be involved in this process and how? In the Diageo story, drawn from interviews with Phil Radcliffe and Marion Devine's account in her book on successful mergers, integration teams were part of the answer.

Learning

Another reason for not delegating risky moves to external consultants is the learning benefit to be gained from a well thought through participation strategy. Members of the integration teams are engaged in action on problems and situations that are new and unfamiliar. As they create the new organization, they must find ways of engaging meaningfully and effectively with the line managers and operational staff. These are the perfect conditions for action learning.

Where action and learning are flourishing, this creates dialogue opportunities between the implementation teams and the overall leadership team. In Diageo, these 'stop and think' meetings were about challenge and learning between those at the front and those at the centre, and not about supervision, inspection or monitoring by the top on the bottom.

The Diageo story

Initial talks between the Chief Executives of Guinness and Grand Metropolitan on the integration of the drinks businesses took place in early 1997. These talks convinced them that a consolidation of the global spirits industry was inevitable and that they should go for 'first mover advantage'. Shareholder approval was given in December 1997 and the integration process began in January 1998, lasting for most of that year.

The aim from the beginning was to create Diageo as a decentralized organization to preserve the local strengths which existing in both Guinness and Grand Metropolitan. A critical decision was taken to create the new company not by the more usual top-down model but through encouraging local participation in the integration effort. This required significant devolution of power and authority to implement local solutions and required nerve from the leadership team because this felt risky and was less controllable from the centre.

However, there were clear benefits to this decentralized approach. Apart from the recognition that you can hardly build a decentralized operation via a highly centralized process, what the company wanted was for … our managers to feel that they had driven the integration process and that it was their job to fix any problems that might arise (Radcliffe, in Devine, 2002, p. 111).

As the process got under way, it was led by a steering group of senior managers who developed the overall strategy and set business targets for the integrated operation. They also described a new desired culture in the *UDV Way of Working*. Reporting to this steering group was an integration programme team which oversaw the detail of 11 work streams in procurement, sales, human resources and so on, which aimed to reduce costs through eliminating duplication and look for synergies and growth opportunities. Also in support was a human resources effort especially in recruiting the 50 or so managing directors who would head the various country markets around the world. Working hard to make this a strictly merit-based process not only helped to get the best people in post but also to dispel any concerns about whether this merger was actually a takeover.

The integration process was then largely devolved to the regional market teams. The central integration team offered the local teams various tools to help them do their work, especially the 'integration road map', which was designed to break a long journey down into small steps. This framework for integration offered ideas for arriving at a new organization structure and on how to manage the whole project, was but it was left up to the local teams to decide whether to use these resources or not.

Opportunities and encouragement to learn from local action was designed into the integration process. The central team proposed a 'workshopping' of the process, emphasizing facilitation and coaching to develop the thinking of the local team. One aspect of this was the 'stop and think' reviews with senior managers. These meetings were not seen as being about inspection or monitoring, but as learning spaces to take stock, review progress and consider options for next steps. By asking questions and encouraging debate rather than managing the project, senior managers could offer practical help and coaching based on a wider experience while gathering useful local knowledge to take back to the central team.

The risks inherent in this devolved strategy became clear when all the local integration projects were pulled together in the company-wide plan. It emerged that the local market implementation plans would not add up to the desired growth targets set by the leadership team. At this point, overall marketing plan targets were imposed on the local teams. A management conference in September 1998 allowed the 'robust discussion' of these targets but they were not negotiable. However, this did force out the issues and make them public.

Despite this imposition, it did not negate the positive effects of the integration process. As far as the new company was concerned, the process built up support for the merger. Thousands of employees had participated in the integration, including some of those who eventually lost their jobs as a result of the merger. Phil Radcliffe believes that, even for these people, there was a positive side:

> People felt that they had learned a lot, that they were trusted and given useful tools ... . A good number of the people who lost their jobs saw their involvement as a positive means to sell themselves to a new employer. Ultimately, everyone knew that the new strategy was a winner.
>
> (Devine, 2002, p. 114)

Although this claim appears heroic, actively participating and learning from the experience of merger is arguably better than having your fate determined far away and in secret. The importance of handling the downside aspects of mergers is vital, not just for those who leave but also for the morale and confidence of those who stay:

> If employees feel they were treated fairly and the managers were well prepared, had the documentation to hand and treated them as human beings, they should leave the company with few hard feelings. For the staff remaining in the company, if they see departing employees treated with respect ... then they know their company is one that values people.
>
> (June Rothwell, quoted in Devine, 2002, p. 189)

An integration road map

The Diageo story is that of a well thought through and well managed merger. Perhaps the quality of the organization development resources and advice available to the merger leadership made a major contribution to ensuring that the synergies were achieved and the losses minimized. Critical to this success were the transitional arrangements put in place. A common error in some circles is to hand over your merger to 'merger specialists'. According to McCann and Gilkey (1988, p. 155), the best transitions are internally managed and do not rely upon external consultants. However, unless there is confidence in the internal organization development capacity and because of the political and turf problems likely to be encountered, an external support can be helpful.

During any merger, everything is more fluid than usual and, to encourage constructive action and learning during this period, some sort of scaffolding is useful – a temporary structure which will support the building of the new organization. This parallel organization, consisting of steering groups, task forces, transition teams and so on, provides the temporary bridge between the existing organizations, so that both carry on unaffected until handover.

The temporary organization for a merger will usually have three levels of structure:

- *Leadership Group*: The senior team which visibly leads the process, describing the new organizational culture, which sets the targets, timetables and performance criteria and is on hand to resolve any conflicts that arise.
- *Integration Team*: A core design group of 6–12 drawn from different specialisms to oversee the integration. This groups plans, co-ordinates the task teams, coaches on local action and learning and facilitates organizational learning exchanges between the leadership group and the task teams.
- *Task Teams*: Local project groups responsible for working out how best to implement the integration on a particular patch or specific area, for taking action and for learning from this action.

Whereas the Leadership Group takes on the considerable responsibility of leading the process, including sanctioning the 'headroom' and local autonomy for the Task Teams to get on with the work, the Integration Team has particular responsibility not only for co-ordinating and facilitating this work, but also for seeking to maximize organizational learning. The middle position of this team gives them unique access in both directions and their facilitation is crucial in circulating intelligence around the system.

Activity: an integrations road map

The integration road map (Table 22.1) will help you manage any merger situation. Like any road map, it conceals a lot of useful detail to be developed *en route*. Wherever there is the capacity – and there is always more of this than you think – use your internal people to develop this detail. For example, although it is tempting to try and buy a merger toolkit off the shelf, this will not work well. These tools for local application should be developed to fit your context, by the people who will be charged with implementation.

Table 22.1 An integration road map

Stage	Need to consider
1. Define 'end state vision' – 'where are we going?'	• Business case – the underlying corporate purpose around synergies, efficiencies, costs savings, etc. – but also the … • 'To create a better organization' case – the changes to the way we will work and be together
2. Agree style of merger process	• How are we going to conduct this journey? • What are the key stages, e.g. getting ready, planning for integration, going live • Is the style consistent with the philosophy of the new organization? (e.g. can't do network organization in a centralized way)
3. Manage stakeholder expectations	• What are their views? • What will they support/resist? • How will they be involved in the process?
4. Plan transition organization	Determine the overall parallel structure to act as scaffolding during the merger
5. Define and build the leadership group	Define the membership, roles and remit of this group, e.g. to: • set overall targets, sustain the holding framework and monitor progress, but also to … • visibly model and lead the changes Also define consultancy or coaching support to this team
6. Define role and remit of integration group	Define the membership, roles and remit of this group, e.g. to: • oversee the integration plan • devolve the integration work • design toolkits and workshops • facilitate local progress • act as conduit and connector of learning
7. Develop integration plan	What, by when? Who and what are the teams and projects that will deliver the integration?
8. Design the remit of specific projects	How will the overall plan be accomplished?
9. Create local merger toolkit	• Specify 'end state principles' and 'new ways of working' • Offer 4 or 5 key tools for local application, e.g. 'thinking tools' around e.g. business strategy, creating a new model organization, common working language, etc.
10. Design communications plan and processes	How will we keep people informed of progress?
11. Provide workshop and meetings process to support the work of the task teams	Design processes for taking teams through key tasks and questions, e.g.: • How will task teams be briefed on integration goals, tools, etc.? • How will they get their ideas 'signed off' for action? • How will they be supported in action? • How will they share their learning?, etc.

(continued)

Table 22.1 (continued)

Stage	Need to consider
12. Facilitate the work of local project teams or task forces	This involves managing on various dimensions, e.g.: • Do teams have the authority to act or just to make recommendations? • Are the required changes about continuous improvement or radical step-jumps? • How can local autonomy and diversity be balanced with overall targets?
13. Track commonalities and synergies across and between projects	• Gather intelligence from task teams • Create a network for sharing what works in terms of local implementation • Create forums for leadership team to dialogue about progress with task teams

14. Evaluation and feedback	• How will results be measured and reported?
	  – on business synergies and efficiencies?
	  – on progress on new ways of working and becoming a 'better organization'
	• How will we 'beat the plan'? (i.e. over-deliver)

Conclusion: learning from the merger

This chapter – and this book – assumes that leading involves acting in situations where you know something needs to happen even when you do not know exactly what to do. In the case of a big merger, you will not be on your own with this responsibility and there are many sources of support, help and advice for embarking on the process. However, most mergers do not involve global brands, but are much more local integrations. They come about as a result of public service changes or of one company taking over a part of another's operations. What all these mergers have in common is that people are coming together from previously different situations. Most of them will be at least anxious and some of them will be very fearful of the future. Developing an inclusive approach to integration with the aid of the road map will help to turn this tide of anxiety into a going forward movement.

The lessons from the Diageo story apply to all mergers and integrations. Here are some of the useful lessons.

Develop new meaning and purpose – Recognize the loss of meaning and purpose inherent in merger situations. Work to create a vision of the new organization that emphasizes its cultural quality as much as its business targets. Lead from the front on the vision, the values and the conflicts; take a back seat on implementation.

Avoid the project management trap – Project management is a useful tool but a bad master. Experienced leaders do not use external consultants to manage merger processes because they know that this means that the 'project management boys' will move in, structure the process down to the nth degree and drive all diversity and innovation out of it.

Create a holding framework – Rather than bringing in the 'project management boys' to drive it through, create a temporary structure with clear targets, time-frames and processes to allow people to learn how to implement the integration of the different people and organizations.

Be inclusive and empowering – Develop a process which allows as much participation as is possible and sensible given the demands of the timetable. Empowering people implies allowing them to work out their own understandings and to experiment with options rather than having these imposed.

Maximize learning opportunities – Teach reflection and the learning cycle to task teams so that they can learn from their actions and experience. Create networks for the sharing of good practice and of what works. Facilitate meetings between the parts and levels of the parallel organization to generate organizational learning.

Work with the energies – Synergy will come from the energies of the people involved rather than the structures that eventually emerge. Focus on these energies from the outset, be aware of them and what can be done or needs to be done at particular times. How can these energies be channelled into positive movement for personal development and for the new purposes?

Further resources

Is a merger different from other types of change? Yes. Does it resonate with other forms of change? Yes. For example, there is a lot of overlap between how to get the best out of a merger, how to make a major change and how to develop a lean or learning organization. Although each of these has its own unique flavour, you will find other helpful material and tools in the chapters on the other challenges in the 'change cluster'.

Marion Devine's *Successful Mergers: Getting the People Issues Right* (referenced below) is a practical and down-to-earth book containing straightforward advice on the merger process viewed from a people perspective. McCann and Gilkey's *Joining Forces: Creating and Managing Successful Mergers and Acquisitions* (referenced below) is a more academic text from the USA which is very well referenced and has a useful annotated bibliography.

More advice can be found in sources which focus more on getting the best from more general alliances. Amongst the best here is Yves Doz and Gary Hamel's *Alliance Advantage: the Art of Creating Value Through Partnering* (Harvard Business School Press, Cambridge, MA, 1998), which has a very detailed 'road map' of questions about the various stages of the evolutionary process of building an alliance over several years.

References

Devine, M. (2002) *Successful Mergers: Getting the People Issues Right,* Profile Books, London.

KPMG (2001) *Creating Shareholder Value through Mergers and Acquisitions,* KPMG, London.

McCann, J. and R. Gilkey (1988) *Joining Forces: Creating and Managing Successful Mergers and Acquisitions,* Prentice Hall, Englewood Cliffs, NJ.

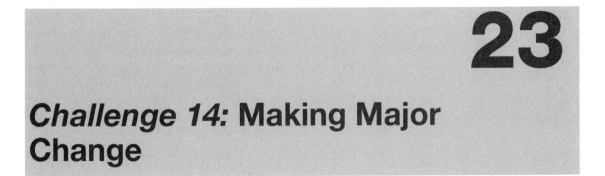

Challenge 14: Making Major Change

Change is required. There is a process of change just as there is a process of manufacturing or for growing wheat. How to change is the problem
W. Edwards Deming

Introduction

Overseeing change and helping people through it are a leadership hallmark. Change is the most common differentiator between managing and leading and yet the evidence of success is unconvincing. Despite their popularity, top-down, rolled-out change programmes start with great fanfares but tend quickly to run into the sands. It is time for some new thinking.

Ideas about change are changing. The three-stage model bequeathed us by Kurt Lewin over 50 years ago:

Present state $\longrightarrow$ Transition $\longrightarrow$ Desired state

looks less and less adequate as a description of what actually happens. This depiction of a smooth linear passage from one state to another has been disputed for many years, but it is the insights of systems thinking that are leading to a new approach to the implementation of change.

Lewin's model assumes that we can bring about the desired future as a new steady state, and that other things can be held steady whilst this is done. This grandfather model is still highly influential, but neither of these assumptions holds up in a rapidly transforming world, where the ground shifts under our feet even as we stand thinking about the changes we want to make. In the complex collaborations of alliances, value chains, multi-agency partnerships and networks that characterize the contemporary organizational world, such control is illusory. In this world there is much that is not under any one person's control. As the string of corporate disasters and scandals illustrates, those who think that they are in charge in such circumstances can be very dangerous.

Leadership will ever be about purpose, clarity of vision and direction setting, but in the face of complexities, the best response is openness about the uncertainty and ambiguity and the commitment to share the responsibility for choosing the next step. Recruiting others to share in the decisions, planning and implementation of change is a new priority for leadership. This is leading through *the power of relationships*:

> *The only way to lead when you don't have control is you lead through the power of your relationships. You can deal with the unknown only if you have enormous levels of trust, and if you are working together and bringing out the best in people.*

(Margaret Wheatley, 2002)

Relational leadership is less grand, but more authentic. It entails letting go and keeping faith in others, which is particularly difficult for 'control freaks'. Being effective and profitable in addition to being socially accountable and environmentally sound requires this sort of engagement and a more inclusive approach. There is little here to be gained by those who portray themselves as heroes, much more for those concerned to encourage the heroism in others.

This chapter contains:

- some principles for managing change
- danger: mad management virus!
- an antidote: complex adaptive systems
- the importance of leadership in change processes
- storytelling: a tool for helping with change
- mapping the change architecture
- further resources.

Managing change

The organizational development (OD) movement, which grew out of the ideas of Lewin and his contemporaries and flourished first in the 1960s and 1970s, was richly prolific in its thinking and practice. Its leitmotif was the principle of 'planned organizational change', but even then many things did not go to plan. There were many questions: How does OD deal with power? How does the theory apply in the multi-agency situations of the public services? How is intervention linked to change?

These questions endure, and OD lives on especially through the use of its models of learning, change and development. Most major change initiatives will borrow from ideal type models for their picture of the desired organization, such as McKinsey's '7 S' (Peters and Waterman, 1982) or Hammer and

Champney's 'Diamond' (Hammer and Champney, 1993), and will continue to reflect this linear sequence:

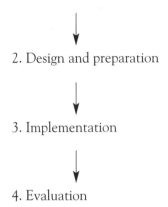

1. Diagnosis and analysis

2. Design and preparation

3. Implementation

4. Evaluation

Major change initiatives will include a detailed and well-planned programme of change management, incorporating:

Diagnosis – What kind of change is it – incremental, radical, crisis or long-term transformational?

The business case for the change –

- How does it contribute to strategic goals?
- Is it a knee-jerk reaction to a crisis?
- Or is it change for change's sake – perhaps coming from a new boss, or 'churning' – the more or less continual restructuring and reorganizing experienced in some quarters?

Engaging sponsors – Who will commit and support this change?

Engaging stakeholders – Who should be involved? Who supports and who resists this change?

Mobilizing and involving people – Who are the change agents? Who is in the design and project teams? What are the key roles? What training and new skills are needed?, etc.

Project management – What are the targets, milestones and measuring disciplines? How do we prioritize?; set up project teams?; co-ordinate?; encourage sharing between project teams?; etc.

Communications – How will we carry out the imperative: 'communicate, communicate, communicate' – of visions, benefits, targets, progress, etc.? Do we brand the change, e.g. 'Project Storm'?

Visible, tangible leadership – How can we sustain visible and tangible leadership from the top throughout the change process? (one of the more difficult tasks).

Evaluation – (Does anyone ever do this?)

Although these durable principles of the change management process work well for some situations, they are prey to many pitfalls. A particular one is the very power inherent in this disciplined process. Project management is essential for moving house, equipping an expedition and moving an army overseas; in other words, where there is no real disagreement about the goal or the means of achieving it. In these situations, a powerful discipline of project management, allied with an overall and accepted command structure, works brilliantly well.

In change situations requiring people to change their behaviour or the way they do things, individually and collectively, project management is still necessary but certainly not sufficient. Any behavioural or cultural change requires learning by individuals, teams or even whole organizations, and this cannot be project managed. However, such is the seductive power of strong project management that people are misled into thinking that it can. Mad management virus (MMV) is a particularly virulent form of this affliction.

Mad management virus

According to Attwood *et al.* (2003, p. 5), this virus takes hold where systematic strategies of change and performance management are being imposed on people in organizations. MMV takes the form of a belief system promising simple ways to control delivery and outcomes that comes to dominate management style and language. It is characterized by such beliefs as:

- Programmatic top-down approaches always work.
- Targets produce specified results with no unintended consequences.
- The more inspection, the better are the outcomes.
- Change is about engineering systems approaches employing negative feedback and control.
- Quality philosophies are best implemented through paper-based systems and organization-wide bureaucracies.
- Change programmes can be parachuted on to the top of any organization and operated by the remote control of carrots, sticks and levers disconnected from the concrete world of doing and implementing.
- These methods have no bad effect on levels of trust, staff morale, absenteeism or turnover.

The worst thing about MMV is that it worms its way into managerial operating systems and damages the genuine efforts of people on the ground to improve products and services.

An antidote: complex adaptive systems

It is the idea of organizations as living systems that provides the 'patch' and the necessary antidote for MMV and the excesses of project management. The old view of change emerged from the 17th century view of a mechanical universe operating to causal laws as proposed by Newton and Descartes. This deterministic worldview has taken root in our thinking to such an extent that it is often hard to question. Western medicine still sees the body as a machine, to be understood and managed as a set of discrete parts; organizations seen as machines have people who act rationally and fit into roles, in departments that 'mesh together', all of which can be 're-engineered' and changed.

The field of complexity science stems from the critique of the deterministic machine metaphor. The exploration of new metaphors, particularly that of the organization as a living system, allows a paradigm shift in the way we relate to the world. Systems thinking has developed a rich discipline for recognizing the interrelatedness of parts within wholes and for working with these patterns and relationships. In this view, rather than the current tasks or functions of the parts, it is the largely self-organizing capacity to form patterns of relationships that is most important.

Complex adaptive systems (CAS) do not comprise a single theory, but rather the study of living systems that are both complex and adaptive – or able to learn. Organizations can thus be seen as self-organizing living systems, in which life cannot be directed because it organizes itself, but can be disturbed and influenced. The words *complex adaptive systems* denote:

- multiple connectedness between diverse parts (Complex); with …
- the capacity to change and to learn from experience (Adaptive); in …
- an interconnected set of people or agents (System).

In this view, there are three useful principles to guide change efforts: *Minimum Critical Specification; Equifinality; and Simple Rules*. Adopting the first of these means asking, 'What is the minimum (and not the maximum) that we can specify in advance for this change situation?' Equifinality means that there are different, but equally useful, paths to the same place, and is hard to understand because it contradicts much one-best-way advice from management experts. It is particularly hard for planners of major change to get their heads around.

Simple rules are those which can be used by everyone to guide their actions to enable widespread adaptive change. Because a CAS is a densely connected web of agents acting on their own local knowledge and sense of how things work, individual moves are not controlled by any centre but are influenced and co-ordinate on the basis of general rules such as 'observe what your neighbour does' and 'pass it on'. For example, here are five simple rules for 'modernizing' the UK's NHS:

- See things through patients' eyes.
- Find a better way of doing things.
- Look at the whole picture.
- Give frontline staff the time and the tools to tackle the problems.
- Take small steps as well as big leaps.

(Fillingham, in Attwood *et al.*, 2003, p. 24)

If a critical mass of people adopts such rules, then individuals and organizations can change how they do things in a way that can never be achieved by detailed top-down planning and control. Such simple rules can enable rapid learning, through stories of problems, mistakes and solutions transmitted from person to person and communicated organization-wide.

'The fish rots from the head' (Garratt, 1999)

Adopting this approach to change demands a great deal in terms of courage and confidence from the leadership of any organization. Consider the following story.

> The Directors of an advertising agency commissioned a development process to help the agency respond to feedback from its major clients and stakeholders. This involved staff and customer surveys followed by a large conference for all employees where the survey data would be fed back. However, when the consultants submitted the conference design, the Directors removed all references to 'dialogue' between the conference floor and the leadership team. Although they were willing to hear the views of staff, they were not prepared to discuss the issues openly in public.
>
> Not unnaturally in such circumstances, the views expressed from the floor during the conference were not as forthright or explicit as they might have been. The Directors concluded that people were more or less happy with how things were in the agency and that there was no strong case to change their own actions and behaviour.
>
> (Adapted from Attwood *et al.*, 2003, Ch. 9)

In whole systems development approaches, the problem of 'resistance to change' is overcome by including all those who need to have a voice in the change process. This 'big tent' approach, which is common in community organizing and democratic politics, is rarer in the organizational world. To bring it off, leaders have to learn to share their power with other stakeholders in the future of the enterprise. This relieves them of the burden of having to be right all the time, but it demands more visible and committed leadership throughout the process.

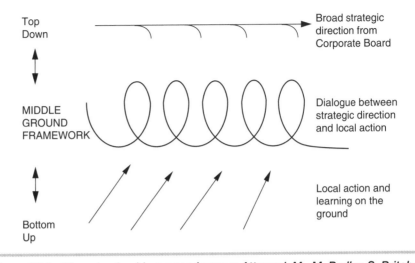

Figure 23.1 Three leadership arenas (source: Attwood, M., M. Pedler, S. Pritchard and D. Wilkinson (2003) Leading Change: a Guide to Whole Systems Working, *Policy Press, Bristol, Ch. 3)*

Surprisingly, perhaps, this is often one of the most difficult things to achieve in any change situation. The leadership of any organization tend to be the guardians of the *status quo* and the currently established order rather than champions of the new. Major change programmes run out of steam as leaders distance themselves and hand over to the project managers. To prevent this, a whole systems development design for change involves the facilitation of leadership in three arenas (Figure 23.1).

The first leadership arena is the creating and sustaining of direction at the strategic level. Where there is a strong corporate team this may be straightforward, but in partnerships, alliances or networks it is often an effort to achieve visible, committed leadership at this level. What is wanted here is a broad sense of purpose, values and direction without too much interference in the details of who does what and when.

The second arena is that of encouraging local leadership on the ground. This involves supporting and developing capacity and leadership in all those individuals, groups and project teams who can contribute to the desired change. All action and learning start locally and it is normal for people in different situations to have different views of how to proceed. This is where the equifinality comes in.

Senior people have a critical job to do here in helping others with their learning to change. Sometimes there is not enough time to allow everyone to learn at their own pace, as dignity demands. At these times especially, the leadership must be there – visible, encouraging and continuing to uphold the optimistic view while acknowledging and accepting the difficulties. Modelling this demands considerable openness and emotional resilience, what Bennis and Nanus (1985) call the 'deployment of self'.

The third arena of leadership is in managing the critical connections between top-down strategic direction and bottom-up action and learning. This is done through the development of frameworks in the middle ground that allow this dialogue and connection. Through forums and other meetings, the Directors tell their story of their strategic thinking and learn from the action and learning on the ground, while local actors feed back their stories and have the opportunity to make sense of the big picture.

Storytelling

Stories are sometimes dismissed as anecdotal, but this misses the point of their ability to pass on and share knowledge between people. This is not about scientific knowledge, but the deep knowledge of beliefs, values and wisdom. Children's stories pass on messages about good actions and good manners, about danger and evil in the world, about fine and noble purposes. These stay with us, deeply embedded, continuing to guide us all our lives.

Stories have always been one of the best ways to learn about what is going on in organizations, and storytelling has an especially important part to play in times of change. The poor performance of many top-down change programmes is leading to a new popularity for storytelling as a way of engaging people at deeper, more intuitive and imaginative levels. Stories are a natural part of life, they are entertaining and energizing, they spark the imagination. As we wonder, fantasize, worry and question about the future, our perceptions and assumptions can shift and re-form. As the imagination is freed, both options and optimism can flourish. In situations of major change, and given the freedom and space to do so, these willing workers can transform the otherwise lacklustre grind from State A to State B.

The new plant

In a new industrial plant, the managers and employees had all signed up to a set of guiding principles emphasizing trust and partnership working. One symbol of this was an open cash box, from which anyone could borrow, as long as they left an IOU. One morning, the plant manager arrived to find the plant buzzing with stories about someone who had taken $60 without an IOU. A quick end to the high-trust policy was predicted. After a short management meeting, the plant manager spoke to all staff. He said he regretted the loss and hoped it would soon be returned. In the meantime, he wanted to put it right, and he then took $10 from his own pocket and put it in the box. At this, several other people followed suit. This story was widely told in the plant thereafter and served to demonstrate the high-trust style of leadership.

(Morgan, 1989, pp. 161–162)

Critical incidents like this are rare, but everyday stories possess great dramatic force. The strange behaviour of a new employee; the enterprising person who shows initiative only to be told that it is against company policy; the manager who really helps someone in trouble: all of these are the stuff of great stories.

In action learning, telling your story is the first step in the journey. Each person shares their narrative of what is happening to them, what they would like to happen, where they would like to go and what perils and dangers may be stopping them. Over time, new episodes are added and the narrative moves on, being rewritten and reinterpreted. These stories lead into dialogues and reflections with colleagues, who can provide us with the support to change ourselves and what goes on around us.

Activity: co-creating a change story

Stories help us deal with changes and encourage us to innovate. Personal stories can be told in groups but they can also be co-created – generated and developed by the group as a whole. Here is a story writing and telling activity that can be done in any group of, say, 5–12 people.

Step 1 – Choose a relevant theme from the current change situation and ask each person to think about some experience of this that was significant for them in some way. For example, the theme might be safety, or working in a team or merging with another department. Ask everybody to think of a story and write some notes on:

- When and where did this take place?
- What happened?
- Who was involved?
- Why have I remembered this?

Step 2 – Ask each person to tell their story. If the group is large, it may be best split into smaller groups or continue over more than one session. Whilst the storyteller is speaking, everyone else should:

- listen without interruption
- ask questions, if they wish, when the story is finished
- clarify their understanding
- show appreciation but not pass any judgements on other people's personal stories
- join in discussion afterwards on general issues.

Step 3 – After all the stories have been told, ask everyone to join in co-creating a story of this theme in the future organization. This can be done in many ways such as drawing pictures or brainstorming ideas and then getting people to write stories in pairs. A fun way to do it is to write joint stories in a writers' circle:

(i) Ask each person to start off a story by writing two or three sentences about this theme in the future company, say, in 5 or 10 years time.
(ii) When everyone has done this, pass the paper to the right and ask the next person to add two more sentences to the story. Encourage people to be imaginative – creative, funny, pessimistic – however they feel, but also to be serious by adding what they think is important.
(iii) Pass the story on to the next person and ask them to add two more sentences. Repeat until the story comes back to the originator. This person should now add the final sentence.
(iv) Each person reads out 'their' stories in turn. Enjoy them and allow them to settle briefly before moving on.
(v) When all the stories have been read, ask: What are the common themes arising from these pictures of the future? What would we like the future to be like?

This storytelling tool can be used at different points in any change process. If used early in the process, it may help to assuage anxieties and allow people to contribute to ideas about the change programme. Once a programme is under way, storytelling can help people deal with the personal consequences for themselves and again to provide feedback to the change managers. Storytelling is also a very valuable way of qualitatively evaluating any change effort; these critical incidents and glimpses can often catch the essence far better than pages of graphs or statistics.

Facing the feelings

Telling and co-creating stories is a very good way of create the space to acknowledge and learn from the feelings and emotions aroused by change. Change creates heightened feelings and senses are enhanced. We become more sensitive to bereavement as old things are dispensed with, and more angry as things happen to people without due cause.

Managers trained in change management at Business Schools are often ill-prepared for this sensitivity, and unable to learn from these feelings. This is a big loss because feelings are an important source of information, energy and learning in change situations. With some corporate emotional intelligence they can help to anticipate grief and prepare for the ground for optimism and hope. In any major change situation, apply the following.

Face up to the feelings

Talk about them in planning meetings – how will people feel? How do I feel? How will we acknowledge and take account of these feelings? How can the energy of those feelings be put to good use rather than despair?

Acknowledge and build on the past

The biographies of those who have worked here is the history of the company. This is the prime source of values and beliefs and the stories, legends and myths that carry them. What are the stories that should be told? How can we create space for these stories? What new stories shall we tell?

Engage people in creating the future

Most of us feel better when we have something to do. What is the plan for engaging people in thinking about the future and working on tasks to bring it about? How can you engage everyone on the change process?

Keep communicating

Too much information is probably better than too little. If it is absent we make it up; information gives us lots to talk about, speculate over and respond to. Face the tough issues up front: 'We are closing Mansfield Road on October 1st and moving to John Street. The implications of this will be discussed with everyone one-to-one with their manager'. This bluntness is better than having the rumour mill grind out a more lurid version of the story. What is the plan for keeping everyone informed? What can be said with certainty? What can be said about what is not clear?

Publish the change architecture and stick to it

It helps to know that there is a plan, even if the details are unclear and the content is yet to be worked out. Make public the road map or change architecture and show people what will happen and when. How will we get from here to the new organization? What will happen when? Who will be involved and how?

A change architecture

It is implementation, and not vision or strategy, that is the biggest challenge in any change process. A change architecture creates the space for sustainable change by specifying the process of involvement by which all those who are part of the problem, are engaged in creating and implementing the solutions (Figure 23.2).

The aim of the change architecture is to create spaces for action and learning at local levels, and then for the sharing of this learning in a system-wide process of creating meaning and direction. It allows for the emergence of good ideas and important learning on the way to implementing any change.

Conclusion

Change management advice is usually based on rational planning and a linear model. To drop these ideas altogether would be to throw out the baby with the bath water. Planning helps, but recent thinking suggests that change

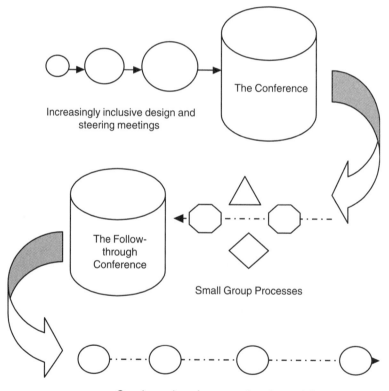

Figure 23.2 A change architecture (source: Attwood, M., M. Pedler, S. Pritchard and D. Wilkinson (2003) Leading Change: a Guide to Whole Systems Working, *Policy Press, Bristol, Ch. 3)*

management processes should create space for the emergence of new ideas, new options and new directions along the way.

In change situations, the telling of stories is a particularly important way of communicating ideas, actions and learning. The heightened atmosphere surrounding major change programmes makes them ideal theatres for tales of daring escapades and hilarious disasters.

Reg Revans, the founder of action learning, preferred to tell stories and resisted attempts to overdefine. 'There are no such things as "truths", only half truths,' he said, 'and it is our job to find out more about those other halves.' Storytelling and action learning encourage people to act and learn on the basis of their ideas about what might work. This counteracts the project managers' one-best-way, and invokes the equifinality principle of generating many paths to desired ends.

> *Action Learning is to make useful progress on the treatment of problems/ opportunities, where no solution can possibly exist already because different managers, all honest, experienced and wise, will advocate different courses of actions in accordance with their different value systems, their different past experiences and their different hopes for the future.*
>
> (Revans, 1998, p. 28)

Further resources

There are many recent books on storytelling as a way of helping with change, one of which is Steve Denning's apparently incendiary *The Springboard: How Storytelling Ignites Action in Knowledge-Era Organizations* (Butterworth-Heinemann, London, 2000). According to his website, in November 2000, Steve was selected as one of the world's 10 Most Admired Knowledge Leaders along with Jack Welch (GE) and John Chambers (CISCO). The recent rise of storytelling books should not obscure Gareth Morgan's valuable books *Images of Organisation*, 2nd edn (Sage, London, 1996) and *Imaginisation* (Sage, London, 1993) which remain useful for their imaginative and creative use of metaphor and story in helping to understand organizational change.

Margaret Attwood, Mike Pedler, Sue Pritchard and David Wilkinson's book *Leading Change: a Guide to Whole Systems Working* (referenced below) gives more detail on whole systems development and provides the tools for this way of working.

References

Attwood, M., M. Pedler, S. Pritchard and D. Wilkinson (2003) *Leading Change: a Guide to Whole Systems Working*, Policy Press, Bristol.

Bennis, W. and B. Nanus (1985) *Leaders: Strategies for Taking Charge*, Harper and Row, New York.

Hammer, M. and J. Champney (1993) *Re-engineering the Corporation*, Harper Business, New York.

Morgan, G. (1989) *Creative Organisation Theory: a Resourcebook*, Sage, London.

Peters, T. and R. Waterman (1982) *In Search of Excellence*, Harper and Row, New York.

Revans, R. W. (1998) *ABC of Action Learning*, Lemos and Crane, London.

Wheatley, M. (2002) *The Servant Leader from Hero to Host – An Interview with Margaret Wheatly*, Greenleaf Centre for Servant Leadership.

Index